CRITICAL THINKING

Critical Thinking provides language teachers with a dynamic framework for encouraging critical thinking skills in explicit, systematic ways during their lessons.

With the proliferation of fallacious arguments, "fake news," and untrustworthy sources in today's multimedia landscape, critical thinking skills are vital not only in one's native language, but also when engaged in the task of language learning. Written with the language teacher in mind, this book provides a springboard for teaching critical thinking skills in multicultural, multilingual classrooms. Suitable for graduate students, in-training teachers, and language curriculum developers interested in purposeful applications of critical thinking pedagogy for the second-language classroom, this volume presents classroom activities, suggestions for lesson planning, and ideas for researching the impact of critical thinking activities with second-language learners.

This book is ideal as an invaluable resource for teacher-directed classroom investigations as well as graduate dissertation projects.

Gregory Hadley is a Professor of Cultural Studies and Applied Linguistics at Niigata University, Japan. He received his PhD in Applied Linguistics from the University of Birmingham, UK, where his primary focus was in the Sociology of English Language Teaching. A Visiting Fellow at the University of Oxford, UK, he is the author of *English for Academic Purposes in Neoliberal Universities: A Critical Grounded Theory* (2015) and *Grounded Theory for Applied Linguistics: A Practical Guide* (2017).

Andrew Boon is a Professor in the Global Communications Department of Toyo Gakuen University, Japan. He holds a PhD in Applied Linguistics from Aston University, UK, and has published numerous articles on methodology, motivation, and teacher development. He is also author and co-author of several writing, listening and speaking, and news media ELT textbooks and scores of graded readers for English language learners.

Research and Resources in Language Teaching
Series Editors: Anne Burns, University of New South Wales, Australia and Jill Hadfield, Unitec Institute of Technology, New Zealand

Research and Resources in Language Teaching is a groundbreaking series that aims to integrate the latest research in language teaching and learning with innovative classroom practice. Books in the series offer accessible accounts of current research on a particular topic, linked to a wide range of practical and immediately usable classroom activities.

Communicating Identities
Gary Barkhuizen and Pat Strauss

Extensive Reading
The Role of Motivation
Sue Leather and Jez Uden

Digital Literacies 2e
Mark Pegrum, Nicky Hockly, and Gavin Dudeney

Sustaining Action Research
A Practical Guide for Institutional Engagement
Anne Burns, Emily Edwards and Neville John Ellis

Initial Language Teacher Education
Gabriel Diaz Maggioli

Critical Thinking
Gregory Hadley and Andrew Boon

For more information about this series, please visit: www.routledge.com/Research-and-Resources-in-Language-Teaching/book-series/PEARRLT

CRITICAL THINKING

Gregory Hadley and Andrew Boon

NEW YORK AND LONDON

Cover image: Getty Images

First published 2023
by Routledge
605 Third Avenue, New York, NY 10158

and by Routledge
4 Park Square, Milton Park, Abingdon, Oxon, OX14 4RN

Routledge is an imprint of the Taylor & Francis Group, an informa business

© 2023 Taylor & Francis

The right of Gregory Hadley and Andrew Boon to be identified as authors of this work has been asserted in accordance with sections 77 and 78 of the Copyright, Designs and Patents Act 1988.

All rights reserved. No part of this book may be reprinted or reproduced or utilised in any form or by any electronic, mechanical, or other means, now known or hereafter invented, including photocopying and recording, or in any information storage or retrieval system, without permission in writing from the publishers.

Trademark notice: Product or corporate names may be trademarks or registered trademarks, and are used only for identification and explanation without intent to infringe.

Library of Congress Cataloging-in-Publication Data
Names: Hadley, Gregory (English language coordinator) author. | Boon, Andrew, author.
Title: Critical thinking / by Gregory Hadley and Andrew Boon.
Description: New York : Routledge, [2022] | Series: Research and resources for language teaching | Includes bibliographical references and index. |
Identifiers: LCCN 2022011456 (print) | LCCN 2022011457 (ebook) | ISBN 9780367181673 (hardback) | ISBN 9780429059865 (ebook)
Subjects: LCSH: Critical thinking--Study and teaching. | English language--Study and teaching--Foreign speakers. | Thought and thinking--Study and teaching. | Language and languages--Study and teaching.
Classification: LCC LB1590.3 .H34 2022 (print) | LCC LB1590.3 (ebook) | DDC 370.15/2--dc23/eng/20220622
LC record available at https://lccn.loc.gov/2022011456
LC ebook record available at https://lccn.loc.gov/2022011457

ISBN: 978-0-367-18167-3 (hbk)
ISBN: 978-0-367-18171-0 (pbk)
ISBN: 978-0-429-05986-5 (ebk)

DOI: 10.4324/9780429059865

Typeset in Bembo
by Deanta Global Publishing Services, Chennai, India.

CONTENTS

List of Figures   *xi*
List of Tables   *xii*
Preface   *xiii*
Acknowledgments   *xv*

PART I

From Research to Implications   **1**

Introduction – What Is Critical Thinking?   1
A. Common Questions about Critical Thinking in English
   Language Teaching   2
   A.1 I'm a Language Teacher: Why Should I Be Concerned
      about Teaching Critical Thinking?   3
   A.2 Isn't Critical Thinking Something Best Taught in the
      Students' First Language?   7
   A.3 My Students Are So Unmotivated: How Could I Ever
      Get Them to Study Critical Thinking?   8
   A.4 Isn't Critical Thinking Something That Students Pick
      Up on Their Own as Part of Getting a Good Education?   10
   A.5 Aren't We Just Forcing Our Students to Adopt Western
      Styles of Thinking?   12
   A.6 Do You Really Need a Book on Critical Thinking in ELT?   16
B. Focusing on Critical Thinking   17
   B.1 Argumentation   18
   B.2 Logical Fallacies   21

      B.3 Externalizing Critical Thinking Through Problem-Solving   23
C. Teaching Critical Thinking Skills to Second-Language Learners   27
D. Implications   30

PART II
From Implications to Application   32
Introduction   32
Section 1: The Critical Thinking Cycle   34
A. Developing Dispositions   34
    Activity 1: Prove It!   35
    Activity 2: Supporting Opinions: The 'Why' Game   36
    Activity 3: Challenging Beliefs   38
    Activity 4: Create a Profile: Understanding Biases   41
    Activity 5: Bias in News Headlines   43
B. Receiving   46
    Activity 6: Paying Attention   47
    Activity 7: Show Me You're Listening: Body Language   48
    Activity 8: Show Me You're Listening II: Backchanneling   52
    Activity 9: Picture What I'm Saying   55
    Activity 10: Listen. Don't Interrupt!   57
C. Reasoning   60
    Activity 11: Categorize It!   60
    Activity 12: Rank It!   63
    Activity 13: Persuade Me!   65
    Activity 14: Spot the Problem!   67
    Activity 15: Sloppy Sophistry   71
D. Responding   73
    Activity 16: Reflecting   73
    Activity 17: Summarize This   75
    Activity 18: Critical Conversations   79
    Activity 19: Correct Me!   81
    Activity 20: The Critical Thinking Cycle: A Review   85

Section 2: Logical Fallacies   88
A. Logical Fallacies: An Introduction   88
    Activity 21: Introduction to Logical Fallacies   88
B. Logical Fallacies: Faulty Conclusions   93
    Introduction   93
Non Sequitur
    Activity 22: Does It Follow?   96
    Activity 23: Spot the Non Sequitur   98
    Activity 24: Non Sequiturs in Politics   101

Probability Fallacy
 Activity 25: How Probable?   103
 Activity 26: Drawing the Conclusion   104
 Activity 27: Fearmongering with Probability   108
Begging the Question
 Activity 28: Which Is the Better Reason?   111
 Activity 29: Don't Beg the Question!   114
 Activity 30: To Beg or Raise the Question   118
Post Hoc Fallacy
 Activity 31: Does A Cause B?   121
 Activity 32: Fallacious Connections   123
 Activity 33: Correlation not Causation   128
Hasty Generalization
 Activity 34: All Students in This Class …   132
 Activity 35: Don't Be Hasty!   135
 Activity 36: Everyday Generalizations   139
Single Cause Fallacy
 Activity 37: Many Causes   141
 Activity 38: A Popular Restaurant   144
 Activity 39: How Many Causes?   147
False Equivalence
 Activity 40: Comparing Apples to Oranges   148
 Activity 41: They're Not the Same   151
 Activity 42: Wronger than Wrong   155
Sunk Cost Fallacy
 Activity 43: What Should They Do?   158
 Activity 44: Is It a Good Decision?   161
 Activity 45: What Would You Do?   164
C. Logical Fallacies: Questionable Reasons   168
 Introduction   168
Ad Hominem
 Activity 46: Don't Attack Me!   171
 Activity 47: Attack the Argument!   174
 Activity 48: Guilt by Association   177
Red Herring
 Activity 49: Avoiding the Question   180
 Activity 50: Don't Distract Me!   183
 Activity 51: Red Herrings in Politics   186
Circular Reasoning
 Activity 52: Don't Go Round in Circles   189
 Activity 53: You Gotta Do What You Gotta Do!   193
 Activity 54: Is Circular Reasoning Begging the Question?   196

Straw Man
    Activity 55: Don't Exaggerate!   199
    Activity 56: Family Arguments   202
    Activity 57: Countering a Straw Man Argument   206
Either/Or
    Activity 58: The Third Option   209
    Activity 59: Either A or B But What About C?   212
    Activity 60: It's Not So Black and White!   215
Stacking the Deck
    Activity 61: Half the Picture   218
    Activity 62: The Full Picture   221
    Activity 63: Fair Play or Stacking the Deck?   224
Equivocation
    Activity 64: Homonyms   227
    Activity 65: Changing the Meaning   231
    Activity 66: Equivocation in Politics   234
Appeal to Emotion
    Activity 67: How Does It Make You Feel?   236
    Activity 68: Be Afraid, Be Very Afraid   239
    Activity 69: So Many Emotions   242
D. Logical Fallacies: Mistaken Assumptions   246
Gambler's Fallacy
    Activity 70: Heads or Tails?   250
    Activity 71: Monte Carlo   252
    Activity 72: What Would You Do (Part 2)?   254
Logical Paradox
    Activity 73: Is It a Contradiction?   257
    Activity 74: The Abilene Paradox   261
    Activity 75: What's the Paradox?   263
Unwarranted Assumptions
    Activity 76: Is It Warranted?   265
    Activity 77: This Morning's Assumptions   268
    Activity 78: What Have the Romans Ever Done for Us?   271
Genetic Fallacy
    Activity 79: Which Is the Better Reason? (Part 2)   274
    Activity 80: Who Said It?   277
    Activity 81: Origins   279
Common Belief Fallacy
    Activity 82: True or False   283
    Activity 83: Accept or Reject   285
    Activity 84: The Things We Believed   288

Slippery Slope Fallacy
    Activity 85: Negative Chains   290
    Activity 86: Can I Have a Chocolate?   292
    Activity 87: Countering Slippery Slope Arguments   294
Ignorance Fallacy
    Activity 88: Evidence of No Evidence?   298
    Activity 89: No Evidence Is No Evidence!   301
    Activity 90: No Evidence Is Evidence!   305
Naturalistic Fallacy
    Activity 91: Is It Good For Us?   307
    Activity 92: What Is to What Ought to Be!   311
    Activity 93: That's Just the Way It Is!   314

PART III
From Application to Implementation   **317**
Introduction   317
A. Creating a Critical Thinking Course   317
    A.1 Making Your Own CT course   318
    A.2 Negotiating a CT Course   320
B. Using the Activities to Supplement a Course   321
C. Implementing Critical Thinking Activities into Your Classroom   321
    C.1 Using the CT Cycle Activities as an Introduction   321
    C.2 Using Activity 21 as a Needs Analysis   322
    C.3 Using the Logical Fallacy Activities   322
    C.4 Returning to the CT Cycle   323
    C.5 Reflecting on Learning   323
    C.6 Keeping a CT Diary   324
D. Going Beyond the Activities in the Book   324
    D.1 Researching CT   324
    D.2 Finding More Fallacies   325
    D.3 Creating Your Own CT Activities   325
E. A Final Note   325

PART IV
From Implementation to Research   **326**
Introduction   326
A. Integrating Methodologies   326
    A.1 Action Research   327
    A.2 Mixed Methods Research   328
    A.3 Putting It Together   329

B. The 'PEAR' Approach 331
    B.1 Progressive Exploratory Action Research 331
    B.2 Progressive Explanatory Action Research 337
C. Final Caveats and Suggestions 344
D. Making a Contribution 345
E. Concluding Thoughts 345

References *347*
Index *354*

FIGURES

1.1	A Visual Metaphor for the Parts of an Argument	18
1.2	Argument Structure	20
1.3	Sample Questions for Analyzing Arguments in Critical Thinking	21
1.4	Example of a Formal Fallacy	22
1.5	Systematic Process for the Teaching of Critical Thinking in This Volume	29
4.1	Action Research Process	328
4.2	Synthesizing the Rationale of Mixed Methods with Action Research	330
4.3	Progressive Exploratory Action Research Process	332
4.4	Example of a Coded Diary Study Entry	333
4.5	Sample Critical Thinking Test Question	334
4.6	Sample of Critical Thinking Test Question with Space for Qualitative Responses	336
4.7	Progressive Explanatory Action Research Process	340
4.8	Template for Creating Research Questions	343

TABLES

1.1	Common Logical Fallacies	24
1.2	Comparing the Sequencing of Critical Thinking Instruction	27
2.1	Developing Dispositions: Activity Titles and Aims	34
2.2	Receiving: Activity Titles and Aims	46
2.3	Reasoning: Activity Titles and Aims	60
2.4	Responding: Activity Titles and Aims	73
2.5	Logical Fallacies: An Introduction: Activity Titles and Aims	88
2.6	Logical Fallacies: Faulty Conclusions: Activity Titles and Aims	94
2.7	Logical Fallacies: Questionable Reasons: Activity Titles and Aims	169
2.8	Logical Fallacies: Mistaken Assumptions: Activity Titles and Aims	247
3.1	Example CT Syllabus	318
4.1	Example Joint Display after First Stage of Exploratory Cyclical AR Investigation	335
4.2	Sample Joint Display from Second Cycle	338
4.3	Sample First Stage of Data Display from Hypothetical Study	342

PREFACE

About the Series

Research and Resources in Language Teaching is a ground-breaking series whose aim is to integrate the latest research in language teaching and learning with innovative classroom practice. The books are written by a partnership of writers, who combine research and materials writing skills and experience. Books in the series offer accessible accounts of current research on a particular topic, linked to a wide range of practical and immediately useable classroom activities. Using the series, language educators will be able both to connect research findings directly to their everyday practice through imaginative and practical communicative tasks and to realize the research potential of such tasks in the classroom. We believe the series represents a new departure in language education publishing, bringing together the twin perspectives of research and materials writing, illustrating how research and practice can be combined to provide practical and useable activities for classroom teachers and at the same time encouraging researchers to draw on a body of activities that can guide further research.

About the Books

All the books in the series follow the same organisational principle:

Part I: From Research to Implications

Part I contains an account of current research on the topic in question and outlines its implications for classroom practice.

Part II: From Implications to Application

Part II focuses on transforming research outcomes into classroom practice by means of practical, immediately useable activities. Short introductions signpost the path from research into practice.

Part III: From Application to Implementation

Part III contains methodological suggestions for how the activities in Part II could be used in the classroom, for example, different ways in which they could be integrated into the syllabus or applied to different teaching contexts.

Part IV: From Implementation to Research

Part IV returns to research with suggestions for professional development projects and action research, often directly based on the materials in the book. Each book as a whole thus completes the cycle: research into practice and practice back into research.

About This Book

Most language teachers would readily acknowledge the importance of critical thinking, but few are able to address it in explicit, systematic ways during their lessons. Especially given the pervasive effects of our multimediated world and the space it provides for transmitting fallacious and uncritical arguments to untold millions, having a critical thinking component to our language lessons is becoming increasingly important. Written with the language teacher in mind, this book focuses on teaching critical thinking skills in multicultural, multilingual classrooms. This book is also suitable for graduate students, in-training teachers, and language curriculum developers seeking purposeful applications of critical thinking pedagogy for the second-language classroom. Ideas for researching the impact of critical thinking in this book are also provided, which may aid in teacher-directed classroom investigations and research for graduate dissertation projects.

Anne Burns and Jill Hadfield (Series Editors)

ACKNOWLEDGMENTS

Writing a book is rarely, if ever, a solitary act. It is created in community, and represents the voices, struggles, and hopes of those who both stimulate and support the authors as they put their ideas into written form. We would like to acknowledge some of the many who encouraged us during this writing of this work. For my part (Gregory Hadley), I am sure that Andy Boon will join me in thanking Chuck Sandy for introducing me to Jill Hadfield during the 2015 Japan Association of Language Teachers (JALT) international conference held in Shizuoka. It was then that I learned of her then-recent Research and Resources in Language Teaching series that she was co-editing with Anne Burns. I thought the series concept was both practical and attractive, but at the time I did not have any ideas for a contribution. Fast-forward to 2018, where on social media, television, and in face-to-face life, issues such as Brexit, the US Presidential elections, and socio-political uncertainties in many parts of Asia kept so many of us in a state of constant mental turmoil. The level of discourse and lack of critical thinking often displayed, both online and in our second-language classrooms, convinced me that a book on critical thinking might be a helpful contribution to the Research and Resources in Language Teaching series. My thanks to Jill Hadfield for encouraging me to follow through, as well as for the ideas that emerged from our early correspondence on this topic. Also, sincerest thanks to Anne Burns for her astute editorial input on the parts of this book that I wrote (Part I and Part IV), as well as to Amy Laurens, Harry Dixon, and the rest of the Editorial Team at Routledge, without whom this book would not be possible. In addition, many thanks to Ze'ev Sudry. During his tenure at Routledge, Ze'ev was an immense help and source of encouragement during those times when the unexpected calamities of life got in the way of writing. To Andy Boon, a special word of thanks, as he allowed me behind the scenes to get a view of how much hard graft goes into the art of creative genius. On a more personal note, I would also like to thank my wife, Hiromi, who despite having her own busy schedule as a university language teacher, constantly worked to create a space for me at home where I could think and write.

I (Andy Boon) would like to thank Gregory Hadley for inviting me to be a part of this project and for being an ever-present sounding board and source of motivation during the writing of the critical thinking activities. I would like to thank Anne Burns and Jill Hadfield for their comments, direction, and patience throughout this project. I would also like to give my thanks to Amy Laurens, Harry Dixon, and the Editorial Team at Routledge for their great support. Finally, I would like to give a special thank you to my wife, Yitzha for taking the time to read through and comment on every activity as I wrote them, for listening to my ideas as they took shape during our many 'pandemic' walks around the river, and for being the sparkle that brings me light.

PART I

From Research to Implications

Introduction – What Is Critical Thinking?

For many of us in the world of English Language Teaching (ELT), embarking on a consideration of 'critical thinking' can feel just a little bit intimidating. While 'most teachers believe that developing critical thinking in their students is of primary importance' (Duron et al., 2006, p. 161), many are unsure as to how to teach it. In study after study (Ketabi et al., 2013; Marin & de la Pava, 2017; Mok, 2010) researchers report that critical thinking is viewed by many teachers as unclear, difficult to pin down, and often contradictory in the way it is described. Such uncertainty makes it easier to avoid the hassle and just stick to running second-language lessons in ways that are more comfortable.

Simply put, critical thinking (CT) is a teachable mental skill that enables a person to uncover the underlying beliefs and assumptions behind the messages they encounter during their daily lives. It means paying careful attention to the words of others, mentally assessing the validity of statements, and considering the potential ramifications of the conclusions. CT empowers a person to respond in a way that is organized, respectful, and logical. Proficiency in CT is enhanced by such dispositions as a willingness to be open-minded, an awareness of the limits of what one really knows about a subject or issue, and an inclination toward polite skepticism when presented with information that is new, potentially life-changing, or that argues for a certain side on controversial subjects. Critical thinkers are persistently curious. They avoid jumping to conclusions until they can determine what can be reasonably known about a certain topic.

We believe that anyone can become a better critical thinker with time, training, and practice. This book is intended to assist you and your students in that process. CT has a lot to offer those of us involved in the task of ELT – in-service teachers,

DOI: 10.4324/9780429059865-1

teachers in training, graduate students of applied linguistics, and, of course, the learners attending our classrooms. This part of the book starts out by wrestling with questions that language teachers often raise about whether CT is feasible for their students. We will draw from research in education, sociology, psychology, and, whenever possible, applied linguistics in our answers to these common concerns. Then we will lay the groundwork needed for later and discuss the basics of critical thinking. We will construct a framework for teaching it within second-language learning environments and think about some of the implications all of this might have for your teaching practice.

In Part II, you will find a wealth of enjoyable and engaging activities, which range from beginner-level activities to those intended for more advanced students. All are intended to help both you and your learners reflect critically on the limits of what you know about a topic, and guide both you and your learners in developing an argument, identifying mistaken thoughts or assumptions, organizing your ideas, and engaging in rational problem-solving.

We foresee these activities acting as either a supplement to your existing in-class teaching materials or a springboard for creating your own second-language–based course in CT. Therefore, in Part III of this book we consider some of the ways to implement the activities in this book in your classes. We will suggest how you could create your own second-language CT course, but we also recognize that many language teachers must work in courses where the content and textbooks have been predetermined by administrative management, so there will also be strategies for introducing CT to enhance such situations.

Part IV will introduce you to methods for investigating whether your second-language learners have become better critical thinkers and for improving future lessons. We think this is important so that you can share your discoveries with the rest of us and contribute to CT in second-language education.

Finally, as we begin, we don't consider ourselves to be 'experts' in CT, but instead, avid students of the craft. There is always more to learn, and in this book we are excited about the opportunity to share with you some of what we have learned – and to do it in a way that we hope you will find to be friendly, intelligent, and accessible. Picture us sitting with you amidst the bustle of a teachers' common room, or maybe at a corner table in a happily humming campus coffee shop. Our sleeves are rolled up, and we're ready to discuss with you how we can get your second-language learners thinking more critically. With this as the backdrop, keep in mind that we do not expect you to slavishly follow the ideas and principles that we will present. Think with us, build on our suggestions, and innovate. Above all, be critical! Now, let's get started!

A. Common Questions about Critical Thinking in English Language Teaching

It is safe to assume that since you are reading this book, you are among those who accept the idea of CT as a worthwhile pursuit, though maybe you are equally just as curious as to how it might fit into your language classes. As you begin to explore the possibility of incorporating CT into your lessons, you may discuss your ideas with a group of colleagues or peers. You may even enthusiastically show them this book that you have bought (or borrowed from the library). Then you may receive a variety of responses. Some people may be positive, wishing you the best of luck with your endeavor and asking you to let them know later how you got on with it. Others may argue that CT is not really appropriate for their students. Or they may question why you need this book when CT is already included in the course material they use. The following is a possible list of questions and objections that you may encounter from your colleagues or peers:

1) I'm a language teacher. Why should I be concerned about teaching critical thinking?
2) Isn't critical thinking something best taught in the students' first language?
3) My students are so unmotivated. How could ever I get them to study critical thinking?
4) Isn't critical thinking something that students pick up on their own as part of getting a good education?
5) Aren't we just forcing our students to adopt Western styles of thinking?
6) Do you really need a book on critical thinking in ELT?

Let's now respond to each of these questions in turn.

A.1 I'm a Language Teacher: Why Should I Be Concerned about Teaching Critical Thinking?

Understanding why, as language teachers, we should be concerned about the teaching of CT requires that we first look at some of the far-reaching social dynamics that are affecting our modern lives in the 21st century. This will help contextualize our call for giving CT a more prominent place in English language education.

For many years, scholars and commentators have warned about a number of sociological and technological dynamics contributing to a loss of common ground necessary for people to believe in the notion of truth, which has led a decline in our collective proficiency to think critically. Barkun (2003), for example, has documented several decades of disenchantment with long-standing pillars of power, such as democratic governance, organized religion, academia, and the media, which has resulted in ever-increasing numbers of people around the world distrusting once-respected institutions of knowledge. Denzin (1991) and Harvey (1990) forewarned us about these trends early on, explaining that the corrosive effects of long-term mistrust in the authority of science and expert knowledge would lead to the displacement of truth as a universal concept, and replace it with the notion of *personal truth* – one that is validated either through feelings, group membership, or individual preferences. This makes the teaching of critical thinking skills even more important because, presently, these social processes have intensified to the point that, for many people, operating in the echo chambers of social media and group identity:

> there is a sudden absence of any authoritative perspective on reality. In the digital age, that vacuum of hard knowledge becomes rapidly filled by rumours, fantasy, and guesswork, some of which is quickly twisted and exaggerated to suit a preferred narrative ... we inevitably end up placing more trust in sensation and emotion than in evidence. Knowledge becomes more valued for its speed and impact than for its cold objectivity, and emotive falsehood often travels faster than fact.
>
> *(Davies, 2019, p. xi)*

Our world is currently experiencing a crisis of the mind. In 2016, Oxford Dictionaries announced the word *post-truth* as the international word of the year to describe our present predicament. A year later, on the cover of *Time* magazine's April 3, 2017, edition, the question 'Is Truth Dead?' was posed, in stark red letters, to highlight how, with growing intensity, our agency in critically discerning truth from error is under constant attack. In our multi-mediated world, 'speaking your truth' has become a watchword for justifying what one already believes, and even more often, for justifying what one simply *wants* to believe. Zollo and Quattrochiochi (2018) explain that this phenomenon is actively encouraged by social media companies, whose algorithms seek to group us into micro-markets, whereby we are fed, moment by moment, the type of news and content that will strengthen our worldview while, at the same time, increasing our engagement on their platforms. While once, for many of us, the main task was getting access to information, now an important skill for both us and for the students in our classrooms is to discern whether the current overflow of information that we have at our disposal is in any way trustworthy.

At this point, skeptics might counter with the observation that scholars have always sounded the alarm about a crisis in society's ability to think critically. And indeed, to a certain degree, they are correct. Fears about society's diminished capacity to think critically is an enduring theme in the texts on CT pedagogy (Bowell & Kemp, 2015; Cottrell, 2005; Davies & Barnett, 2015; Fisher, 2005; McPeck, 1981; Naiditch, 2016), and educators have often bemoaned problems related to critical thinking in their schools and societies. Over 30 years ago, Kurfiss (1988) complained that students only began to show signs of critical thinking after entering a graduate study program. Given the relatively small number of graduate students, when compared to the total population, the implications of this complaint are clear. Go back over 100 years, and we find Dewey (1910) lamenting how the 'scope for thinking' was, in his words, 'pallid and remote' (p. 138) among the ordinary people of his time. Head back even further to 400 years in the past, and there we find Francis Bacon protesting the 'idols of the mind' that have prevented most from thinking clearly and logically on a subject (Ivie, 1989).

What is dramatically different from these earlier times, however, is the pervasive nature of communication technology in today's world. Without a doubt, a significant number of messages we encounter during the day are intended to instruct, assist, or inform. At the same time, whether online, on the street, at home, or in the marketplace, we encounter arguments and propositions intended to prey upon those with an underdeveloped sense of critical thinking. During times of social stability, underequipped thinkers may merely suffer separation from their money in the purchase of some item falsely claiming to give them better health, lower weight, or greater sex appeal. However, during times of crisis, the steady toxicity of being inundated with a torrent of messages, via social media, television, podcasts, radio, and signage, that expose us to lies, myths, half-truths, and wishful thinking, can have cataclysmic effects on society. This can be seen in the disinformation, both foreign and domestic, that has plagued democratic elections in many countries recently. A lack of critical thinking skills contributed to the mass purchase of subprime loans, which were a direct cause of the disastrous world recession of 2008. Poor critical thinking in vast swathes of society can even be life-threatening, as we saw during the COVID-19 global pandemic, where shortfalls in evidence-based critical thinking skills allowed for the rapid spread of conspiracy theories, quack cures, the panic buying of toilet paper, the politicization of science, and instinct-based proclamations from non-experts. All of this put the health and economic well-being of untold millions in danger, and many hundreds of thousands have died due to decisions made as a result of poor critical thinking.

Earlier generations have faced similar challenges but these were on a much smaller scale: The immediacy, global spread, and sheer intensity of today's public discourse is of a type never experienced before in human history. 'It is human irrationality, not a lack of knowledge,' writes Kurfiss (1988, p. 1), 'that threatens human potential.' If we as a civilization are going to survive and ultimately improve, one important feature is that we must all become better critical thinkers.

These dynamics are experienced most intensely by young people around the world. They have grown up literally swimming in the streams of digital interaction. As teachers, we often find ourselves working with learners, and sometimes managers of educational institutions, who operate within what Viner (2016) has called 'viral modernity' – a world where 'facts don't work.' Educational institutions today no longer emphasize critical thinking in their curricula, favoring topics aimed at future career development. Educational institutions, according to Rider (2018), have become increasingly 'vulnerable to … "truthiness", "wikiality", and "alternative facts"' (p. 29). 'Criticality,' according to Peters (2018, p. 148), 'has been avoided or limited within education, and substituted by narrow conceptions of standards and … instrumental and utilitarian pedagogies.'

The results are indeed troubling. Arum and Roksa's (2011) investigation of over 2,300 students at 24 universities found that critical thinking skills were no longer being explicitly taught, and, if explicit in the curricula at all, were only included within elective courses. Using the Collegiate Learning Assessment (CLA) test of academic knowledge and critical thinking, Arum and Roksa (2011) found that, after four years of instruction, nearly half of the students in their study showed no significant improvement in critical thinking and added that this percentage was significantly higher than in similar studies conducted in the 1980s.

In response to these issues, teachers from all disciplines, both in secondary and higher education, have called for a renewed emphasis on the explicit teaching of critical thinking (Bergdahl & Langmann, 2018; Quantz, 2016; Thompson, 2019). This brings us back to the question of whether we, as language teachers, should be concerned about addressing CT in our lessons. Do we as a community of educators sit on the sidelines and focus upon only teaching the technical aspects of the language? Or do we join with other educators in responding to the current challenge?

We understand that conditions are increasingly difficult for many of us as English language educators. Over the years, we have experienced significant increases in workloads, crippling decreases in classroom freedom, and onerous constraints on time, (Cowie, 2011; Hadley, 2015; Johnston, 1997; Varghese et al., 2005). These challenges make it easier to forego CT – especially if we are tired or simply unsure of how to introduce CT to our students. And yet, regardless of where we work, whether at a university, school, or private institute, the current assault on our students' capacity to think critically is as relentless as it is remorseless. Our second-language classrooms cannot somehow be walled off from what is taking place around us. By focusing on the technical aspects of teaching language, and by sidestepping the question of whether we should be enabling learners to think about the implications of what is being communicated, we, as language teachers, run the risk of becoming little more than 'instrumental and utilitarian' (Peters, 2018, p. 148) language technicians in our institutions.

On this point, Ding and Bruce (2017), who have built upon the work of earlier scholars (Allman, 2001, p. 71; Varghese et al., 2005, p. 22), highlight how many university teachers of English for Academic Purposes (EAP) today are being steadily relegated to the fringes of academic life. Instead of being seen as full-fledged educators in their own right, many are treated more as word mechanics tasked with fixing the broken language of international students. To regain their standing as educators who have as much to offer as their discipline-specific colleagues, Ding and Bruce (2017) call upon EAP teachers to seek out opportunities to collaborate with and support the work of colleagues in other fields. If you incorporate a CT component into your language lessons, we believe that you and, eventually, all of us as second-language teachers, can build bridges of collaboration with colleagues. By sharing in the task of teaching students to think critically, we can make a significant contribution to the quality of education offered in our schools and universities.

Not only could this improve our professional standing but by adding CT to our lessons we are making a lifelong contribution to our students' well-being. Butler's (2012) landmark study of 137 adults and university students found that those who scored higher on tests of critical thinking also had fewer negative life events stemming from poor judgment or flawed personal decisions. In other words, it can be argued that people who learn to become better critical thinkers have better lives. In addition, by purposefully including a CT element in English language instruction, we are working to combat the current social dynamics that are waging war on critical thinking and, as Bluedorn and Bluedorn (2015, p. 15) state, to 'exercise our minds so that it does not hurt anyone when we try to use it' (p.15).

Something that we will touch upon again later is that you do not need to treat critical thinking pedagogy as somehow alien to second-language learning. CT can run alongside our learners' need to improve their communicative competence. As Kramsch (2006) states, 'Today, it is not sufficient for learners to know how to communicate meanings; they have to understand the practice of meaning making itself' (p. 251). In this respect, CT requires students to listen more analytically, read more thoughtfully, and to speak, as well as to write, more logically. Shirkhani and Fahim (2011, p. 112), based on their review of studies investigating CT in the second-language classroom, argue that students get practice not only in decoding the meaning of messages in the second language, but also that CT enables them to consider the deeper implications of what is being communicated, thus making the experience of language learning more meaningful in the process. Elfatihi (2017) adds that since problem-solving tasks feature prominently in second-language instruction, the integration of critical thinking skills moves such activities away from a puzzle-solving activity to one where students must reflect more deeply on what they are doing and work for solutions in a rational and empathetic manner.

A.2 Isn't Critical Thinking Something Best Taught in the Students' First Language?

Often an objection that is raised to teaching CT is that the English proficiency of 'my students' is so low that they won't be able to handle anything as complex as critical thinking. We believe this may be considered an example of an informal fallacy known as a 'false dilemma.' False dilemmas are 'either/or' forms of binary thinking that position only two possibilities when many options are in fact available. Here the objection could be restated as: 'Either my students should be able to study critical thinking in English as easily as they could in their native language, or they shouldn't be asked to learn it at all during their English language classes.' The first thing that should be remembered is that, depending on their education and other life experiences, beginners in the second language may already have well-developed CT skills, and simply need instruction on how to express their arguments in the target language. And for those who need more training in CT, we should remember that we do not have to teach such beginners or low-intermediate learners everything about CT. It is possible to teach some of the simpler aspects of critical thinking for students at this level. The Pathways series of textbooks (e.g., Chase & Johanssen, 2012) demonstrates that CT activities and lessons can be crafted for learners of lower levels of English language proficiency. For example, in the Level 1 textbook for Listening, Speaking, and Critical Thinking (Chase, 2013, pp. 66–67), learners must first listen to a radio interview about a new book on meteorology. After completing tasks aimed at identifying the main points of the author's argument, students engage in a groupwork task in which they critically assess the claims made in the interview. This serves as a springboard for teachers to assess the students' critical awareness and to suggest further ways to help them become aware of the implications and validity of what is being introduced in the textbook.

Moreover, there are numerous ELT situations throughout the world where the teacher also speaks the same language as the learners. These teachers have the opportunity to explain aspects of CT in their own language before practicing the principles in classroom-based target language activities. As an example of this, Lin (2018) reports on the success she had in teaching critical thinking to rural Chinese students in mixed-level English language classes. She suggests that non-native teachers of English in monolingual environments can and should be at the forefront of introducing their learners to CT within second-language classrooms.

We admit that the degree to which you choose to introduce CT to your learners will depend, in part, on their language proficiencies. Learning CT skills in another language will be more difficult than learning it in one's own language. However, the question of whether students would benefit from learning how to think critically by receiving instruction in their native language does not have to be framed in terms of 'all or nothing.' Students may be able to improve their critical thinking in both the L1 and the L2. Furthermore, we, as language teachers, should not see ourselves as teaching CT in isolation. It is possible that other colleagues in our schools and universities are also teaching aspects of critical thinking. Why not seek out such teachers and cooperate with them, whenever and wherever possible, in the shared task of educating our learners? Instead of avoiding the teaching of CT, we could investigate the possibilities that are available and make use of them with our second-language learners.

A.3 My Students Are So Unmotivated: How Could I Ever Get Them to Study Critical Thinking?

We have all had that class in which we feel our students are not motivated enough to do anything; that one class in which the students were unresponsive and seemingly unwilling to participate. So, how can we introduce CT in such a situation?

Often, what may seem to be students' lack of motivation may, in fact, be resistance to the challenging of their assumptions. Kurfiss (1988, p. 63) explains that few of us enjoy the process of questioning our suppositions and belief systems

– stop and think about a time you argued with a friend or colleague about something you truly believed in and how you resisted them. When encountering such reluctance, it often helps to lessen the sense of threat by reminding your students that you are not trying to force them to change their minds, and that they themselves will always have the power to decide whether to accept new perspectives. Assure them that you only wish to introduce new viewpoints for them to consider. Cottrell (2005) explains:

> Critical thinking does not mean that you must abandon beliefs that are important to you. It means giving more consideration to the evidence that supports the arguments based on those beliefs so you do justice to your point of view.
>
> *(p. 11)*

Another approach is to reframe motivation. If we are honest, many of us, as language teachers, tend to look at student motivation as the 'oil' of language teaching. It might be down there under the surface but getting to it requires that we use various pedagogical tricks in order to drill down far enough to cause it to gush forth from our learners. Motivation is treated as a natural resource for powering our students' attempts at mastering the English language, so some language teachers spend a considerable amount of time finding ways to motivate their students, that is, to get them to 'do something' in the classroom. This constant quest for ways to 'motivate' often dissolves into an exhausting struggle to coax students into doing things they really do not want to do.

As an alternative, we find Bonny Norton's (Norton, 1997, 2001; Norton-Peirce, 1995) notion of *investment* to be very helpful for moving forward. Norton (2001) argues that learners tend to weigh up quietly whether the investment of time, effort, and resources are likely to yield enough of a return for their efforts. In this sense, a return represents something that brings the learner closer to actualizing their idealized self, or achieving a desired result such as gaining greater acceptance into the target language community or fulfilling certain values that they hold as important. Norton (1997, 2001) explains that investment is different from instrumental motivation, which she describes as static and transactional. Investment is a dynamic process by which language learners are constantly striving to improve in the target language so that they may further develop their social identity within a wider community. Norton's context was that of migrants wishing to integrate into Canadian society. For your classes, it may be your students' wish to become global citizens, to be able to achieve discreet goals, or to become a member of a wider community that is 'in the know,' so to speak, on how powerful people and organizations attempt to deceive the masses, and to join those who resist being manipulated.

Viewed in this light, introducing learners to CT involves explaining how it would both protect them from those who would attempt to take advantage of them and empower them to learn how to communicate more effectively in the target language. When the material, social, and affective benefits are presented to learners, the case for investing in CT may be compelling. At the same time, if your students have decided that CT within English language study is simply not worth their investment, it may be better to wait until later for an opportunity to demonstrate the importance of CT. Sometimes, that chance may never come, but then magical moments do happen, which is one of the reasons why many of us persevere as language teachers.

A.4 Isn't Critical Thinking Something That Students Pick Up on Their Own as Part of Getting a Good Education?

This is an important question, because the way one answers it determines not only how one will teach CT, but also whether one will teach it at all. Some see critical thinking as a talent that develops naturally through regular scholarly interaction. Others view critical thinking as an attainable skill. Still others search for a middle ground. Let's look at these perspectives in greater detail so that we can better stake out the position taken in this book.

The understanding of critical thinking as a natural disposition or talent that develops out of nurture and exposure to new ideas has a long tradition stretching back at least as far as Francis Bacon, who in 1604 described himself as

> fitted for nothing so well as for the study of Truth, as having a mind nimble and versatile ... being gifted by nature with desire to seek, patience to doubt, fondness to meditate, slowness to assert, [and] readiness to reconsider.
> *(Bacon, 1868/2011, p. 85)*

Educationalists who uphold this view (Ennis, 1991; Facione, 2000; Paul & Elder, 2006) see critical thinking in terms of a person's mental attributes, such as 'Inquisitiveness, Open-mindedness, Systematicity, Analyticity, Truth-seeking ... Self-confidence, and Maturity' (Facione et al., 1995, p. 4). This inventory is not exhaustive, and the literature features long lists of dispositions linked to critical thinking (e.g., Ennis, 1985, 1996). Many of these scholars, however, are not simply saying that critical thinkers are 'born, not made,' but rather, that one's natural aptitude as a critical thinker develops through interaction within a specific scholarly community. For them, critical thinking cannot be taught; it must be acquired through nurture and by being immersed in the scholarly discourse of a specific field of study (Dewey, 1910; McPeck, 1981, 1990; Moore, 2011). Unlike musical talent, where some will be virtuosos while others will be no more than average, the view of critical thinking as a disposition claims that most people can become better critical thinkers if they persist in reading the scholarly literature and participating in academic discourse with others in their field.

At the other end of the spectrum are those who frame critical thinking as teachable sets of abilities or skills (Bowell & Kemp, 2015; Cottrell, 2005; Judge et al., 2009). Critical thinking results from training learners into being able to identify issues, conclusions, and reasons for a person's argument. Students are presented with opportunities to identify ambiguous language, assumptions, and logical fallacies. CT also entails the assessing of evidence, the consideration of other causes, and the search for alternative conclusions. The outcome is not simply 'the ability to analyze and evaluate information' (Duron et al., 2006, p. 160) but also to learn how to structure one's ideas in order to communicate in ways that are logical, justified, and trustworthy. Those who approach CT as a skill are at the vanguard of developing curricula and courses for teaching it, since they believe that critical thinking improves through the regular practice of techniques and awareness-raising activities.

Empirical research tends to support the notion that important aspects of CT *can* be explicitly taught to and retained by students. Fong et al. (1986) reported on a project in which a class of university learners were taught critical thinking skills in the context of a statistical reasoning course. Six months later, students who passed the course were contacted by a researcher pretending to give a phone survey that had fallacious reasoning couched within the questions. At significant levels, the students used what they had learned in their class to question the underlying assumptions and logical errors given by the researcher. Kosonen and Winne (1995) replicated this study with even greater results.

In their experiments, Marin and Halpern (2011) found that explicit instruction of CT skills was retained by secondary-school students at a low-performing US inner-city high school. Within the ELT context, Lin (2018) taught CT skills to a group of Chinese secondary students. After 14 weeks, students in the experimental group showed significant gains, especially in their persistence to seek the truth within a particular given issue, while students in the control group showed no statistical improvement (Lin, 2018, pp. 74–75). Similarly, Davidson and Dunham (1997) found that an experimental group of Japanese university students who received instruction in CT embedded within their regular English language instruction scored far higher in CT skills than the control group that received no CT instruction.

Therefore, we believe the indications to be clear – critical thinking skills can be taught in second-language learning environments, provided that our learners receive repeated exposure. Learners need frequent opportunities to explicitly practice what they have learned. Kurfiss (1988) states that this works best when colleagues join forces:

> While individual faculty frequently emphasize critical thinking in their courses, students' thinking abilities will remain limited unless faculty combine forces to cultivate critical thinking skills throughout the curriculum.
>
> *(p. 91)*

We need to be careful, however, because teaching CT as a set of skills or communicative strategies can still fail if it is taught merely in a mechanistic manner.

Paul (1981) and Browne and Keeley (2007, p. 10) both warn that a shallow application of CT as a rhetorical toolbox can result in creating a generation who learn to manipulate aspects of critical thinking in order to strengthen their pre-existing beliefs. Critical thinking must start as a reflective process of evaluating our own beliefs before we can engage with others. This requires a willingness to persevere in the painful process of critical self-reflection, which of course draws us inexorably back toward a discussion of dispositions.

As a way of getting off this conceptual merry-go-round, other scholars have sought middle ground by combining what they see as the strengths of natural talent and skills positions on CT, while also seeking to mitigate the weaknesses (e.g., Glaser, 1941, pp. 5–6). A good example of this is Halpern (2014), who in combining the notion of skills learned through nurturing dispositions and pragmatic use, sees CT as:

> the use of those cognitive skills or strategies that increase the probability of a desirable outcome. It is used to describe thinking that is purposeful, reasoned, and goal directed … Developing a critical thinking attitude and disposition is at least as important as developing the skills of critical thinking. The skills are useless if they are not used. The attitude of a critical thinker must be cultivated and valued.
>
> *(p. 52)*

This is the position that we take in this book, and it is embedded within our definition of CT at the beginning of this chapter. Our response to the question at the beginning of this part of the book, then, based on our reading of the literature, is that CT may not come naturally to our learners through implicit instruction. It must be taught explicitly and exercised reflexively. Students need regular practice and reinforcement in order to make CT an enduring feature in their lives, both for inside and outside the classroom.

A.5 Aren't We Just Forcing Our Students to Adopt Western Styles of Thinking?

Let's shift to consider the concerns that we are imposing Western values on our students via the medium of critical thinking. Proponents of this view argue that 'critical thinking is cultural thinking' (Atkinson, 1997, p. 89), and state that it should not be introduced to second-language learners (Fox, 1994, p. 63). This is because, as Ramanathan and Kaplan (1996) explain, critical thinking runs counter to the cultural values and thought processes of many non-Western cultures:

> Not all cultures value individualism to the extent that North American culture does; neither do all cultures promote the ability to be sceptical or think critically.
>
> *(p. 28)*

Culture is usually treated as a general sociological dynamic, but Ramanathan and Kaplan (1996) do single out Asian, Native American, and Islamic cultures within their critique, arguing that when we require people from these cultures to adopt Western thinking skills, we, as language teachers, are guilty of 'intellectual imperialism' (1996, p. 28). Atkinson (1997) adds that the logic that drives CT prevents second-language learners from fully expressing their emotions, thereby causing them instead to interact in a manner similar to the conflicted character of Mr. Spock from the science-fiction series *Star Trek* (Walters, 1994). In the series, Spock, who is half human and half Vulcan, can deduce many things through logical thought, but at the cost of sublimating his emotional human side. This not only causes him private personal pain but it also makes him prone to making mistakes when placed in temporary command of missions. As a result, he is distrusted by the rest of the crew because he neither empathizes with their feelings nor does he take chances based on intuition. Ramanathan and Atkinson (1999) state that when the logical thinking of CT becomes a part of our language lessons, we can similarly place students into a Spock-like pressure cooker of mental and emotional turmoil.

The notion of critical thinking as a logically dispassionate Western construct permeates our intellectual landscape. Floyd (2011) and Rear (2017) both offer reviews of scholarly literature citing papers stretching back 20 years, in which language teachers use this notion as the basis for criticizing East and Southeast Asian English language students as uncritical and passive, with a tendency to rely on rote learning or memorization. Given these arguments, it is unsurprising that some may eventually attempt to push back and present CT as incompatible with non-Western, typically East Asian, language learners.

But the problem with this argument is that its underlying premise rests on what Said (1978/2003) has described as 'Orientalism.' Orientalism presents Western culture as masculine, logical, rational, and pragmatic, while Oriental culture is portrayed as feminine, indirect, paradoxical, and esoteric. Critical thinking is construed as a product of Western civilization that represents something that Eastern culture either struggles to adopt or resists in favor of conformity to totalitarian regimes.

We argue that Orientalist arguments against the teaching of critical thinking to students from non-Western cultures are unacceptable, first because they draw a circle around CT as the property of Western culture and implicitly exclude anyone whose culture is deemed to be not Western enough. Second-language learners are especially vulnerable to such 'Othering' or stigmatization (Rear, 2017) that can happen during those moments when a teacher mistakenly assumes their 'Asian' students to be more disadvantaged than 'Westerners' when it comes to critical thinking (Floyd, 2011; Melles, 2009). As we will see shortly, it is a mistake to assume that some students have less critical thinking skills because they are not from the West.

The second reason why we oppose Orientalist attitudes is because the portrayals of *Western* as opposed to *Eastern* thinking can be grossly stereotypical; they overlook the diversity of individuals operating within these cultures. There is no one 'Asian' or 'Western' culture in any meaningful sense. While the cultures of Thailand may share many commonalities with South Korea, an Orientalist mindset ignores the differences, just as it would ignore the differences in 'Western' culture seen between Northern Italy and Texas. The monolithic view of Eastern and Western cultures is unable to account for, or fully appreciate, why a business executive from Shanghai or Tokyo is likely to share far more in common with a financial advisor in New York than with a farmer in central Cambodia. Neither is there any basis for gendering the West as masculine and the East as feminine, especially since there is a sexist implication positing the West as somehow stronger and superior.

Another weakness in the argument of those opposing CT in the second-language classroom is the notion that it somehow comes more naturally to Westerners, who are steeped in an educational environment based on the principles of critical thought. We have already seen from empirical research that CT may not be learned through osmosis or, as Atkinson (1997, p. 73) claims, 'though the pores' (p. 73). CT is learned through constant and purposeful practice. Critical scholars (Sagan, 1996; Shermer, 2011; Specter, 2009) point out that there are many groups or subcultures of people living in the West who cling to paradoxical and uncritical worldviews. These range from post-modernists to anti-vaccination advocates to utopian religious sects. The West does not have a corner on the critical thinking market. Five minutes of watching a debate on a 24-hour news network or a quick scan of comments on social media in the Anglophone world would, we argue, be ample evidence of this point.

If we accept the statement of Norris and Ennis (1989) that, at its core, CT represents 'reasonable and reflective thinking that is focused upon deciding what to believe and do' (p. 3), then such skills and dispositions are active within people throughout the world, even though they may be expressed with different terminology or with different emphases. What we mean here is that critical thinking as a concept is multilayered enough for different cultures, disciplines, and educational systems to approach it from different directions – all of which can be equally valid. As Howe's (2007) comparative investigation of the CT beliefs and teaching practices of Canadian and Japanese secondary-schoolteachers discovered, they had two different methods of introducing CT to their students. Canadian teachers sought critical engagement through questioning and awareness of logical fallacies, while the Japanese path to CT was through introspective analysis of the validity of received knowledge claims.

There are many ways to think critically, and the judgment of some educators and Anglophone schools and universities about silent and uncritical Asian students may be more of a criticism of communication styles than of skill as critical thinkers. Another landmark study (Lun et al., 2010) on the effects of culture on Asian students' critical thinking found, in its comparison of critical thinking scores on several batteries of standardized tests between 110 New Zealand European and 52

Asian students, that after accounting for linguistic issues, Asian students performed as well and even better than the New Zealand students in critical thinking skills such as dialectic thinking.

Next, let us consider the claim that CT harms students by turning them into unemotional, logical entities like Spock in *Star Trek*. This 'Spock Metaphor' was first popularized by the American philosopher Kerry Walters (1994), who referred to CT pedagogy as helping to bring about the 'vulcanization' of students:

> An exclusive concentration on the canons of formal and informal logic ... does not school students in rationality. Instead, it vulcanizes them by overplaying the calculus of justification and underemphasizing – if not outright ignoring – the pattern of discovery.
>
> *(p. 76)*

'Rationality or good thinking,' Walters (1994) contends, 'encompasses both logical and nonlogical cognitive functions' (p. 75). By 'nonlogical,' Walters (1994) means the provision for emotions and gut-feeling intuition.

However, there appears to be no credible empirical evidence of CT causing harm to students. Instead, we find there to be a compelling case for the opposite being true. Many studies suggest that CT instruction provides long-term benefits to learners, such as becoming better problem-solvers, making better personal choices, and getting better jobs (Keeley et al., 1995; Martin et al., 2006; Topping & Trickey, 2015). What Walters (1994) and his supporters seem to be guilty of is what is known as a Straw Man Argument: when, to take down a complex and compelling argument, a person creates a weak caricature of the concept and attacks this instead of the actual argument.

In this book, we are not advocating an exclusive concentration of informal or formal logic in ELT. We are not calling for the suppression of emotions in the service of logic. We understand that the *Star Trek* character of Spock is used here as a metaphor, but we must remember that he is still an imaginary character. In our reading of many critical thinking textbooks made for university students (Bowell & Kemp, 2015; Cottrell, 2005; Dummett & Hughes, 2019; Fisher, 2005; Halpern, 2014; Judge et al., 2009), we have yet to find anyone using Spock as a model for real-life success in CT.

And yet, we agree with Walter's (1994) claim that critical thinking requires a balance between logic and emotions, because this is what is advocated by scholars in the field (Bowell & Kemp, 2015; Cottrell, 2005; Davies & Barnett, 2015; Halpern, 2014; Hunter, 2009) and even more because clinical research supports this position. In a groundbreaking book on the role of logic and emotion, Antonio Damasio (1994), a neuroscientist at the University of California, tells the story of a patient (with the pseudonym of Elliott), who suffered damage to an area of his frontal lobes vital to the processing of emotion. A battery of tests confirmed that Elliott's logical reasoning, language skills, and understanding of ethics were all intact. However, because of the damage to his brain, Elliott was unable to experience emotions. The tragic problem for Elliott, according to Damasio, was that he was unable to come to a decision, either about abstract issues or about choosing the best possible solution to a certain problem. The point, according to Patrick Grim (2013), professor of philosophy at the State University of New York at Stony Brook, is that 'both emotion and what we think of as pure logic have important parts to play. We need both cool rationality and hot thought' (Grim, 2013, p. 38). Critical thinking, then, is not the absence of emotions. It is the practice of channeling our thought and emotions through rational discipline so that we can come to the best possible conclusion about a problem or pressing issue.

A.6 Do You Really Need a Book on Critical Thinking in ELT?

There are already many critical thinking ELT resources out there. In any given year, the major conferences in ELT and applied linguistics are likely to feature several presentations on various aspects of CT, and some educational organizations have special interest groups (SIGs) devoted to CT in second-language instruction. Dummett and Hughes (2019) note that many features of critical thinking are already implicitly embedded within ELT classroom-based activities, such as when learners are taught to synthesize different sources of information in an essay, or where students must consider the underlying assumptions of different statements on a controversial subject. CT appears in some coursebooks under the umbrella of the 4 Cs of 21st-century skills (critical thinking, collaboration, creativity, and communication). Moreover, over years, ELT has seen language textbooks that explicitly address critical thinking within second-language learning environments (Maher & Haugnes, 1998; Najafi & Fettig, 2014; Numrich, 2010; e.g. Scull, 1987); and at the time of our writing of this book, there are at least two major series of textbooks: *Pathways* (Chase, 2013), which actualizes critical thinking within a multilevel four-skills set of learning materials, and *Unlock*, the second edition of another multilevel four-skills series (White et al., 2019). In addition, over the past 10 years, numerous resource books for language teachers interested in teaching CT have appeared (Dummett & Hughes, 2019; Goodwin & Sommervold, 2012; Houston, 2009; Naiditch, 2016; Schuster, 2014). So, why do you need this book you're reading?

Most of the CT resources are produced by small publishers, as evidenced by the fact that the majority of the books cited above are out of print. The relatively short shelf life of critical thinking materials in ELT (and indeed, of most language textbooks) forces language teachers interested in CT to cobble together what they can from multiple sources – often outside of ELT. Not only is this time-consuming, it is also risky because teachers may not have time to trial their materials beforehand.

Also, while it is true that presentations on critical thinking and special interest groups in some language teacher organizations can be found, many of these feature limited numbers of scholars and teachers working alone in their institutions with small-scale classroom projects. This does not invalidate what they are doing – we are only observing that work in CT underway in ELT may often stand in the shadow of other interests that garner greater attention, such as learner autonomy, translanguaging, materials development, or global issues.

Gann's (2016) survey of the actualization of critical thinking in several global English language textbooks raises another important issue in relation to CT and ELT coursebooks. Gann (2016) found that while numerous textbooks claim to encourage CT, most of this is implicit to the point of invisibility. His conclusion is that the application of CT in ELT materials seems to be insufficient in most cases.

What we are saying is that while efforts to increase the explicit integration of CT into ELT represents a good start, more work is needed. We must expand the reach of CT in our second-language classrooms. Critical thinking is a concept that allows for different emphases, so we need a greater variety of materials in order to meet the needs of students and teachers. This is one reason why, in other applied educational fields, we find a vast corpus of books from a period of well over 30 years that cover almost every aspect of teaching CT (Fisher, 2005; Holmes et al., 2015; Moore, 2013; Paul & Elder, 2002; e.g., Powers & Enright, 1987). Even more important, we need more books that will relate theory to practice, which is what this book does.

What we have discussed so far represents some common questions and misgivings that may be encountered when discussing the feasibility of CT in the second-language classroom. We have argued that research supports the idea that CT can be taught as a mental skill, and when applied in an informed manner, is appropriate for second-language learning environments. For the remainder of this part of the book, we shall shift attention to the aspects of CT that will feature prominently in Part II.

B. Focusing on Critical Thinking

A closer look at CT requires making choices. In this book we have chosen to focus on *informal logic*, which is an important facet of critical thinking. Informal logic is concerned with recognizing and constructing truthful, rationally defensible statements, listening for logical fallacies, and justifying better solutions to problems as well as alternative ways of framing an issue. Informal logic is exercised through a process of listening for main ideas, careful thinking about the implications, and asking questions in an interactive manner. We think that a focus on informal logic has more potential for second-language learning environments, because these sorts of collaborative activities complement what many of us already do in our classes. Let's study the features of informal logic in greater detail by first considering argumentation, followed by logical fallacies and problem-solving.

B.1 Argumentation

In CT pedagogy, an argument is different from the popular use of the word, where people shout at each other or write irrational statements to one another in anger on social media posts. Instead, an argument in CT consists of the following:

- **Conclusion:** Sometimes also called a proposition, a conclusion is the main message. Its purpose is to change your mind or move you to take certain actions. Conclusions are presented as a decision, prediction, judgment, problem, or as a solution.
- **Reasons:** These are also called premises, and are the ideas, empirical facts, interpretations of data, logical statements, observations, received knowledge, and expert opinions crafted together in support of the conclusion.
- **Assumptions:** These are beliefs based on experience, data, or earlier logical arguments believed to be firmly established. They are facts that a person assumes to be so basic that they are often not mentioned at all. The notion of *underlying assumptions* works well here, because they lie under the surface of daily discourse, but are fundamental support for the reasons and the conclusion.

Cavender and Kahane (2010, p. 6) explain that it is important to keep in mind that for an argument to be acceptable, or *cogent*, the assumptions must be *plausible*, that is, they must be based upon what we know or believe to be true through theorization and thought experiments. The reasons must be *valid* in that they should be relevant to the issue at hand and not twisted to only appear on the surface as supporting the conclusion. They should be as free as possible from bias, logical fallacies, and misinterpretation of any observations, evidence, or other data. The conclusion needs to be a *fair representation* of its accompanying parts (see Figure 1.1).

If the assumptions are faulty, then the reasons based on the assumptions may also be insufficient, and some of the support for the conclusion falls away. If enough of the assumptions and/or reasons are discovered to be weak, then, like

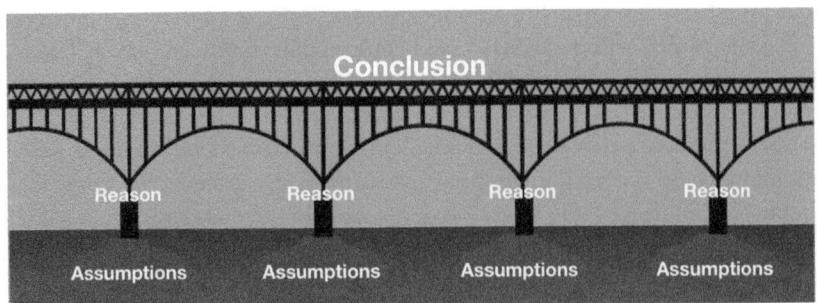

FIGURE 1.1 A Visual Metaphor for the Parts of an Argument

a bridge with major structural problems, the whole argument collapses. It is regarded as fallacious.

When we think about something, our ideas are scaffolded by an interlocking matrix of multiple arguments that we have accepted as facts, and we may encounter arguments from others throughout a regular day, often without even realizing it. Here is a simple example of how something as mundane as a decision to go shopping can be represented as an argument. Picture in your mind a husband and wife sitting at the breakfast table. It is a crisp November morning, and the sun is streaming through the window. The couple have finished eating. The wife is reading the newspaper. After reading an advertisement, she looks up and says, 'We should buy some apples at the farmers' market. There's an autumn harvest sale going on today.' Viewed critically, this could be expressed as:

- **Conclusion:** We should buy apples at the farmers' market today.
- **Reason:** There is an autumn harvest sale going on.
- **Assumptions:** Apples are fruit that ripen in the autumn. The farmers will be selling apples. The newspaper is a reliable source of information.

These are only a small sample of possible premises. More could be found through questioning, such as whether the person has been to the market in the past and has seen apples being sold there, thereby explaining the expectation of seeing apples again in future autumn markets. One could, of course, pick apart the assumptions by questioning the trustworthiness of the newspaper, or state that one's past experiences of apples at the farmers' market does not always guarantee that apples will be sold there this time, but the focus in critical thinking is upon *reasonable* and *plausible* statements based on the best available information.

Of course, most arguments are far more complex than this simple example and will have more reasons and assumptions. Quality, however, is more important than quantity. Consider another example with our married couple, who are considering the purchase of a pet for their young child. Sitting again at the breakfast table, the husband states, 'I think the best idea is to get a dog instead of a cat. I mean, dogs are friendlier and more faithful. They get along with children better and can protect them when we're not looking. And cats ... you know ... I mean, I heard from someone that cats can steal a baby's breath. Don't you think it's too risky?' In Figure 1.2, we can see a way of structuring this argument.

There are many more possible assumptions than these, and by laying them out visually, the assumptions do not always match up neatly with the reasons. Instead, they form the unseen basis for interconnecting reasons. Mapping it out in this way helps us to understand that assumptions, reasons, and conclusions within an argument need to be made more explicit before critical thinking can start. Discussions that continue without knowing these or proceed further without knowing if one has reasons that are supported by evidence or logical thought, reduce us to the

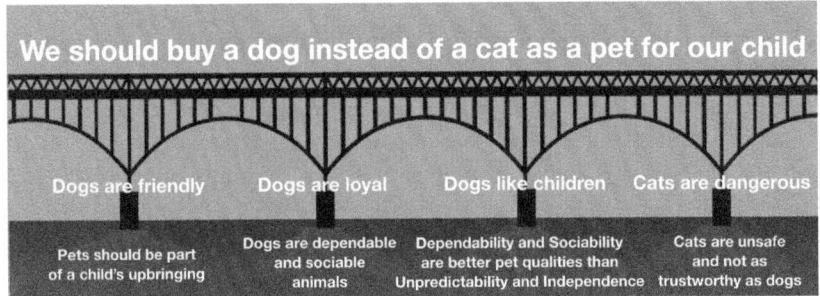

FIGURE 1.2 Argument Structure

world of competing opinions. The opinion of 'Let's get a dog because I like dogs,' is not the same as having an argument. In low-stakes situations, as many of us have learned from social media, there is little point in arguing about opinions because they either lack a logical, empirical basis for truth, or may be even devoid of reasons. An argument cannot be created without reasons. In times of crisis or greater personal risks, opinions may be very risky as solutions.

It is important to note that parts of an argument can be upfront and explicitly stated, but more often, aspects of an argument are left implicit. Sometimes this vagueness results from the speaker or writer not having clearly thought out their ideas. At other times, the ambiguity is intentional. Elder and Paul (2013, pp. 18–20) explain that it is up to us to ask questions that lead to greater clarity, relevance, coherence. To gain a broader perspective and uncover deeper meanings, we must probe carefully. For example, in clarifying a conclusion, you could ask the person speaking to you (or if you are reading something, ask yourself) to complete such phrases as, 'So, this means that ....,' 'Hence, it follows that ...,' 'Consequently, for these reasons ...,' or simply 'Therefore ....' Similarly, many of the reasons for the conclusion will be presented explicitly, making it a case of listening for or looking for markers such as 'because,' 'based on,' 'due to,' 'as a result of,' and so forth. Finding the implicit reasons, however, may require you to ask all manner of 'who, what, when, where, why, and how' questions. Even then, implicit reasons might end up presenting themselves as smaller, separate conclusions. Eventually, by asking more questions, you may be able to drill down to the level of assumptions. Figure 1.3 shows an example of how critical questioning helps to unpack the earlier argument about dogs being better than cats. Later in this book, there will be several activities that will help your learners ask the types of questions that can gauge the validity of the reasons, premises, and conclusions of an argument. Seeking clarity and consistency within the messages that we and our learners encounter throughout the day is not intended to short-circuit other forms of cognition (i.e., abstract, artistic, intuitive). It is intended to help us become more aware of unfounded opinions and logical fallacies.

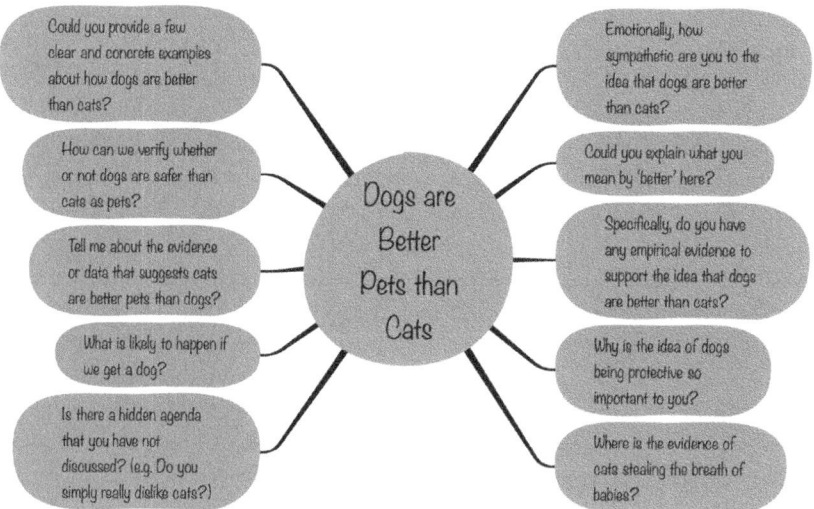

FIGURE 1.3 Sample Questions for Analyzing Arguments in Critical Thinking

B.2 Logical Fallacies

Earlier when mentioning the 'Either/Or Dilemma' and the 'Straw Man Argument,' we were referring to *logical fallacies*. As a basic rule of thumb, any argument (conclusions, reasons, and/or assumptions) that prevents you from getting closer to the truth, whether it is by directing your attention to another topic, putting forth groundless reasons, or basing one's reasons on questionable assumptions, is a logical fallacy. It is important to develop a sensitivity to logical fallacies in the arguments of others as well as ourselves. This is not always easy because, at face value at least, many logical fallacies seem convincing. Most people engage in fallacious thinking unintentionally, but when one consciously uses logical fallacies to distract the listener or reader from finding out if their reasons really support the conclusion, this should be treated as an attempt at deception. When someone refuses to change their mind even after a fallacy has been pointed out, this is looked upon as either pseudo-reasoning (Bowell & Kemp, 2015, p. 219) or (more uncharitably) as 'junk cognition' (Enfield, 2017). More positively, when a person unknowingly uses logical fallacies in their argument, this becomes a springboard for learning to think more critically. But it is also important to remember that many valid arguments can contain a logical fallacy here or there. You and your students should remember that finding a few fallacies in someone's argument does not necessarily mean that it is invalid. Listening only for fallacies is not really listening at all. Simply looking for fallacies with the hope of having a 'gotcha' moment, while ignoring the plausible strengths of what someone has stated, is also a form of fallacious thinking. Nevertheless, returning to our bridge metaphor (Figure 1.1), if, in the process of discussion, you find many fallacies, this will allow you to question the validity of an argument and to show where it falls apart.

Logical fallacies feature prominently in books written to improve one's informal logic (Almossawi, 2013; Bowell & Kemp, 2015; Cavender & Kahane, 2010; Davies & Barnett, 2015; Fisher, 2005; Hunter, 2009; Judge et al., 2009), and the Internet is full of sites dedicated to explaining and categorizing them. Even though there is a wealth of resources readily available for understanding logical fallacies, the subject can also be confusing, partly because the same fallacy might be widely referred to by three or four different names. Philosophers and logicians have tried to impose greater coherence on this profusion of fallacies by classifying them within different groupings (Schmidt, 1987). The simplest of these has been to divide fallacies into 'Formal Fallacies,' which were pointed out by the philosopher Aristotle and are based on logical errors in which the premises do not support the conclusion (Figure 1.4) and 'Informal Fallacies,' which focus on faults in relevance and ambiguity and omission of reasons supporting the conclusion. Even if one takes this approach, classifying the informal fallacies in reasoning has proven to be especially difficult, because many tend to overlap with each other.

With this in mind, taking as inspiration a synthesis of Cavender and Kahane (2010) and Browne and Keeley (2007), we have chosen to minimize the importance of names and classes of fallacies in order to focus more on how logical fallacies work to distort the conclusions, reasons, and assumptions used in constructing an argument. We classify logical fallacies within three areas:

- Those that further faulty conclusions,
- Those that engage in questionable reasoning, and
- Those that rely on mistaken assumptions (see Figure 1.1).

We believe that you and your students will find logical fallacies easier to work with by checking whether the conclusion has some structural or logical error, of if it has some sort of disconnection from the reasons. Looking for fallacies in the reasons becomes more manageable if you can find out where someone has tried to shift your attention away from relevant information toward something else. This can entail attacks on the person making the argument, using ambiguous

Premise 1:	All English teachers carry pens.
Premise 2:	All doctors carry pens.
False conclusion:	All doctors are English teachers.

FIGURE 1.4 Example of a Formal Fallacy

language, hiding key information that could refute the conclusion, or enflaming passions as a smokescreen. Helping your students to question assumptions helps them to find out if their connections with the reasons are convoluted, if they are based in factual evidence, or if they have a firm foundation on earlier arguments that are reasonable and sound.

Every classification system has its strengths and shortcomings, and ours in Table 1.1 is no exception. We hope you will find this helpful, as not only will it serve to structure later activities in this book but will also help you remember that the fallacies underpinning faulty conclusions, for example, might be used as a reasoning strategy, or as an assumption (especially if it is based on an earlier argument). There are other ways of classification that are equally valid, so long as they help you to identify faulty reasoning and suspicious conclusions.

The last point that needs mentioning is that there are literally hundreds of logical fallacies. For example, see the following:

i) When a person says or writes that since someone else has done something wrong, they cannot be blamed for doing the same thing (Tu quoque),
ii) When someone states ambiguously that 'a lot of people are saying' something without any proof (The Bandwagon Fallacy), or
iii) When someone uses the testimony of well-known people to support a subject in which they have little or no expertise (Appeal to Improper Authority),
iv) When someone uses a broad general rule to mistakenly conclude about a specific case (Sweeping Generalizations).

Table 1.1 presents other examples that your students are likely to encounter on social media and elsewhere. These will form the bulk of activities that you will find in Part II. The activities based on these and other fallacies will be fun for you and your students, and they will provide opportunities for them to start to spot fallacies outside of the classroom.

B.3 Externalizing Critical Thinking Through Problem-Solving

So far, we have learned that critical thinking operates within a heightened consciousness of the techniques used to persuade, deceive, and/or divert attention away from a problem or issue. It is learned through practice and expressed through successfully presenting cogent viewpoints that are structured, logical, and balanced through a cautious consideration of a certain subject or issue. Critical thinking should not be misconstrued as 'cynical thinking' – one in which all statements are treated as untrue until proven otherwise. Rather, to borrow a phrase from Cottrell (2005, p. 2), critical thinking entails the exercise of 'polite doubt' (p. 2) – the conscious choice to suspend one's judgment until thoroughly investigating what can be known about a certain topic or statement, all the while maintaining a humble appreciation of one's own limitations.

TABLE 1.1 Common Logical Fallacies

Faulty Conclusions	Questionable Reasons	Mistaken Assumptions
Non-Sequitur: The conclusion does not follow from the reasons. *Antonio got a high score on his TOEFL test. He must have many friends.*	**Ad Hominem:** Attacking a person rather than dealing with the facts of the argument. *Professor Smith states that global warming is real, but don't listen to him. He cheated on his wife last year.*	**Gambler's Fallacy:** Assuming that something is more likely or less likely to happen based on the frequency of past events. *I need to sell my stock. The market has been going up for three years. It's bound to crash soon.*
Probability Fallacy: Thinking something will happen because is it possible. *There might be a terrorist attack in that country. We shouldn't go because there is going to be one.*	**Red Herring:** Sidestepping the real topic and replacing it with something else. *I know that gun control laws are an issue, but the real problem is mental illness.*	**Logical Paradox:** Assuming an idea is valid without realizing that it is contradictory and illogical. *We all know that we really don't know anything.*
Begging the Question: Stating that conclusion is true because it is assumed to be true. *Therefore, it is important to use appropriate grammar because people need to write properly.*	**Circular Reasoning:** Like Begging the Question, Circular Reasoning contains the conclusion in the reason. *Aliens don't exist because there isn't any evidence of their existence. Any evidence of aliens is nonsense, because aliens don't exist.*	**Unwarranted Assumptions:** Some truth or condition is believed to exist when in fact it does not. *My mobile device is broken. I press the power button but nothing happens. (Actually, the device only needs recharging.)*
Post Hoc Fallacy: Concluding that an earlier unrelated event caused a second event to happen. *After my child got his immunization shots, he was diagnosed with autism. Immunizations cause autism.*	**Straw Man:** Creating an exaggerated version of someone's assertion and attacking this exaggerated version. *Prime Minister: I want to streamline immigration. Opposition: You won't be happy until you throw all foreigners out of our country.*	**Genetic Fallacy:** Assuming something is true (or false) because of its origin. *Those findings came out of England, so the research must be reliable.*

(*Continued*)

TABLE 1.1 Continued

Faulty Conclusions	Questionable Reasons	Mistaken Assumptions
Hasty Generalization: Coming to a conclusion based on insufficient proof. *Grandpa drank half a bottle of brandy every night until he died at the age of 100, so it is clear that brandy will help you live longer.*	**Either/Or:** Only two choices are given when many more exist. *You are either for us, or against us.*	**Common Belief Fallacy:** Because everyone believes something to be true, it must be true. *Over 60% of people in Iceland believe that elves exist. There must be something to it. I mean, they can't all be wrong.*
Single Cause Fallacy: The conclusion that there is only one cause for an event. *Ever since that new teacher was hired, the students have been getting better grades.*	**Stacking the Deck:** Presenting only the reasons and data that support the conclusion. *All of the data points to the conclusion that Grammar-Translation is infinitely superior to Task-Based Language Teaching.*	**Slippery Slope Fallacy:** The assumption that a small action will lead to a huge negative outcome. *If I help you, then I will have to help everyone. Then the whole system will break down and we will have rampant corruption everywhere.*
False Equivalence: Concluding that because some things share some characteristic, they are the same. *We all cry, we bleed, and we die. We're all the same, you and I.*	**Equivocation:** Using a key word in two different ways to insert ambiguity into an argument. *Critical thinking will help us to argue better, but should we be arguing? We need more peace in today's world.*	**Ignorance Fallacy:** Assuming something is true because it has not been proven false. *They have not offered proof that language course books are bad for language learners, so we can assume that course books are effective language learning tools.*
Sunk Cost: Deciding to continue with a plan of action even though continuing may not be the best thing to do. *Our government has invested so much into the Olympics that we must hold them no matter what happens next year with the current world crisis.*	**Appeal to Emotion:** Justifying reasons by using emotionally charged words or explanations rather than facts. *We need to protect our glorious country from those murderous foreigners. Think of the children!*	**Naturalistic Fallacy:** Assuming that is natural is good and unnatural is bad. *Letting students learn English on their own while abroad is much better than studying English in an artificial classroom environment.*

Yet, if your inward journey does not take you outward, something is wrong. In terms of CT, this means that if your study of the subject fails to find outward expression in a meaningful way, then learning has not taken place. In order to put CT into practice, educators usually begin by presenting principles and discussing specific aspects of critical thinking with students before providing application tasks (Bluedorn & Bluedorn, 2015; Bowell & Kemp, 2015; Browne & Keeley, 2007; Elder & Paul, 2013). These can take the form of short readings in class followed by discussion or writing tasks assigned as homework, where learners identify fallacies, refute weak argumentation, and suggest better alternatives. Written feedback from the teacher assesses the students' critical thinking and suggests ways to further internalize the concepts and principles being taught. This is usually followed by students then engaging in further discussion and problem-solving tasks where, based upon their training, they logically assess each other's proposed opinions and solutions, and collaborate in the development of critically informed ideas.

It needs to be pointed out though that providing students with the opportunity to engage in problem-solving tasks or writing responses to controversial issues is only that – an *opportunity*. People often make the mistake of equating CT with problem-solving or other cognitive functions such as creativity, intelligence, or scholastic performance (Bailin et al., 1999; Lau, 2011; Lipman, 2003, pp. 36-37; Tsui, 2002, p. 744). Empirical research finds that critical thinking – as it is measured on psychrometric tests – is not the same as intelligence, academic performance, problem-solving, compare/contrast thinking, and the like (Kurfiss, 1988; O'Hare & McGuinness, 2009; Stanovich & West, 2008). While studies indicate there to be a slight overlap with CT and other cognitive functions, critical thinking operates in ways that researchers are still struggling to delineate. It seems, though, that CT acts as a conscious set of cognitive tools that enhance creativity or scholarly pursuits. However, even though a student or scholar may be able to complete a certain task, and even if they are what some might characterize as 'book smart,' just because someone is creative and intelligent does not necessarily make them a good critical thinker. The converse can also be true: there are those assessed as being of average intelligence and as having received only limited educational opportunities but who can, with training, become superior critical thinkers.

What this means is that critical thinking is actualized *through* problem-solving; it is activated first through our interaction with and creation of language. It then involves training people to question assumptions and conclusions in a more purposeful manner. Critical thinkers learn how to sense when something is not right in an argument and persevere until they can gain a better understanding of the issue(s) at hand. Although this is not as important as being able to recognize something is, in fact, fallacious, it may then be possible to identify the logical fallacy at play.

C. Teaching Critical Thinking Skills to Second-Language Learners

Helping people to become better critical thinkers is the ultimate aim, but how do we go about teaching these skills to our second-language learners? Part of the answer can be found in the way that CT skills have been traditionally introduced to learners in the L1.

Table 1.2 shows a sample of three CT textbooks for L1 learners. There is a discernable overall pattern to the sequencing of instruction, starting with understanding the nature of an argument. This prepares the way for understanding how an argument can go awry (logical fallacies). Attention then shifts to assessing reasons and evidence. Some books then follow up by suggesting ways to respond in a more critically aware manner.

We have already seen in the previous section that when specifically addressing each skill, the typical approach tends to focus on receptive comprehension before moving on to production. Logical fallacies, the parts of an argument, and other aspects of CT are presented first as reading or listening assignments. After the parts of an argument, problems, or ambiguities are pointed out by the teacher, learners then respond, usually first individually in a writing task and then later in group discussions.

TABLE 1.2 Comparing the Sequencing of Critical Thinking Instruction

Browne and Keeley (2007)	*Norris and Ennis (1989)*	*Cavender and Kahane (2010)*
Identifying Issues and Conclusions	Focusing on a Question	–
Identifying Reasons	Analyzing Arguments	Reviewing Good and Bad Reasoning
Identifying Ambiguous Words and Phrases	Identifying Terms and Judging Definitions	Focusing on Language Use
Uncovering Assumptions	Identifying Assumptions and Assessing Value Judgments	–
Uncovering Contradictions	Asking and Answering questions that clarify and challenge	–
Discovering Logical Fallacies	–	Identifying Fallacious Reasoning
Assessing Evidence	Judging the Credibility of a Source	–
Presenting Alternative Causes and Conclusions	Assessing Deductions Evaluating Inductions	Deduction and Induction
Pointing out Data Omissions	Interacting with Others and Deciding on an Action	Writing Cogent and Persuasive Essays

However, we feel there are many ways of teaching CT that can be just as effective as any other – depending upon the skill of the teacher and the degree of student investment. For example, you could encourage your students to respond to a cleverly constructed logical fallacy in a warm-up activity and point out at the end how they had been tricked. For example:

> Start the class by telling the students a story. Tell them your friend is a famous doctor and she told you that if you hit your head gently three times with your pen or pencil it helps you to think more quickly or to remember the answer. Start to review last week's lesson, forget something, hit your head three times with your pen, and magically remember what you wanted to say. Repeat this throughout the lesson and pay attention to how many students gently hit their heads with their pens. At the end of the lesson, ask them why they hit their heads with their pens. When they answer, remind them not to believe everything that people tell them even when they support the claim with a 'so-called' authority.

This would allow for a transition to activities that unpack the fallacy through providing further examples and presenting ways they could respond in pair-work practice or whole-class activities. Students could then be faced with the fallacy again in the subsequent class (e.g., my friend the doctor said ...), but this time allowing them the opportunity to apply their new knowledge and respond accordingly. The element of surprise at the beginning might help learners to move forward through the training to learn how to protect themselves in the future. On the mean streets of public discourse, fallacious arguments and the need to construct sound responses take place quickly, so you could decide that it is necessary to slow down the process in the classroom in order for students to develop their awareness of the ways that people can push an argument off center, and then to practice response strategies. Or you could decide that since your learners are developing CT skills in the L2, it would be reasonable to start with reception and then move steadily toward production.

> Start the class by explaining the appeal to authority fallacy. Get students to list and rank different authorities for believability (e.g., teachers, doctors, politicians). Tell the story of your friend the doctor who told you that hitting your head gently with your pen helps you to think more quickly. Ask students how believable the statement is. Have them think of research or other examples in which people may appeal to authority.

If you take this approach, fallacies can be stripped of their rhetorical camouflage right away so that students can see them for what they are. This allows fallacies to be spotted more easily when encountered outside of the classroom, which, in turn, enables your learners to internalize ways to structure and develop an argument. By reading and listening first, then shifting toward writing and speaking, learners can be encouraged to think more deeply and formulate more thoughtful responses.

Regardless of the approach you take, it is vital that CT is addressed frequently, explicitly, and systematically. We have frequently stressed the point that for your students to become better critical thinkers, they will need plenty of classroom practice. The research we have cited so far strongly suggests that CT instruction has a more lasting effect when it is explicitly taught as a regular feature of our lessons. This means, for example, presenting different types of fallacies during class, and then having learners find examples outside of class in commercials, social media memes, or everyday interaction to develop their awareness of each particular fallacy. Level-appropriate essays may be assigned, where students can respond to controversial issues that have different viewpoints. This allows learners to study the conclusions, reasons, and assumptions of different positions, to assess the valid points of both sides, and to explain their own conclusions, together with their reasons, as well as the strengths and weaknesses of their arguments. Consciously and consistently helping your learners to develop their argumentation will help to give them the skills they need later for problem-solving tasks that require listening and spoken interaction.

In terms of making the teaching approach to CT systematic, our vision is of a cyclical process (Figure 1.5). This is also the way the next part of this book will be structured to help your learners toward developing their personal critical thinking skills.

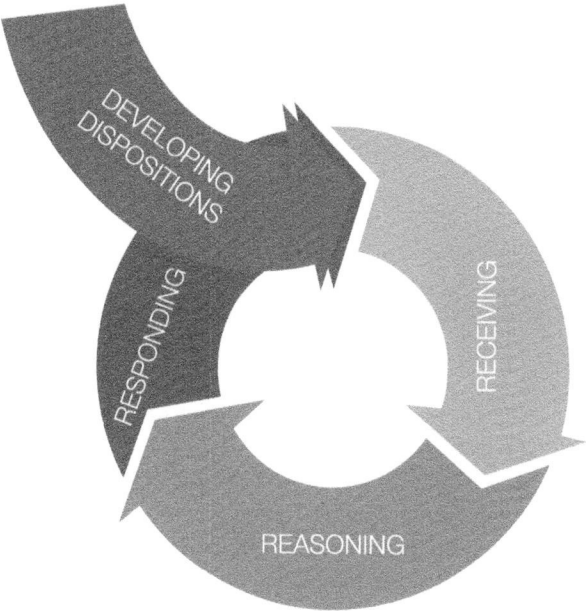

FIGURE 1.5 Systematic Process for the Teaching of Critical Thinking in This Volume

In the entry stage to the process of becoming better critical thinkers, teachers can introduce consciousness-raising activities aimed at helping students to develop a CT disposition; to become both aware and more critical of their own biases and preferred beliefs. Teachers can also help learners to look deeply into themselves and question the degree to which they know what they think they know is true to avoid becoming closed-minded and combative. Learners develop the mental stamina needed to search, question, and be cautious until they can find more evidence that will either support or refute what they believe.

Next, during the receiving stage, learners should study how to listen or read thoughtfully, not in order to respond or identify fallacies but to understand what the other is saying in a respectful and curious manner. The third stage, reasoning, involves thinking about the strengths of another person's argument, and pointing out logical fallacies, misused data, or other issues that may have been overlooked. After this, comes the response stage, which is not intended simply to refute or deconstruct the argument of the person they have thoughtfully listened to. Responding requires learners to be able first to restate the argument of their partners in a way that is fair and respectful, and makes their partners feel that they have been truly heard. It is only then that our learners can engage in activities and tasks aimed at pointing out any perceived weaknesses in their arguments which may lead to deeper thinking, improved questioning, and better conclusions. This process is then repeated by having learners reflect on the exercise so that they can reorient themselves to further developing their CT dispositions, to determining what they have learned, and to identifying gaps in their knowledge that require further study. After this, the process of critically assessing a similar or separate issue would begin again.

The activities in Part II are intended to complement this process cycle, but you should feel free to experiment and explore alternative ways of sequencing activities and tasks if you feel that doing so can make CT more accessible to your specific group of learners.

D. Implications

We have covered a lot of ground in this part of the book, and as we move toward practical applications, this is a good place to recap the main implications as they relate to CT in ELT.

- Critical thinkers are 'made, not born.' Critical thinking is a mental skill that can be taught. The dispositions for learning to think critically can be encouraged though non-threatening exercises of self-reflection.
- We do not have to teach everything about critical thinking to contribute to the development of our students' skills. Simply focusing on argument construction, logical fallacies, and logical thought organization can be enough.

But it may help if we can work in conjunction with other teachers so that our learners can get exposure to CT from multiple sources.
- Despite the objections of some, CT can be successfully taught in a second-language learning context, so long as it is taught explicitly in an orderly manner, and provided that our learners can get enough practice.
- CT can be a painful process of growth, but it does not do damage to a person. In addition, CT is neither the legacy nor the property of a certain group of people or culture. CT is for everyone who wishes to acquire it. This is especially true for today, because the predatory practices of corporations, governments, powerful social elites, often have a vested interest in keeping people in a state where they are easy to fool.
- By introducing CT in your language lessons, your students gain the skills needed to preserve not only their own intellectual well-being, but also to help create better societies later. We think this is a worthwhile goal, and one that we should not do on our own. If possible, we should work with like-minded colleagues. Find out what they are doing and complement it in your lessons.

Since you have read this far, you might as well continue now to the next part of this book – if only to find out why this statement is a logical fallacy! Let's now explore a wide selection of practical activities aimed at getting our learners to become better critical thinkers. Here we go. The best is yet to come!

PART II
From Implications to Application

Introduction

In Part I, we presented a cyclical process (Figure 1.5) that can be used as a means of giving our learners repeated exposure to critical thinking, helping them to develop their personal CT skills both inside and outside the classroom. By developing a CT disposition, learners can increase awareness of their own beliefs and biases and remain open to questioning themselves and seeking evidence to support or challenge what they know. While receiving information from others, learners can learn to listen respectfully, listen to understand, and show others that they are truly listening. In the reasoning stage, learners can begin to consider the strength and validity of the information they have received, watch out for fallacious or weak arguments, and come to new understandings. Then, when responding, learners can show they have understood the information they have heard before engaging in polite and meaningful discussions about any possible weaknesses within the argument. As learners reflect on activities, they are able to reorient themselves and add to their evolving CT dispositions.

Part I also outlines the three parts of an argument within CT pedagogy; an argument consists of a conclusion, reasons, and assumptions. Using the metaphor of a bridge (see again Figure 1.1), we illustrated that an argument must be well structured to support its conclusion. As learners become more disposed to critical thinking, they may become more adept at noticing arguments that are intentionally or unintentionally faulty and fallacious. Understanding logical fallacies can help learners to question the validity of the arguments they hear and draw attention to any weaknesses within them. It can also help them when structuring their own verbal or written arguments.

Thus, the first 20 activities in Part II, Section 1, aim to ready our learners on the journey of becoming better critical thinkers, to illustrate practically and orient our learners to the four-stage cyclical process of critical thinking that we have advocated (see Figure 1.5), and to provide our learners with a solid foundation for CT that can be made use of not only when tackling the remaining 73 activities of this book, but also in their everyday lives.

In Section 2, Activity 21 provides learners with an introduction to 25 common logical fallacies; it focuses on Tu quoque and the 24 logical fallacies that are outlined in Table 1.1. This activity can be used as a needs analysis. Educators can determine the fallacies that their learners are already familiar with, obtain information about the fallacies that their learners would like to learn more about, and involve their learners in negotiating their learning experience (Boon, 2011).

Activities 22 to 93 aim to help learners understand and be aware of the 24 common logical fallacies that are outlined in Table 1.1. These activities are divided into three sections; eight logical fallacies in which the arguer has a faulty conclusion, eight logical fallacies in which the arguer has questionable reasons, and eight logical fallacies in which the arguer has mistaken assumptions. For each logical fallacy, there are three activities that cater for different learner proficiency levels (Level 1, Level 2, Level 3):

1. The first activity is aimed at the elementary to pre-intermediate level (A2–B1)
2. The second activity is aimed at the intermediate to advanced level (B1–B2)
3. The third activity is aimed at the high-intermediate to advanced level (C1–C2)

Please note that the assigned levels are only an estimated guide, and you may find that you wish to use parts of an elementary to pre-intermediate activity with advanced students or you may wish to use an advanced activity with lower-level students and provide learners with additional L1 support when necessary.

The 93 activities are structured as follows:

1. A short introduction provides some background information about the activity.
2. The aim explains the specific aims and objectives of the activity.
3. The level provides a guide to the suitability of the language and material in relation to the proficiency level of your learners.
4. The time provides an estimate of how long it may take for learners to complete the activity.
5. Information about materials and preparation, if any, that you will need to prepare to facilitate the activity with your students is also provided.

6. A box describes the activity's language practice in relation to functions, skills, and area or a brief explanation and example of the logical fallacy being focused on.
7. The procedure offers a step-by-step guide of how to conduct each activity. It also includes optional activities that you may wish to include depending on your teaching context, available time, and preferences. Answers or suggested answers to specific tasks are also provided within the procedure section.
8. Each activity ends with the opportunity for learners to reflect on the activity and to share with their classmates what they have learned about CT.
9. The final section includes materials, such as sentences, worksheets, and cards that are needed for the activity.

And one final point to remember – each activity is a possible road map to help your learners acquire a greater knowledge of CT whilst improving their language proficiency. There are always many possible ways to reach this destination. With this in mind, please feel free to adapt the procedure and materials according to your particular teaching context and to the needs of your learners.

SECTION 1: THE CRITICAL THINKING CYCLE

A. Developing Dispositions

TABLE 2.1 Developing Dispositions: Activity Titles and Aims

Activity:	Title:	Aim:	Level:
Activity 1	Prove it!	To raise learner awareness about the need to check facts for reliability. To break the ice in the first class.	Elementary upwards
Activity 2	Supporting opinions: The 'why' game	To raise learner awareness about the need to support one's opinions. To have students consider more deeply and question their everyday opinions.	Elementary upwards
Activity 3	Challenging beliefs	To raise awareness of and challenge core beliefs.	Pre-intermediate upwards
Activity 4	Create a profile: Understanding biases	To be aware of and identify personal biases and assumptions.	Pre-intermediate upwards
Activity 5	Bias in news headlines	To be aware of and identify bias in news headlines.	Intermediate to Advanced

Activity 1: Prove It!

Introduction

This activity helps learners to explore what they know to be true about themselves and how they may support this with reliable evidence. It also encourages learners to not always believe other people's facts and statements without checking for reliable evidence.	
Aim	To raise learner awareness about the need to check facts for reliability; to break the ice in the first class
Level	Elementary upwards
Time	20–30 minutes
Materials	Sample sentences
Preparation	Prepare five sample sentences to model the activity to learners

Language Practice	
Functions	making statements, challenging
Skills	listening, speaking, writing
Language Areas	simple present, simple past

Procedure

1. Before class, prepare five true sentences about yourself and ways you can prove them (see sample sentences for examples).
2. Pre-teach the words, 'proof' and 'prove.' Explain to students the importance of checking facts to see if they are reliable and true.
3. Read out the five true sentences to the class about yourself. Encourage students to ask you to 'prove it!' after each sentence. Prove your sentences, e.g., show a photo of your sister from your smartphone.
4. [Option] Have students consider how reliable your proof is, e.g., a photo of your sister – 'Is it really your sister? You might be trying to trick us?'
5. Put students into groups of four. Have each student in the group write five sentences about themselves in a notebook or on a separate piece of paper.
6. Have each student take turns reading their sentences and the other three students in the group challenge the student to prove each fact (or to say how they could prove each fact).
7. [Option] Have students consider how reliable the proof is that is given to support each fact.
8. Have students work in new groups and repeat the game.
9. [Option] Have students repeat the game in new groups. Have them write new sentences about themselves, but one or two statements are false. Students in the group must guess which of the statements are false.
10. Have students reflect on the activity and discuss what they have learned about the need to check facts for their reliability.

Sample Sentences

Topic: Statements about myself

1. I was born in the United Kingdom.
2. I have an older sister.
3. I am a teacher at this school.
4. I can play the guitar.
5. I can name five countries beginning with the letter 'F.'

When students ask you to prove the facts about yourself, show them or tell them reliable evidence that supports each statement. For example: (1) Show your passport or nationality on your identity card, (2) Show a picture of your sister, (3) Show your photograph on the school website, (4) Show a YouTube video of you playing the guitar, (5) Demonstrate it – France, Finland, Fiji, Faroe Islands, Falkland Islands.

Activity 2: Supporting Opinions: The 'Why' Game

Introduction

This activity helps learners to examine their beliefs and opinions, to think more deeply about them, to question their everyday opinions, and to be able to support their beliefs and opinions with a variety of reasons.	
Aim	To raise learner awareness about the need to support one's opinions; to have students consider more deeply and question their everyday opinions
Level	Elementary upwards
Time	20–30 minutes
Materials	Dice or online die roller
Preparation	None required

Language Practice	
Functions	making statements, questioning, challenging
Skills	listening, speaking
Language Areas	simple present, 'Wh' questions, simple past

Procedure

1. Elicit many topics from students and write them on the board, e.g., Hobbies, Food, Sport, Music, Destinations, Seasons and so on.
2. Pre-teach the word 'opinion' – a belief that you have about someone or something; other people may disagree with you. Have students choose a

topic from the board and give an opinion about it – e.g., Food – Spicy food is the best.
3. Put students into pairs. Student 1 chooses a topic from the board for Student 2. Student 2 gives an opinion about the topic. Student 1 then rolls a die (alternatively Student 1 can use an online die roller). Student 1 reads out the number on the die and asks Student 2 the corresponding amount of 'why' questions. Student 2 must answer each question to support his or her opinion.

For example:

Student 1:	The topic is sport.
Student 2:	I think soccer is the most popular sport in the world.
Student 1 rolls a die.	Okay, the number on the die is 3. That's three questions. Why do you think soccer is the most popular sport in the world?
Student 2:	Well, many people watch it around the world.
Student 1:	Why do so many people watch it around the world?
Student 2:	Well, it's entertaining and fun to watch.
Student 1:	Why is it entertaining and fun to watch?
Student 2:	Well, there is a lot of action in the game. The ball is always moving.
Student 1:	Okay, thank you.

[Option] Model the game with the class before they begin. Have them roll a die and ask you questions about your opinions.

4. Students switch roles. Student 2 chooses a topic from the board. Student 1 gives an opinion about the topic. Student 2 rolls the die, reads out the number on the die and asks the corresponding amount of 'why' questions.
5. Have each pair repeat the game with new topics from the board.
6. [Option] Switch pairs and have them repeat the game.
7. [Option] Have students research facts to support their opinions and then share them with the class. For example – 'According to many sites on the Internet, soccer has around 4 billion fans worldwide.'
8. Have students reflect on the activity and discuss what they have learned about supporting opinions. For example:
   • Did the activity help you to understand more deeply about the opinions and beliefs that you hold?
   • Did you find it difficult to support some of your opinions?
   • Did any of your opinions change during the activity?
   • Where do our opinions come from? Are they always true?

Activity 3: Challenging Beliefs

Introduction

This activity again helps learners to be aware of, examine, and clarify their beliefs. It also encourages learners to give evidence to support what they believe in and to consider opposing beliefs that others may have and the reasons for holding these beliefs. By doing this, learners may be able to strengthen or challenge their beliefs and be more open-minded and tolerant of those with opposing beliefs.

Aim	To raise awareness of and challenge core beliefs
Level	Pre-intermediate upwards
Time	60–75 minutes
Materials	Copies of worksheets for all class members
Preparation	Prepare a list of three beliefs to give the class as examples. Be prepared to expand on these beliefs, give evidence to support them, and be familiar with the opposing beliefs

Language Practice	
Functions	making statements, supporting beliefs, questioning, challenging
Skills	listening, speaking, writing
Language Areas	simple present, questions, conditionals

Procedure

1. Pre-teach the words, 'beliefs' and 'believe.' Write on the board three things that you believe, e.g., 'I believe that it is important to study English, I believe that Brazil has a great soccer team, I believe in hard work.'
2. Hand students the worksheet (Task 1). Have them work individually to write down three of their beliefs.
3. Point students to the clarification questions on the worksheet (Task 2). Have students ask you to clarify your statements by asking 'What do you mean when you say that ...? Can you explain why you believe ...?'
4. Answer students' clarification questions, e.g., 'It can help you to communicate globally.'
5. Put students into pairs. Have students read out their three statements to one another and ask each other clarification questions to explain more about their beliefs.
6. Point students to the giving evidence questions on the worksheet (Task 3). Have students ask you to give three pieces of evidence to support your beliefs, e.g., 'About 1.2 billion people speak English around the world. That's 20% of the world's population.'
7. Have students research evidence to support their beliefs.
8. Have students work in new pairs. Have students read out their statements to one another and ask each other for evidence to support their beliefs.

9. Point students to the challenging beliefs questions on the worksheet (Task 4). Have students ask you the challenging questions. 'What is the opposite belief? Why would someone believe this?' E.g., 'It is not important to study English.' Some people may believe this if they do not plan to travel, do not need it for work, can use the Internet easily in their own language, or can watch foreign programs with subtitles.
10. For each of their three belief statements, have students ask each other the challenging belief questions.
11. Have students work individually to choose one of their three beliefs (Task 5). Students write down the opposite of their beliefs and think of reasons to support the belief. E.g., 'I don't believe in hard work – luck is very important to be successful – you can work hard and be unlucky.'
12. Put students in new pairs to argue for the opposite of what they believe in.
13. Have students reflect on the activity as a class and discuss what they have learned about their beliefs. Has the activity made their beliefs stronger or weaker?

WORKSHEET

1. **My beliefs**: Write down three things that you believe

1.
2.
3.

2. **Clarification questions**

   Student A: Share your beliefs with a partner.
   Student B: Listen to each belief statement. Ask Student A to clarify their beliefs.

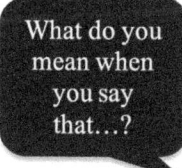

Switch roles

3. **Giving evidence questions**
    Student A: Repeat your belief statements.
    Student B: Listen to each belief statement. Ask Student A to give evidence to support their beliefs.

> What evidence do you have to support your belief?

> Do you have any more evidence to support your belief?

> How else can you support your belief?

Switch roles

4. **Challenging beliefs questions**
    Student A: Repeat your belief statements.
    Student B: Listen to each belief statement. Ask Student A questions to challenge each belief.

> What is the opposite belief?

> Why would someone believe this?

Switch roles

5. **Opposite beliefs**: Look again at Step 1. Choose one of your beliefs. Write the opposite belief. Think of three reasons to support this belief:

Opposite belief	
Reason 1	
Reason 2	
Reason 3	

Work with a new partner. Share the opposite beliefs. Give reasons to support the belief.

Activity 4: Create a Profile: Understanding Biases

Introduction

This activity helps learners to be aware of, examine, and understand the possible biases they may have, to question them, and become more critical of them.	
Aim	To be aware of and identify personal biases and assumptions
Level	Pre-intermediate upwards
Time	45–60 minutes
Materials	Worksheet
Preparation	Copies of the worksheet for each student. Think of five example occupations that people tend to have stereotypes about

Language Practice	
Functions	comparing and contrasting, discussing bias, researching
Skills	listening, speaking, writing
Language Areas	simple present, questions, simple past

Procedure

1. Make a list of five occupations on the board, e.g., English teacher, firefighter, scientist, nurse, politician.
2. Put students into groups of five and assign a different occupation from the board to each member of the group. E.g., in one group there should be a student assigned the occupation of English teacher, firefighter, scientist, nurse, politician.
3. Hand students the worksheet. Pre-teach the words 'gender,' 'race,' and 'marital status.' Instruct students to work individually to complete the profiles in Task 1 using their imagination. Have students include a drawing of their person in the space provided. [Option] – Have students search profile images on the Internet, choose an image they feel is appropriate, and copy and paste into the space provided on an electronic worksheet.
4. Have students present their profiles to their groups. [Option] – Have students interview each other – What's your person's name? What's your person's job? How old is your person? – and so on.
5. Put students into new groups according to occupations, e.g., an English teacher group, firefighter group, scientist group, nurse group, politician group. Have them share their profiles with the new group members. Have students take notes on each other's profiles (Task 2 – Worksheet).
6. Have groups discuss the similarities and differences of the profiles. E.g., 'Everybody had female for the gender of the nurse. That was the same.'

7. Introduce the idea of 'bias' to students. Give an example of bias e.g., 'This is the best class of the school.' Ask students to give reasons why the statement is biased.
8. Discuss the 'create a person/profile' activity as a whole class activity. Why did you make the choices you made in the create the person activity? What does this say about your hidden biases? What does this say about some of the stereotypes you may hold?
9. Have students research information on the Internet to challenge or confirm some of the assumptions that have been made in the activity. E.g., 'There are 63,000 male nurses in Japan. However, this is only 6% of the total number of nurses in Japan.'
10. Have students share their research with the class.

WORKSHEET

Create a person

Task 1: You are going to use your imagination to create a person. Complete the profile below and get ready to share your answers with your group:

Picture

(Draw a picture of your person)

Profile

Full name: _____

Job title: _____
(Write the job title given by your teacher)

Age: _____

Gender: _____

Race: _____

Marital status: _____

City of residence: _____

Share your person with your group.

Task 2: Listen to each person in your group share their profiles. Take notes on each profile:

Profile

Full name: _____

Age: _____

Gender: _____

Race: _____

Marital status: _____

City of residence: _____

Activity 5: Bias in News Headlines
Introduction

The final activity in learners developing a CT disposition focuses on being aware of and identifying biases that learners may encounter in everyday life that can affect their own biases and beliefs. In this activity, learners can be aware of biases in news headlines and how the news is presented to its consumers.	
Aim	To be aware of and identify bias in news headlines
Level	Intermediate to advanced
Time	45–60 minutes
Materials	Sample headlines
Preparation	Search the Internet for some current news headlines that you consider to be biased to introduce to students

Language Practice	
Functions	understanding headlines, discussing bias, researching
Skills	reading, analyzing, listening, speaking
Language Areas	newspaper headlines, biased language

Procedure

1. Pre-teach the word 'bias.' Give an example of bias e.g., 'This is the best class in the school.' Ask students to give reasons why the statement is biased.

2. Pre-teach the word 'headlines' and elicit from students the purpose of a headline in a news article. Accept different answers. Possible answers are:
   A) To get the reader's attention
   B) To give an immediate overview of the story
   C) To encourage a reader to keep reading the article
   D) To help to organize the article
3. Put students into pairs. Have them discuss how the news media can be biased. Have pairs share their answers with the class.
4. Put students in small groups. Have them read and analyze the three sets of headlines. Have them discuss the differences in each headline for Set A, B, and C. Have them discuss how each headline could bias the reader of the article. Possible answers are:

   Set A   In the first headline, the perpetrators are identified as gunmen. In the second headline, the perpetrators are identified as terrorists. In the third headline, the perpetrators have been omitted. One bias is in the lexical identification of perpetrator – a 'gunman' can be defined as a criminal who uses a gun to commit a criminal act; a 'terrorist' being a much stronger and 'loaded term' – a person who commits violent acts for extreme political or religious purposes. Another bias is through omission of the perpetrators in the third headline. This may lead the reader to focus on the victims and lead their thoughts away from the perpetrators.

   Set B   In the first headline, there may be no bias. The word 'female' added in the second headline is gender bias – if the scientist were 'male,' the writer would not include the word 'male.' The third headline is another example of gender bias in which the writer takes the focus away from the individual scientist to focus on her 'famous' movie star husband and thus reduce her achievement for the reader.

   Set C   In the first headline, the perpetrator is identified as a 'Texan' and the family is identified as 'immigrants.' There is racial bias as the family is labeled as immigrants and yet they may have been living in Texas much longer than the perpetrator. Also, the nature of the attack is implied rather than overtly stated for the reader, i.e., a racist attack. There is also racial bias in the second headline as the perpetrator is identified as a business owner, which may lead the reader to think of the perpetrator in a more favorable light. The third headline identifies the attack as 'racist' – which may bias the reader as it is a loaded word. The perpetrator has also been omitted from the headline. However, the description of the family is much more neutral in the third headline.

5. [Option] Divide the students into groups of three. Assign each set of headlines to different groups to read and analyze (Set A group, Set B group, and Set C group). After an appropriate period, put the students into new groups of three. Divide students so that there is a member from the Set A group, Set B group, and Set C group in each new group of three. Have A group students share their headlines and discussions with B group and C group students. Then, have B group students share their headlines and discussions. Finally, have C group students do the same.
6. Have groups share their ideas with the whole class about how the headlines are different and may bias a reader.
7. Introduce some current news headlines that may be biased. Have students discuss how they may bias a reader.
8. Put students into pairs. Have them search the Internet for current news headlines. Have them find an example of a biased headline and a neutral headline. Have them share their two headlines with another pair and explain why one headline is biased and the other headline is neutral.
9. [Option] Have students rewrite the biased headlines to make them more neutral.
10. For homework, have students keep a record of biased news headlines they read over the following week and share the headlines in the subsequent lesson.
11. Have students reflect on the activity and discuss what they have learned about bias in news headlines.

Notes
If one has lower-proficiency learners who are studying English in monolingual environments, students may wish to carry out Step 7 in their native language. They may then translate the headlines they have found on the Internet into English.

Sample Headlines

Set A

| Gunmen kill three in downtown shooting |
| Terrorists kill three in downtown shooting |
| Three people killed in downtown shooting |

Set B

| Scientist wins Nobel prize |
| Female scientist wins Nobel prize |
| Famous movie actor's wife wins Nobel prize |

Set C

Texas man arrested for attack on immigrant family
Business owner arrested for attack on immigrant family
Arrest made in racist family attack

B. Receiving

TABLE 2.2 Receiving: Activity Titles and Aims

Activity:	Title:	Aim:	Level:
Activity 6	Paying attention	To raise learner awareness about paying attention when listening. To raise learner awareness of how much we actually hear and remember when listening to others.	Elementary upwards
Activity 7	Show me you're listening: Body language	To raise learner awareness about positive body language to show that you are listening carefully to another speaker.	Elementary upwards
Activity 8	Show me you're listening II: Backchanneling	To raise learner awareness about positive non-verbal and verbal backchanneling techniques that can be used to show that you are listening carefully to another speaker.	Elementary upwards
Activity 9	Picture what I'm saying	To help learners focus on the message being communicated to them by another speaker.	Elementary upwards
Activity 10	Listen. Don't interrupt!	To raise learner awareness about listening respectfully to other speakers. To demonstrate the potential negative impacts of interrupting other speakers.	Pre-intermediate upwards

Activity 6: Paying Attention

Introduction

During the receiving stage, learners need to learn how to listen and pay attention to what the other person is saying. This activity raises awareness of how easy it is to become distracted, not pay attention, and only half listen to another speaker during the listening process.	
Aim	To raise learner awareness about paying attention when listening; to raise learner awareness of how much we hear and remember when listening to others
Level	Elementary upwards
Time	20–30 minutes
Materials	Chalkboard or whiteboard
Preparation	None

Language Practice	
Functions	giving directions, discussing listening habits
Skills	listening, speaking, writing
Language Areas	simple present, questions

Procedure

1. On the board, write the names of three or four restaurants in your town or city.
2. Explain to students the types of restaurants and have them choose one they would like to visit.
3. Give students directions from the nearest station to the restaurant of their choice. Make sure your directions have several steps to them. For example –

   'You come out of the station and turn right. Go down the escalators and walk straight. You'll see a pharmacy on your left. Turn right and cross over the road. You will see a store selling smartphones. Go past that store. Then, you will see a bank on your left. After the bank, turn left. Keep walking straight and you will come to a big supermarket. The restaurant is across from the supermarket on the second floor.'

4. Draw a stick figure on the board. Write the word 'Station' and have students repeat the directions of how to get to their chosen restaurant. Draw a map as students give you the directions. It is expected that students will only be able to give the first few directions.
5. [Option] Put students in pairs. Students make a list of their favorite restaurants. Students use the L1 and take turns to give directions from the station to the restaurant.

6. Ask students, 'When listening to the directions, how much did you really hear?' 'Did you hear 100%, 50%, 25% or less?' Once you have elicited replies ask students for reasons why.
7. Explain to students that a lot of research has shown that people tend to be poor listeners. We often listen to, comprehend, and remember about 25% of what someone has told us. Put students into pairs or groups to reflect on the 'directions' activity. Have them discuss what the activity has shown them about their own listening. Students may also discuss –

- Do you think you are a good or bad listener? Why?
- Do you find it easy to pay attention when someone is speaking to you?
- How can you become a better listener?

8. Have pairs or groups share their answers with the class.

Activity 7: Show Me You're Listening: Body Language

Introduction

This activity raises awareness of the importance of body language when listening to a speaker. Learners can determine and practice ways that show they are listening carefully to someone as they speak.	
Aim	To raise learner awareness about positive body language to show that you are listening carefully to another speaker
Level	Elementary upwards
Time	30–40 minutes
Materials	Worksheet
Preparation	Copies of the worksheet for each student

Language Practice	
Functions	analyzing, discussing, and observing body language
Skills	listening, speaking, writing, note-taking, observing
Language Areas	simple present, simple past

Procedure

1. Have students think about when they talk to family members and friends. Ask students for examples of when they know a family member or friend is really listening or not really listening to them. Write the examples on the board.
2. Hand students the worksheet. Have them look at the photographs and check whether they think the person is listening or not listening to the speaker. Have students write a reason why next to each photograph on the worksheet. [Option] Find suitable images on the Internet of positive and negative body language when listening and create your own worksheet.

3. Put students into pairs or groups. Have students share their answers together.
4. As a class, go through each photograph and discuss the answers. (Answers may vary):

   Photo 1: Not listening: multi-tasking and checking messages. The listener is not focusing 100% on the speaker.

   Photo 2: Listening: stroking chin may show thinking deeply about what the speaker is saying.

   Photo 3: Not listening: arms crossed and no eye contact with the speaker. The listener may be defensive or disagrees with the speaker and has stopped listening.

   Photo 4: Not listening: pulling ear and no eye contact with the speaker. The listener may be thinking about something else.

   Photo 5: Listening: leaning in shows that the speaker is interested in and trusts the speaker. They want to hear more about what the speaker is saying.

   Photo 6: Not listening: hand on cheek and no eye contact with the speaker. This shows the listener is thinking about something else and not listening to the speaker.

   Photo 7: Listening: reacting, surprised. The listener is listening to the speaker and showing appropriate reactions.

   Photo 8: Not listening: both hands to the face. The listener looks bored and wants to be somewhere else. This does not show the listener is listening to the speaker.

5. Put students into groups of three. Assign roles of 'Speaker,' 'Listener,' and 'Observer.' Have Speakers talk for two minutes about a chosen topic (e.g., what they did on the weekend). Have listeners listen to the speakers. Have observers observe the body language of the listeners. Observers take notes on what they see. After two minutes, have both observers and speakers in each group share their feedback about the listener and their body language. Observers can share what their notes and Speakers can talk about whether they felt listened to or not.
6. Repeat Step 5 and rotate the roles in each group. Repeat the activity again so that each student has had the opportunity to undertake the three roles of Speaker, Listener, and Observer.
7. Have students reflect on the activity and discuss what they have learned about positive and negative body language and the importance of showing that one is listening to someone when they are speaking.

50 From Implications to Application

8. For homework, have students take notes on positive and negative body language they experience or observe during the week. Students can report back their findings in the subsequent lesson.

WORKSHEET

Look at the photographs below. Do you think the listener is listening to the speaker or not? Check the box:

Photo 1:

Listening	
Not listening	

Why? _____
_____
_____

Photo 2:

Listening	
Not listening	

Why? _____
_____
_____

Photo 3:

Listening	
Not listening	

Why? _____
_____
_____

Photo 4:

Listening	
Not listening	

Why? _____
_____
_____
_____

Photo 5:

Listening	
Not listening	

Why? _____
_____
_____
_____

Photo 6:

Listening	
Not listening	

Why? _____
_____
_____
_____

Photo 7:

Listening	
Not listening	

Why? _____
_____
_____
_____

Photo 8:

Listening	
Not listening	

Why? _____
_____
_____

Activity 8: Show Me You're Listening II: Backchanneling

Introduction

This activity raises awareness of the importance of using short verbal (backchanneling) or non-verbal responses (gestures) when listening to a speaker. By using backchanneling and gestures, learners can show that they understand and are listening carefully to someone as they speak.

Aim	To raise learner awareness about positive non-verbal and verbal backchanneling techniques that can be used to show that you are listening carefully to another speaker
Level	Elementary upwards
Time	40–50 minutes
Materials	Worksheet
Preparation	Copies of the worksheet for each student

Language Practice	
Functions	using backchanneling gestures and expressions
Skills	listening, speaking, reading, writing
Language Areas	various

Procedure

1. Put students into pairs. Have each student choose a photograph to show from their smartphones. Have students select roles as 'Speakers' and 'Listeners.' Have each 'Speaker' explain their photograph to a 'Listener' for two minutes and then switch roles. If your students often use backchanneling gestures or expressions in your classroom, you may wish to prompt listeners not to react during Step 1 of the activity. Backchanneling is a short verbal or non-verbal response in a conversation which shows that the

listener is paying attention and understanding the talk (e.g., 'uh-huh' or nodding one's head).
2. [Option] If students are unable to use smartphones in the classroom, have students talk about a past vacation.
3. Hand students the worksheet (Task 1). Have them work individually to rate how well they felt their partner listened to them and why.
4. Elicit responses from the students.
5. Point students to the non-verbal and verbal backchanneling gestures or expressions that we use to show we are listening (Task 2). Have students add other examples they may know to the list.
6. Have students work in pairs or small groups to read the dialog (Task 3) and rewrite it with more backchanneling (gestures or expressions) from the listener.
7. Put pairs or small groups with another pair or small group to present their answers to each other.
8. [Option] Have pairs or small groups perform their dialogs in front of the class. Give feedback on backchanneling or encourage feedback from other groups.
9. Put students into new pairs and repeat Step 1. Have each student choose a photograph to show from their smartphones. Have each partner explain their photograph to each other for two minutes each. Encourage listeners to use the gestures and expressions they have learned in Task 2 of the worksheet.
10. Have students work individually to rate how well they felt their partner listened to them and why (Task 4).
11. Elicit responses from the students.
12. Have students reflect on the activity and discuss why it is important to show that one is listening to someone when they are speaking

---

WORKSHEET

1. How well do you feel the 'Listener' listened to you?

    - 5. Very well   ____
    - 4. Well   ____
    - 3. Okay   ____
    - 2. No so well ____
    - 1. Badly   ____

    Give reasons for your answer:

2. When we listen to people, we use gestures or expressions to show that we are listening closely to what we are saying. For example, you:

Gestures	Expressions
Nod your head	Say 'Uh-huh'
Smile	Say 'Mmm'
Frown	Say 'Right'

Can you add two more gestures or expressions to the list?

3. Read the following dialog. The speaker is showing the listener a photograph:

Speaker: This is a photograph of me in Jakarta, Indonesia. I went there in the summer of 2018. I stayed at a hotel in the center of the city. It was very close to many sightseeing spots. In fact, I was about ten minutes on foot from the National Monument which is called 'Monas.' This is very famous in Indonesia. In this photo, you can see the monument behind me. You can go up the monument and get a great view of Jakarta. There is an elevator that takes people up to the top. However, there's always a long line of people. So, on this day, I decided not to wait. It was very, very hot. It was about 32 degrees. I walked around the monument and then I got a coffee at a local coffee shop. The coffee shop had lovely air-conditioning!

Listener: I see!

Rewrite the dialog so that the 'Listener' reacts more to what the speaker is saying. For example:

Speaker: This is a photograph of me in Jakarta, Indonesia.

Listener: [Nods head]

Speaker: I stayed …

4. This time, how well do you feel the 'Listener' listened to you?

    5. Very well   ____
    4. Well   ____

3. Okay ____
2. No so well ____
1. Badly ____

Give reasons for your answer:

```
┌─────────────────────────────────────────────────────┐
│                                                     │
│                                                     │
│                                                     │
└─────────────────────────────────────────────────────┘
```

Activity 9: Picture What I'm Saying

Introduction

This activity helps learners to listen, pay attention to, and fully focus on the message being communicated to them by another speaker. By summarizing each message through pictures, it is a fun activity to check how well we listen and to reflect on reasons for misunderstandings.

Aim	To help learners focus on the message being communicated to them by another speaker
Level	Elementary upwards
Time	45–60 minutes
Materials	Question cards and paper
Preparation	None

Language Practice	
Functions	making questions, answering, supporting answers
Skills	listening, speaking, writing, drawing
Language Areas	simple present, questions

Procedure

1. Put students into groups of three to four. Give students eight to nine blank question cards (alternatively use some paper and have students fold and rip the paper into eight to nine pieces).
2. Write some example questions on the board related to favorites. For example:
   - What is your favorite day of the week?
   - What is your favorite city?
   - What is your favorite sport?

Have students work together to write eight to nine 'favorites' question on the question cards. They can use the questions from the board and come up with their own questions. Have students shuffle the cards and place them face down on the table.

3. Make sure each student has paper in front of them. They will need the paper to draw pictures on.
4. Student 1 picks up the first question card from the top of the pile. Student 1 answers the question and gives three reasons to support their answer. Student 1 speaks for one minute or so. Students 2, 3, and 4 listen carefully to what Speaker 1 is saying. After Student 1 has finished speaking, they draw a series of pictures on their paper to summarize what Student 1 has said. For example:

Student 1 says:

> 'Well, my favorite day of the week is Sunday and I have three reasons for this. The first is, I can sleep in. I don't have to get up early to go anywhere. I can sleep until 11am. The second reason is, I get to hang out with my friends. We often play soccer in the park. And the third reason is I don't have to catch a train to get to school.'

One student may draw:

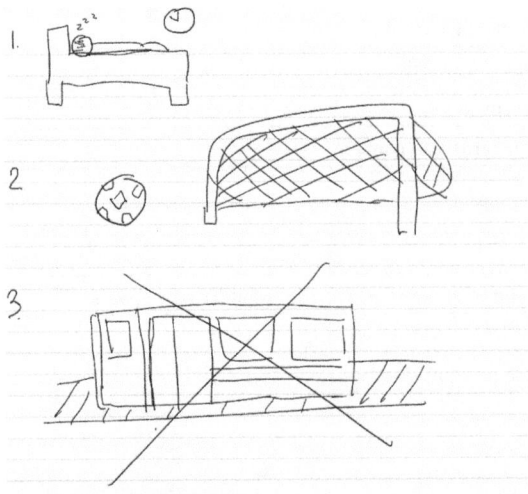

5. Students 2, 3, and 4 compare their pictures to check how well they listened to Student 1. For example:

    'Picture 1 is sleeping in until 11, right?'

6. Student 2 picks up the next question card from the pile and answers the question. This time, Students 1, 3, and 4 draw the pictures.

7. Repeat Steps 4 to 6 of the activity until all question cards have been answered or the time you have set for the activity elapses.
8. Have students reflect on the activity and discuss why it is important to focus on what a speaker is saying. They may also reflect on reasons for any listening mistakes or incomplete information that may have resulted from distractions or mind-wandering.

Activity 10: Listen. Don't Interrupt!

Introduction

This activity helps to raise awareness of ways to listen respectfully to another speaker. It demonstrates the potential negative impacts of interrupting other speakers when they are in the middle of speaking and gives learners the opportunity to consider when is appropriate for a listener to speak during the receiving stage and why.	
Aim	To raise learner awareness about listening respectfully to other speakers; to demonstrate the potential negative impacts of interrupting other speakers
Level	Pre-intermediate upwards
Time	45–60 minutes
Materials	Prompts cards – interruptions and example preference
Preparation	Print out cards for students

Language Practice	
Functions	giving preferences, agreeing, disagreeing, interrupting, describing feelings
Skills	listening, speaking
Language Areas	simple present

Procedure

1. Pre-teach the words 'preference' and 'prefer.' Elicit preference topics from students and write them on the board, e.g., coffee vs. tea, winter vs. summer, Seoul vs. Busan and so on.
2. Choose one topic from the board and provide an example to the students of giving a preference and supporting it with reasons. For example:

    'I prefer summer to winter because I don't like cold weather. I really feel the cold, and it makes me very unhappy. I much prefer to be warm. Also, in winter, it is too dark. It gets dark around 5pm. In summer, the days feel much longer, and I can do more with my time.

58 From Implications to Application

Finally, I live near the ocean, and I love swimming. In winter, the water is too cold for swimming. In summer, I can go swimming every day. That is why I prefer the summer.'

3. Put students into pairs. Have each student choose one topic from the board to talk about with their partner. Tell students they will need to give their preference and supporting reasons as per your example in Step 2. Give students some preparation time.
4. Assign each student a role – Student 1 or Student 2. Ask all Student 1s to stand up and leave the classroom for a short time. Explain you will call them back into the room when you are ready.
5. With Student 1s out of the room, distribute the prompt cards to Student 2s. Explain that their task is to interrupt Student 1 as many times as possible when they are in the middle of speaking. Explain that they can use the prompts to help them to interrupt.

For example:

Student 1: I prefer summer to winter because [I don't like cold weather.]
Student 2:   [Actually, I disagree with you.]

[Option] You may wish to model the activity with one student at the front of the classroom.

6. Call Student 1s back into the room. Have them explain their preferences to Student 2s. Each student 2 has already been secretly instructed to interrupt Student 1.
7. After a few minutes, stop the activity and explain to Student 1s that Student 2s have been instructed to interrupt them. Elicit from Student 1s how they felt about being interrupted many times by Student 2s. Their answers will probably be frustrated, angry, upset, irritated, not listened to and so on.
8. Have Student 2s turn over their prompt cards and look at the example preference you gave students in Step 2 of the activity. Have students work together to discuss when would be appropriate for the listener to speak and why. Answers may vary.
9. Elicit answers from pairs. One possible answer is:

'I prefer summer to winter because I don't like cold weather. I really feel the cold, and it makes me very unhappy. I much prefer to be warm.'

[Possible for listener to speak to backchannel (see Activity 8), agree, or ask a question]

'Also, in winter, it is too dark. It gets dark around 5pm. In summer, the days feel much longer, and I can do more with my time.'

[Possible for listener to speak to backchannel (see Activity 8), agree, or ask a question]

'Finally, I live near the ocean, and I love swimming. In winter, the water is too cold for swimming. In summer, I can go swimming every day. That is why I prefer the summer.'

[Possible for listener to speak to backchannel (see Activity 8), agree, ask a question, or disagree – 'Actually, I love the winter …']

10. Have Student 2s explain their preferences to Student 1s. Have Student 1s listen to Student 2s and practice responding at an appropriate time to avoid interrupting Speaker 2s.
11. Have Student 2s give feedback to Student 1s. Did they feel listened to or did Student 1 interrupt them? Elicit some answers from Student 2s.
12. Have students reflect on the activity and discuss the negative impact of interrupting other speakers.

Prompt Card

Front side:

Phrases for Interrupting:

- Yeah, me too. I think…
- Yes, I agree because…
- Actually, I disagree with you, I prefer…because…
- But don't you think…?
- Can I just say…?
- What I think is…

Reverse side:

I prefer summer to winter because I don't like cold weather. I really feel the cold, and it makes me very unhappy. I much prefer to be warm. Also, in winter, it is too dark. It gets dark around 5pm. In summer, the days feel much longer, and I can do more with my time. Finally, I live near the ocean and I love swimming. In winter, the water is too cold for swimming. In summer, I can go swimming every day. That is why I prefer the summer.

C. Reasoning

TABLE 2.3 Reasoning: Activity Titles and Aims

Activity:	Title:	Aim:	Level:
Activity 11	Categorize it!	To increase learners' skills of categorizing information by critically comparing and contrasting data and recognizing links between it.	Elementary upwards
Activity 12	Rank it!	To identify premises and conclusions in other people's arguments; to listen for and evaluate the strength of other people's arguments.	Elementary upwards
Activity 13	Persuade me!	To listen for and evaluate the strength of other people's arguments, to convince others with logic and reason.	Pre-intermediate upwards
Activity 14	Spot the problem!	To raise awareness about, listen for, and identify false, misleading, or unproven claims.	Elementary upwards
Activity 15	Sloppy sophistry	To raise learner consciousness about logical fallacies and sophistic strategies that can be used to distract and deceive.	Elementary upwards

Activity 11: Categorize It!

Introduction

During the reasoning stage, learners consider the strengths of another person's argument. This activity increases the ability of learners to think critically about incoming information, to compare and contrast it, recognize links between it, and categorize it.	
Aim	To increase learners' skills of categorizing information by critically comparing and contrasting data and recognizing links between it
Level	Elementary upwards
Time	30–60 minutes
Materials	Worksheet
Preparation	Copies of the worksheet for each student; a list of pertinent vocabulary and topics that will elicit data from students

Language Practice	
Functions	questioning, categorizing
Skills	listening, writing, speaking
Language Areas	'Wh' questions, simple present

Procedure

1. Think of five categories and three words related to each category from the textbook you are using or words that students have already learned in your lessons. On the board, write the 15 words randomly. Put students in groups to work out what the categories are. For example:

   - spring, summer, fall   (Seasons)
   - textbook, notebook, pen   (Things students bring to class)
   - red, green, blue   (Colors)
   - happy, sad, surprised   (Feelings)
   - Store clerk, bartender, tutor   (University student part-time jobs)
   - dancing, playing tennis, shopping (Free-time activities)

2. Give students a research topic question or have students come up with a research topic question to ask their classmates. For example: 'What do you do in your free time?'
3. Hand out copies of the worksheet.
4. Have students walk around the class and interview as many students as possible in the class. Have students listen carefully to and write the answers they hear in the correct section of the worksheet.
5. Put students into pairs to share the answers they have collected. Have students categorize the answers they received from their classmates. Students write their categories in the correct section of the worksheet. Example categories might be:

   - Free-time activities that people do alone
   - Free-time activities that people do together
   - Free-time activities that cost money
   - Free-time activities that cost no money
   - Free-time activities that people do outside
   - Free-time activities that people do inside

6. Have pairs share their categories with the class and provide supporting evidence for the categories. For example:

   - **Category:** Free-time activities that people do alone: **Supporting evidence:** Reading, video games, watching TV, listening to music

7. [Option] Have students include one piece of supporting evidence that does not fit into the category being shared and have their classmates listen for it. For example:

   - **Student A says:** 'Category: Free-time activities that people do alone: Supporting evidence: Reading, video games, watching TV, play volleyball.' **Student B says:** 'Playing volleyball doesn't fit. You need other people to play with, right?'

8. [Option] Repeat the activity with a new research question and new pairs for Step 6.
9. Have students reflect on the activity and discuss why categorizing information is an important skill for critical thinking.

WORKSHEET

Name:	
Research Question 1:	
Primary data:	Possible categories:
Research Question 2:	
Primary data:	Possible categories:
Research Question 3:	
Primary data:	Possible categories:

Activity 12: Rank It!

Introduction

	This activity again helps learners to think about the strengths of another person's argument. Learners are encouraged to identify reasons (premises) and conclusions in a speaker's argument. They then evaluate the strength of an argument by ranking reasons and explaining why they gave each reason a particular rank.
Aim	To identify premises and conclusions in other people's arguments; to listen for and evaluate the strength of other people's arguments
Level	Elementary upwards
Time	20–60 minutes
Materials	Worksheet
Preparation	Copies of worksheet for each student. Prepare a list of conclusions (see the examples in Step 5)

Language Practice	
Functions	giving reasons, ranking
Skills	speaking, listening, writing, speaking
Language Areas	simple past, 'because' clause (option – 'so' clause)

Procedure

1. Write on the board, 'I didn't do my homework.' Explain that you have given a conclusion but there are no reasons. Now, write on the board, 'I didn't do my homework because …' and elicit a list of five reasons from students. For example:

   - I didn't understand the question
   - I was sick and had to go to hospital
   - I had too much other homework to do
   - I forgot
   - My computer was broken

2. Put students into groups of three or four and give them a copy of the worksheet. Students work together to rank the list of reasons from the board from (5) strongest to (1) weakest. They write each reason from the board

on the worksheet next to the score they have decided upon. They also make notes on why they chose their rankings. For example:

Conclusion:	I didn't do my homework because ...	
Rank:	Reason:	Why this rank?
5 (Strongest)	I was sick and had to go to hospital	If true, good reason. It is difficult to work when you are really sick.
4	I had too much work other homework to do	Being busy is a good reason but manage time better.
3	I forgot	Not good but is a valid reason for not doing the homework.
2	I didn't understand the question	Ask a classmate for help or ask the teacher.
1 (Weakest)	My computer was broken	This is weak – write the homework on paper!

3. Divide the students into new groups so that one or two students from each group in Step 2 work with one or two students from a different group. Have students share their answers and reasons for choosing their rankings.
4. Give the new groups the opportunity to change their rankings if they so wish. Elicit the scores given for each of the five reasons on the board to show which the class members feel are the strongest and weakest reasons.
5. Repeat Steps 1 to 4 with new conclusions. For example:

    You shouldn't watch too much television because ...

    I want to eat the chocolate now and not save it until later because ...

    I believe that critical thinking is an important skill for me because ...

    [Country] is the best place to live because ...

    I will get an A in my next exam because ...

[Option 1] Switch the sentences around to introduce students to the 'so' pattern to introduce a result or conclusion. For example:

    ...., so you shouldn't watch too much television.

[Option 2] Instead of teacher-generated conclusions, elicit new conclusions from the students. When a student gives a new conclusion, write it on the board. Elicit a list of five reasons. Then, repeat Steps 1 to 5.

6. Have students reflect on the activity and discuss what they consider makes a strong or weak reason to support a conclusion in an argument.

WORKSHEET

Conclusion:		
Rank:	**Reason:**	**Why this rank?**
5 (Strongest)		
4		
3		
2		
1 (Weakest)		

*Print as many as you need for the activity

Activity 13: Persuade Me!

Introduction

In this activity, learners listen to each other's persuasive arguments and evaluate which they feel is the strongest and why.	
Aim	To listen for and evaluate the strength of other people's arguments; to convince others with logic and reason
Level	Pre-intermediate up
Time	30–60 minutes
Materials	Paper, timers
Preparation	None

Language Practice	
Functions	questioning, giving reasons
Skills	speaking, listening
Language Areas	questions with should, simple present

Procedure

1. Pre-teach the word, 'persuade.'
2. Write on the board, 'Should we X or Y?' Provide students with an example question and situation – 'Imagine you all live together, and you are deciding what pet to buy. One person asks, "Should we get a dog or a cat?"'
3. Elicit many other questions from students and write them on the board. For example:

   - Should we go to Thailand or Malaysia for our vacation?
   - Should we go out or stay home today?
   - Should we do a part-time job or focus on our studies?

4. Put students into groups of three or four. Give each group some paper and have them fold and rip the paper into six to eight smaller pieces. Have students give each member of the group two pieces of paper.
5. Have students either choose two questions from the board or think of their own questions and write them on their pieces of paper (one question per piece of paper).
6. Have students collect the questions together in their groups, shuffle the paper, and place them face down on the table.
7. Have students prepare a timer on one of their phones for two minutes (groups of three) or three minutes (groups of four).
8. Have Student 1 take the top question, turn it over, and read it for the other students in the group. Have Student 1 start the timer and say 'go.' Students 2, 3, (and 4) are given one minute each to answer the question and support their answers with reasons. For example:

   > 'We should buy a cat. You don't need to walk it and they are not as needy as dogs. Also, they don't chew your shoes.'

9. Student 1 listens carefully to each student's answers. At the end of the turn, Student 1 decides which student they felt had the stronger argument and why. For example –

   > 'I think [Student 2] had the best argument. Dogs do need walking. [Student 3] said dogs are too big. However, I think you can get small dogs.'

10. Student 2 takes the next turn, turns over the next question, and the activity continues with Students 3 (and 4) and 1 giving their answers and Student 2 deciding which student they felt had the stronger argument and why.
11. Repeat until all questions have been answered in turn. [Option] Collect all the questions from each group. Put students into new groups. Shuffle the questions and redistribute them to the new groups so that each group has two questions per member. Repeat Steps 6 to 11.
12. Have students reflect on the activity and discuss what they consider makes a strong or weak argument.

Activity 14: Spot the Problem!

Introduction

In this activity, learners are given more opportunity to improve their reasoning skills by listening to a series of statements to determine which are true, false, misleading, or need greater proof to support the claim.	
Aim	To raise awareness about, listen for, and identify false, misleading, or unproven claims
Level	Elementary upwards
Time	30–45 minutes
Materials	Sample sentences, worksheet
Preparation	Prepare a list of topics that are familiar to the class, such as local restaurants or businesses, famous people in the country, a recent news story of widespread interest, or you as the classroom teacher. Copies of worksheet for each group

Language Practice	
Functions	making statements, asking for clarification
Skills	writing, listening, speaking, dictation
Language Areas	various

Procedure

1. Write a topic on the board, for example, the pizza restaurant next to our school. Read the five sample sentences to students (see example sentences below) and have them listen to each sentence. Tell students that one of the sentences is either false, misleading, or has information that needs greater proof. Read the five sentences again for students.
2. Put students into small groups of three or four. Have students decide which sentence they feel is problematic and why. Have each group share their answers and reasons.
3. Provide a list of topics to each team or have them brainstorm their own topics from which they can choose.
4. Have each team choose one different topic.
5. Give a copy of the worksheet to each group. Have students write their topic on the worksheet and write three to five very positive sentences about the topic in the spaces provided on the worksheet. Tell students that one of the sentences must contain false information, misleading information, or information that needs greater proof.

6. Put two teams together. Each team reads their sentences to the other team. Students listen.
7. After the teams have read all their sentences, have teams pass their worksheets to each other. Teams must decide if the statements are okay, false, misleading, or need more proof by circling the word under each of the sentences.
8. Teams share their answers together and give reasons why they feel any statements to be false, misleading, or needing greater proof.
9. Repeat the activity with new teams.
10. Have students reflect on the activity and discuss what they have learned about false information, misleading information, or information that needs greater proof.

Sample Sentences

Topic: The pizza restaurant next to our school (five sentences)

1. The pizza restaurant is convenient for students because it is open 24 hours.
2. There are always many students in the restaurant, so it is a popular meeting place.
3. According to scientists, people who eat Mediterranean food live a long time, so pizza is good for our health.
4. The pizza restaurant next to our school has been there for 30 years, so it is a successful business.
5. When the school cafeterias are closed during holidays, the pizza restaurant is an important place for hungry students who live far from home.

Sentence 3 is misleading. Even though there are scientific studies of people in the Mediterranean who live a long time, we do not know if the pizza at the restaurant is like the food eaten in Italy, and we do not have any proof that pizza can be called a 'health food.'

Topic: The weather (three sentences)

1. It was sunny yesterday.
2. It is raining now.
3. It's going to rain tomorrow.

Sentence 3 needs more proof. As it stands, this statement is just an opinion and cannot be tested until the next day. If the person has seen many weather reports or is a meteorologist, there is greater weight to the claim

WORKSHEET

Team Topic 1: _____

Team 1: Write three to five sentences about your topic.
Team 2: Read Team 1's sentences and circle if the statement is okay, false, misleading, or needs proof.

1.

      Okay   **False**   **Misleading**   **Needs proof**

2.

      Okay   **False**   **Misleading**   **Needs proof**

3.

      Okay   **False**   **Misleading**   **Needs proof**

4.

      Okay   **False**   **Misleading**   **Needs proof**

5.

      Okay   **False**   **Misleading**   **Needs proof**

Team Topic 2: _____

Team 1: Write three to five sentences about your topic.
Team 2: Read Team 1's sentences and circle if the statement is okay, false, misleading, or needs proof.

1.

    Okay   **False**   **Misleading**   **Needs proof**

2.

    Okay   **False**   **Misleading**   **Needs proof**

3.

    Okay   **False**   **Misleading**   **Needs proof**

4.

    Okay   **False**   **Misleading**   **Needs proof**

5.

    Okay   **False**   **Misleading**   **Needs proof**

Activity 15: Sloppy Sophistry
Introduction

The final activity in the reasoning stage of the CT cyclical process helps learners to be aware of strategies that can be used to distract and deceive listeners when arguing.	
Aim	To raise learner consciousness about logical fallacies and sophistic strategies that can be used to distract and deceive
Level	Elementary upwards
Time	20–30 minutes
Materials	Sample dialog, classroom items, pictures of simple items such as household objects, or concrete nouns from the textbook you are using
Preparation	Make copies of dialog or create something similar to fit your students' interests and/or context

Language Practice	
Functions	questioning, argumentation, clarification
Skills	listening, speaking,
Language Areas	'Wh' questions, simple present

Procedure

1. Pre-teach the word, 'deny.'
2. Ask the class if they have ever seen a person on social media or on a television news program who denied something that was obviously true. Give an example (e.g., some people still argue that the world is flat).
3. Put the class into pairs (and with odd numbered classes, one group of three).
4. Tell the class that they will play a game where one partner will try to deny something which is obviously true.
5. Hand out the sample dialog (see below). Have students read through it in pairs.
6. Ask students to take an item from their bags that they could use for the activity. Alternatively, you could provide pairs with pictures of various objects. Possible objects could be:
   - Smartphone (That's not a smartphone. It's a computer …)
   - Planners (That's not a planner. It's a diary …)

- Chewing gum (That's not gum. It's plastic ...)
- Handkerchief (That's not a handkerchief. It's a takeaway container ...)
- Phone charger (That's not a phone charger. It's a weapon ...)

7. In each pair, have Student A give reasons why the object is what it is, while Student B gives reasons to refute the object and deny what Student A is saying.
8. Set a time limit. After the time is expired, have pairs switch roles and discuss a new item or picture.
9. Have students reflect on the activity and discuss which student won the argument and why. Have them think about the various strategies that they used to distract or deceive each other and share their answers with the class.

Sample Dialog

Student A:	(Holds up a textbook.) This is a textbook.
Student B:	That's not a textbook. It's a tree.
Student A:	What? A tree? Why's it a tree?
Student B:	Because it's made from wood.
Student A:	Many things are made from wood. Paper is made from wood. This is made of paper. But this is a textbook, not a tree.
Student B:	Maybe to you, it's a textbook. I have many friends who say it's not a textbook. They're very smart.
Student A:	Where are these friends? I don't see your friends. Are they experts on textbooks?
Student B:	Oh, I have many friends. They are experts, because they are smart.
Student A:	That is not proof. This is a textbook. It's not a tree.
Student B:	Ok. Maybe it *is* a book, but it's not a *textbook*.
Student A:	Look at it. Inside, it has units. It has homework tasks. It teaches us things.
Student B:	(Holds mobile device) Look. Here's a picture of my cat.
Student A:	Oh, that's a very pretty cat.
Student B:	Yes, she is. And my cat doesn't like textbooks. She sleeps only on regular books. She sleeps on this book. So, it's not a textbook.
Student A:	Your cat does not know the difference between books. Is she an expert?
Student B:	Do you have any proof that this is a textbook?
Student A:	(Holds up the textbook.) Look at the title. Here, it says 'textbook'!

D. Responding

TABLE 2.4 Responding: Activity Titles and Aims

Activity:	Title:	Aim:	Level:
Activity 16	Reflecting	To listen carefully and restate a speaker's argument to show understanding.	Elementary upwards
Activity 17	Summarize this	To identify and restate in one's own words a writer's argument.	Pre-intermediate upwards
Activity 18	Critical conversations	To engage in conversations that are critically aware, fair, and non-confrontational.	Intermediate to Advanced
Activity 19	Correct me!	To be able to correct mistakes and point out weak arguments made by others politely and diplomatically.	Pre-intermediate to High-intermediate
Activity 20	The critical thinking cycle: A review	To be able to review CT activities 1 to 19, to be able to be aware of the CT cycle, to put the CT cycle into practice by discussing CT.	Pre-intermediate upwards

Activity 16: Reflecting

Introduction

During the responding stage, learners can restate a speaker's argument to show that they have understood what the other person has said. This activity helps learners to practice listening carefully to their classmates and reflecting back on what they have listened to and understood.

Aim	To listen carefully and restate a speaker's argument to show understanding
Level	Elementary upwards
Time	45–60 minutes
Materials	Worksheet, timers
Preparation	Copies of the worksheet for each student

Language Practice	
Functions	giving opinions, rephrasing, paraphrasing, note-taking
Skills	speaking, listening, writing
Language Areas	questions, simple present

Procedure

1. Hand out the worksheet to students and have them complete the questions with their own ideas. It is a good idea for the teacher to write some examples on the board. For example:

    What do you think of the city?
    What do you think of K-pop?

What do you think of having lots of friends?
What do you think of the transportation system in this city?

2. Put students into pairs. Have each student show their list of questions to their partner to choose one question to answer.
3. Have students set a timer for one minute. [Option] Negotiate the time to speak with students or increase the time depending on the level of the learners.
4. Have students decide the roles of Speaker and Listener.
5. Each Speaker answers their chosen question and keeps talking until the time on the timer has elapsed. Each Listener listens carefully to the Speaker and takes notes on the worksheet.
6. Each Listener uses the notes to reflect back to the Speaker what they have just said. For example, 'So, what you think is....' Each Listener then checks if their restatement of the Speaker's argument is correct. For example, 'Is that correct?' The Speaker listens carefully to the Listener's reflection and confirms its accuracy or clarifies any misunderstandings that the Listener has made. [Option] For elementary listeners, they may choose to repeat the words of the Speaker rather than restate or paraphrase them.
7. Have pairs switch roles and repeat Steps 4 to 5.
8. Put students into new pairs and repeat Steps 2 to 6.
9. Have students reflect on the activity and discuss what they have learned about listening to each other and reflecting back their understanding to the speaker.

WORKSHEET

Questions:

1. What do you think of	?
2. What do you think of	?
3. What do you think of	?
4. What do you think of	?
5. What do you think of	?

Partner's name:		Partner's name:	
Question chosen:	1 2 3 4 5	**Question chosen:**	1 2 3 4 5
Notes:		**Notes:**	

Partner's name:		Partner's name:	
Question chosen:	1 2 3 4 5	Question chosen:	1 2 3 4 5
Notes:		Notes:	

Activity 17: Summarize This

Introduction

This activity helps learners to read and identify a writer's argument and respond by restating the argument in a fair and respectful way.	
Aim	To identify and restate in one's own words a writer's argument
Level	Pre-intermediate upwards
Time	45–60 minutes
Materials	Worksheet
Preparation	Worksheet for each student, a list of pertinent topics that will elicit different opinions.

Language Practice	
Functions	summarizing, paragraph writing
Skills	reading, speaking, listening, writing
Language Areas	various

Procedure

1. Put the students into small groups of three or four. Hand out the worksheet and have them read the example writing (Task 1).
2. Pre-teach the word 'summary' and have students consider which of the four responses is the best summary and why. Students can discuss in their groups and write their answers in the 'Comments' section on the worksheet.

3. Elicit answers from each group and focus on reasons why 1, 3, and 4 on the worksheet are not good summaries. Possible answers are:

   > Summary 1 is an opinion of the writer's argument and does not summarize the paragraph
   > Summary 2 is the best summary. It contains the main idea of the paragraph.
   > Summary 3 contains only part of the main idea of the paragraph. Also, the paragraph does not explicitly mention that the writer loves new technology, although this can probably be inferred.
   > Summary 4 does not include the main idea of the paragraph. It focuses on a supporting argument of the writer.

4. Elicit from students various topics they can write about and put them on the board. For example –

   - The best pet to have
   - A good place to go on a vacation
   - Paper books versus eBooks
   - The advantages or challenges of learning English

5. Have students choose a topic from the board and write a short paragraph about the topic on the worksheet (Task 3). Set a time limit in which to complete the writing task.
6. In their groups, have each student pass their worksheet to the student on their left. Each student will now have a paragraph that a student in their group has written.
7. Have students write a summary of the writing in the 'Summary 1' section of the worksheet. Set a time limit in which to complete the summary writing.
8. Each student passes their worksheet to the next student on their left. Have students read the original paragraph and write a summary of the writing in the 'Summary 2' section of the worksheet. Set a time limit in which to complete the summary writing.
9. If you have set up groups of four, each student passes their worksheet to the next student on their left. Have students read the original paragraph and write a summary of the writing in the 'Summary 3' section of the worksheet. Set a time limit in which to complete the summary writing.
10. Each student passes the worksheet back to the original writer of the paragraph. Have writers read the summaries and consider which they feel is the best and why.
11. In their groups, students share feedback to each other about the summaries. Students can comment on which summary they felt restated their original ideas in a fair and respectful way and made them feel truly understood.

12. [Option] Repeat Steps 5 to 11 with each student choosing a new topic from the board.
13. [Option 2] Repeat Steps 5 to 11 but do it as a spoken activity. Each student talks about their topic for a short time. Listeners take notes and then have a short time to reflect back to the speaker what they have said.
14. Have students reflect on the activity and discuss what they have learned about identifying and restating each other's arguments in a fair and respectful way.

WORKSHEET

1. **Read:**
   Now, thanks to new technology, the Internet, and social networking sites, it is very easy to keep in contact with the people we know. There was a time not so long ago when people used to have to pick up a telephone to talk to one another or write a letter and mail it. This was expensive and took too long. These days, we can just pick up our smartphones, click on our favorite social media site, type a message to family and friends, and push 'send.'

2. **Read the four responses below. Which is the best summary of the writer's argument and why?**

	Summaries:	Comments:
1	The writer is completely wrong. I hate using social media. It takes too long to communicate to people.	
2	The writer feels that we can communicate quickly and easily to other people these days by using social media.	
3	The writer really loves new technology.	
4	The writer feels that writing letters is not a good way to communicate to people.	

3. **Write:**

My paragraph:

Summary 1:

Summary 2:

Summary 3:

• Activity adapted from Boon (2020)

Activity 18: Critical Conversations

Introduction

In this activity, learners practice discussing current topics, listening carefully to each other's arguments, and responding critically but fairly and respectfully.	
Aim	To engage in conversations that are critically aware, fair, and non-confrontational
Level	Intermediate to Advanced
Time	45–60 minutes
Materials	Worksheet
Preparation	Copy of worksheet for each student, a list of pertinent topics that will elicit different opinions

Language Practice	
Functions	rephrasing, hedging, agreeing, disagreeing
Skills	listening, writing, speaking
Language Areas	simple present, simple past, 'that' as pronoun and relative pronoun

Procedure

1. Ask students to think back to a time when, either on TV, on social media, or among family and friends, there was an angry disagreement about a topic that had different 'sides' or viewpoints. Ask if anything constructive or positive came from those exchanges.
2. Tell students they will practice a more peaceful way to discuss difficult topics. Highlight the following rules:

    A) We should respect other people's opinions and not be rude or indifferent.
    B) We should listen carefully to each other.
    C) We should try and understand why people believe different things.
    D) We should be willing to change our minds about what we believe.

3. Provide a list of topics, either from the textbook that you are using, or from the national news of your country.
4. Hand out copies of the worksheet.
5. Guide students in rephrasing what another person has said. Highlight the point that rephrasing is not repeating word for word. For example: 'I think people shouldn't use their smartphones while walking down the street. They don't pay attention to where they are going, and it is dangerous.' Rephrase: 'So you believe people should put their smartphones away when

walking on the sidewalk because they look down at their screens rather than at their surroundings. It's not safe.'
6. Put students into pairs, and Student A to share their opinion on a chosen topic for about one minute. Student B listens and writes down what they have understood, and shows it to Student A. If Student A feels they have been understood, they can check the 'yes' box. If not, Student B must listen again to Student A, write what they say, and try again until Student A is satisfied that they have been heard accurately and fairly.
7. Have Student A and Student B switch roles.
8. Next, have each student fill out the rest of the worksheet, trying to highlight up to three points in which they agree with their partner, three things they have learned after listening, and three points in which they either disagree or are unsure, due to a lack of evidence, knowledge, or faulty logic.
9. Have students reflect on the activity and discuss what they have learned about listening to each other critically, but fairly.

Notes

1. If one has lower-proficiency learners who are studying English in monolingual environments, it is advised that the students carry out this activity at least once in their native language. This will help them to carry over their expertise as they practice in the target language.
2. This activity can also be expanded towards academic writing by providing learners with a short article and asking them to write a short essay that follows the same general structure as the worksheet.

WORKSHEET

Partner's name:	
Topic:	
What I understood is that you said:	*Partner's response* ☐ Yes ☐ No If no, why? Write what your partner tells you.

I agree with you that:
1.
2.
3.

After listening to you, I learned that:
1.
2.
3.

I also think that:
1.
2.
3.

Activity 19: Correct Me!

Introduction

In this activity, learners will be able to correct mistakes and point out weak arguments made by another speaker politely and diplomatically. In the CT cyclical process, if done well, this can help the other speaker to correct their mistakes, make stronger arguments, and may lead to deeper thinking and better conclusions.	
Aim	To be able to correct mistakes and point out weak arguments made by others politely and diplomatically
Level	Pre-intermediate to High-intermediate
Time	30–50 minutes
Materials	Worksheet
Preparation	Copies of the worksheet for each student

Language Practice	
Functions	Correcting politely
Skills	listening, speaking
Language Areas	various

Procedure

1. Greet students at the start of the lesson and make several mistakes in your greeting. For example, 'Hi everyone. As you know, today is Tuesday (it is Monday), so we will move to a new unit. Let's turn to page 81 (you did page 81 in the last lesson).' Check how students react to the mistakes.
2. If students do not react, explain that you made several mistakes in what you said. Tell students that when we hear mistakes or weak arguments, we may wish to point them out to the speaker, so that they can correct themselves or help them think more about their arguments. However, it is important to do this in a polite way.
3. Elicit from students ways they can politely correct your mistakes in Step 1. For example:

    'I'm sorry, but isn't it Monday today?'
    'You said page 81, right? Actually, I think we did this page last week.'

4. Put students into groups and give them a copy of the worksheet. Have them work through each situation in Task 1 and decide what Speaker B would say. For lower-level students, you may wish to provide four model answers and have learners match them to the correct situation.
5. Elicit answers from each group.
6. Have students work through each situation in Task 2 and decide what Speaker B would say. For lower-level students, you may wish to provide four model answers and have learners match them to the correct situation.
7. Elicit answers from each group.
8. Students think of their own situations in which they make mistakes or have weak arguments (Worksheet – Task 3).
9. Put students into pairs. Students work with a partner and role-play these situations. Speaker A makes a mistake or shares a weak argument and Speaker B corrects Speaker A politely or points out the weakness in the argument politely. After each turn, Speaker A gives feedback to Speaker B about their level of politeness (Worksheet – Task 3) and then switch roles.
10. [Option] Put students into new pairs to repeat Step 9.
11. Have students reflect on the activity and discuss what they have learned about responding to and politely pointing out mistakes to their partners.

WORKSHEET

Task 1. Correcting politely
You are Speaker B. What would you say?

1. Speaker A says: 'I visited the capital of Australia a few years ago. I had a great time in Sydney.' (The capital of Australia is Canberra)	2. Speaker A says: 'I checked with the teacher, and we need to write 200 words for the homework.' (The teacher said write 500 words)
Speaker B says:	**Speaker B says:**
3. Speaker A says: 'It's going to rain tomorrow, so I cancelled the picnic.' (The weather report says it will be sunny)	4. Speaker A says: 'I hear Greg is absent from school today. He's sick or something.' (You just had a class with Greg)
Speaker B says:	**Speaker B says:**

Model answers:

1. 'Australia? I've always wanted to visit there. Isn't the capital city Canberra though?'
2. 'Sorry, but if I'm not mistaken, the teacher told us to write 500 words.'
3. 'Really? The weather report I saw said it would be sunny tomorrow.'
4. 'Actually, he's not absent. I just had Italian with him.'

Task 2. Pointing out weak arguments politely

You are Speaker B. What would you say?

1. Speaker A says: 'We should use yellow for the words on the presentation slides. It's my favorite color.' (You think yellow is not a good color)	2. Speaker A says: 'I don't like critical thinking. I don't need to think this hard.' (You think critical thinking is important)
Speaker B says:	**Speaker B says:**
3. Speaker A says: 'My friend said the movie is bad, so I'm not going to watch it.' (You heard that the movie is good)	4. Speaker A says: 'Hiromi must love sushi because she's Japanese.' (You know Hiromi hates sushi)
Speaker B says:	**Speaker B says:**

Model answers:

1. 'Yellow is a nice color, but don't you think it will be too difficult to read?'
2. 'It is difficult, isn't it? However, there are many advantages to critical thinking. For example, …'
3. 'Really? I read quite a lot of positive reviews about it online. You might want to check them out.'
4. 'Sushi is a popular dish in Japan, isn't it? However, I don't think everyone in the country likes it. I know Hiromi is not a fan of sushi.'

Task 3: Write your own examples below:

Mistakes:	Weak arguments:
Say something that has a mistake. Your partner will correct you.	Say something that has a weak argument. Your partner will correct you.
1.	1.
2.	2.
3.	3.

After each turn, tell your partner how polite they were in correcting you:

5 – Very polite
4 – Polite
3 – Somewhat polite
2 – Not very polite
1 - Rude

Activity 20: The Critical Thinking Cycle: A Review

Introduction

The final activity of orienting learners to the four-stage CT cyclical process gives learners the opportunity to review the activities they have done in Steps 1 to 19. It also helps them be aware of the CT process. It is hoped as learners progress through the remaining activities of the book that they make use of the CT skills they have learned in sections A. Developing dispositions, B. Receiving, C. Reasoning, and D. Responding, during their interactions with others both in and outside of the classroom.	
Aim	To be able to review CT Activities 1 to 19; to be able to be aware of the CT cycle, to put the CT cycle into practice by discussing CT
Level	Pre-intermediate upwards

86 From Implications to Application

Time	20–30 minutes
Materials	Worksheet (See Preparation and Step 3)
Preparation	Make a match-up activity or worksheet that includes the activities you have done with your students (see Step 3)

Language Practice	
Functions	reviewing
Skills	listening, speaking, reading
Language Areas	various

Procedure

1. On the board, draw and simplify, explain, or translate the Critical Thinking Cycle from Part I of this book.

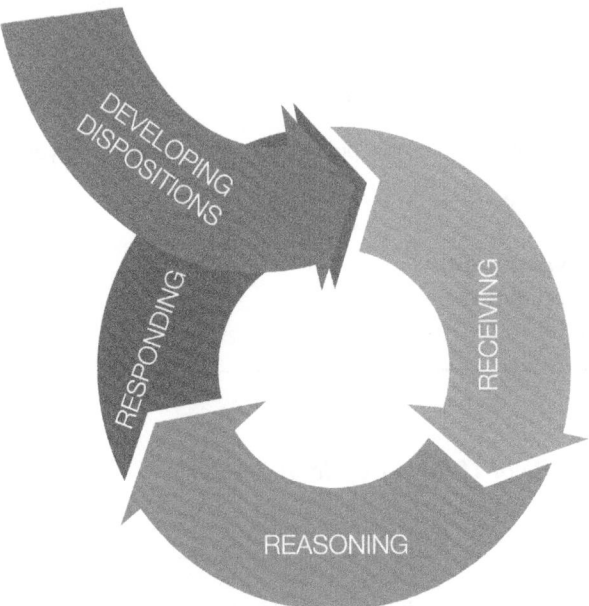

For example:

Developing dispositions = becoming aware and more critical of one's own beliefs and biases, to question oneself and what you think you know.

Receiving = becoming better and active listeners

Reasoning = thinking about and evaluating the strengths of other people's arguments, being aware of false or misleading information.

Responding = restating other people's arguments, making other people feel that they have been listened to and understood, politely pointing out weaknesses in their arguments which may help them to become more critical of their own beliefs and biases.

2. Review the CT activities you have done with your students so far from Activities 1 to 19.
3. Put students into groups. Have them match the activities they have done to each stage of the CT cycle. For example, you may have chosen to do the following eight activities with your students and prepare the following match-up activity for them:

Draw a line to match the CT activities we have done in class to the stages of the Critical Thinking Cycle:

Show me you're listening	**DEVELOPING DISPOSITIONS**
Rank it!	
Spot the problem!	**RECEIVING**
Prove it!	
Reflecting	**REASONING**
Challenging beliefs	
Critical conversations	**RESPONDING**
Paying attention	

4. Have groups discuss how they feel they can become better critical thinkers or how they feel the activities have helped them to become better critical thinkers. Students should take notes of their discussion.
5. Elicit answers from each group.
6. Have students reflect on the activity and how Step 4 may incorporate all stages of the Critical Thinking Cycle – each group member needs to develop CT dispositions, to listen to and receive information from one another, put forward and share ideas, reason by considering the strengths of each other's arguments, and respond fairly as well as respectfully to one another in order for them to engage successfully in the activity.

SECTION 2: LOGICAL FALLACIES

A. Logical Fallacies: An Introduction

TABLE 2.5 Logical Fallacies: An Introduction: Activity Titles and Aims

Activity:	Title:	Aim:
Activity 21	Introduction to logical fallacies	To introduce students to common logical fallacies. To determine which fallacies to focus on in a syllabus.

Activity 21: Introduction to Logical Fallacies

Introduction

This activity introduces students to 25 common logical fallacies. It focuses on Tu quoque (attacking a person's behavior instead of the argument) and the 24 fallacies outlined in Part I of this book (Table 1.1). The fallacies are divided into three sections; fallacies in which the arguer has a faulty conclusion, fallacies in which the arguer has questionable reasons, and fallacies in which the arguer has mistaken assumptions. The activity can be used by educators as a needs analysis, to check which fallacies learners are already familiar with and the fallacies that learners would like to learn more about. The activity also involves learners in negotiating course content and their learning experience. Please note that it is possible to divide this activity into three discrete lessons:

Lesson 1: Introduce students to logical fallacies, Tu quoque, and the eight fallacies related to faulty conclusions.

Lesson 2: Review Lesson 1 and introduce students to the eight fallacies related to questionable responses.

Lesson 3: Review Lesson 2 and introduce students to the eight fallacies related to mistaken assumptions.

These lessons could be taught consecutively or at different stages in a course.

Aim	To introduce students to common logical fallacies, to determine which fallacies to focus on in a syllabus
Level	Elementary* to Advanced
Time	60–180 minutes
Materials	Worksheet
Preparation	Copies of the worksheet for each student

Language Practice	
Functions	analyzing, negotiating
Skills	listening, speaking, reading
Language Areas	various

Procedure

1. Explain to students how logical fallacies are errors in reasoning that will undermine, damage, or challenge the strength of a person's argument. Being aware of fallacies can help us to determine problems in a person's argument and decide if their argument is believable, reasonable, or sound.
2. Provide students with an example on the board:

    Brother 1: Hey, you ate the last cookie. I wanted it.
    Brother 2: Yes, but you ate all the ice cream.

3. Put students into groups to discuss what the problem is in Brother 2's response. Elicit answers from each group.
4. Explain that Brother 2 tries to avoid blame for eating the cookie by stating that Brother 1 has done a similar bad action. The problem is it does not offer a solution to the problem of the last cookie being eaten or provide a reasonable defense. [Option] Explain that this fallacy is called Tu quoque and have students research or come up with other examples.
5. Have students work through the 24 fallacies on the worksheet (see Table 1.1 for the list of Common Logical Fallacies). For each example, students discuss what the problem or error in reasoning is. [Option] First, introduce students to the eight fallacies related to faulty conclusions (Task 1). Then, at a later stage in the course, repeat this activity and introduce students to the eight fallacies related to questionable responses (Task 2) and finally, introduce students to the eight fallacies related to mistaken assumptions (Task 3).
6. Elicit answers from each group. [Option] Teach students the names of each logical fallacy as you work through the answers and have them research or come up with other examples.
7. Negotiate with students which of the fallacies they would like to learn more about in the course. [Option] Pass scrap paper to students to write down five fallacies they would like to learn more about in the course. Collect the paper and write the results on the board.
8. Remind students to keep their worksheets safe as they can use them as a reference for each of the logical fallacies as they work through the subsequent activities in this book.

★Note

If one has elementary or lower proficiency learners who are studying English in monolingual environments, it is advised that students carry out this activity at least once in their native language. This will help students to familiarize themselves with the logical fallacies and carry this knowledge over as they practice in the target language.

WORKSHEET

Task 1: Look at the following eight arguments. What are the problems or errors in reasoning?

Faulty conclusions:

1. Antonio got a high score in his TOEFL test. He must have many friends.
2. There are many earthquakes in Japan. We shouldn't go there on vacation as there may be an earthquake when we are there.
3. This is the best pizza in the world as no one makes a better pizza than this restaurant.
4. My child went out playing in the snow. She got a cold. Playing in the snow causes people to catch colds.
5. My grandpa ate fries every day and lived to 103. French fries must help you live longer.
6. Ever since I got this new computer, I have been getting better scores in my tests.
7. They both need looking after. There's no difference in having a cat or a dog for a pet.
8. I'm bored of this book, but I've read the first two chapters so I may as well keep reading to the end.

Make notes and get ready to share your answers with the class.

Task 2: Look at the next eight arguments. What are the problems or errors in reasoning?

Questionable reasons:

9. This idea for recycling is just a bunch of crazy liberals trying to tell us what to do.
10. Daughter: I want an ice cream. Mother: Oh, look at that cute cat over there.
11. Everybody loves Susan, because she is so popular.
12. Father: You must be home from the party by 10pm. Son: Why do you hate me?
13. Either you get married, or you will spend the rest of your life alone.
14. Advert: This soda now has 10% less sugar. (Hint – the original had 49 grams of sugar.)
15. The sign said, 'fine if I return this book to the library late.' I am late to return the book, so it is fine, right?
16. If we let foreigners into the country, they will take all our jobs.

Make notes and get ready to share your answers with the class.

Task 3: Look at the final eight arguments. What are the problems or errors in reasoning?

Mistaken assumptions:

17. It has been really sunny for the last eight days. It's bound to rain tomorrow.
18. Sorry, I don't speak any English.
19. I pressed the power button, but my phone won't turn on. It must be broken.
20. My teacher told me that you cannot end sentences with prepositions, so it must be true.
21. Most of my classmates think the exam is on Tuesday, so it must be on Tuesday.
22. If you have one cookie now, you will want five cookies tomorrow, and ten cookies the next day. Before you know it, you will have gained weight.
23. Nobody has proved ghosts do not exist, so it makes sense to believe in them, right?
24. It's natural for humans to eat meat, so you should do it.

Make notes and get ready to share your answers with the class.

Answer key:

	Fallacy	Explanation:
1	**Non sequitur**	The conclusion (having many friends) does not follow from the reason (getting a high score in TOEFL).
2	**Probability**	The problem is thinking something will happen (an earthquake), because there is a possibility it will happen (Japan has many earthquakes).
3	**Begging the question**	The reason or premise in the argument (no one makes a better pizza) already assumes that the conclusion is true (the best pizza in the world).
4	**Post hoc**	Believing that an earlier unrelated event (playing in the snow) causes a second event to happen (catching a cold).
5	**Hasty generalization**	Coming to a conclusion (French fries help you to live longer) based on insufficient proof (my grandpa).

6	Single cause	Coming to a conclusion (better scores in my tests) that there is only one cause (a new computer) for an event.
7	False equivalence	Coming to a conclusion something is the same (no difference between cat or dog for a pet) because they share some similar characteristics (they both need looking after).
8	Sunk cost	Deciding to continue a plan of action (reading the book) even though continuing may not be the best thing to do (I'm bored of the book).
9	Ad hominem	Attacking someone (a bunch of crazy liberals) instead of dealing with the facts of the argument (ideas for recycling).
10	Red herring	Avoiding the real topic (ice cream) by replacing it with an unrelated topic (look at that cute cat).
11	Circular reasoning	Similar to begging the question, the reason or premise (she is popular) assumes what it is attempting to prove in the conclusion (everybody loves Susan).
12	Straw man	B makes an exaggerated version (You hate me) of A's assertion, claim, or statement (Be home by 10pm) so that it is easier to attack
13	Either/or	Only two choices are given in the reasoning (get married or be alone) when more choices exist.
14	Stacking the deck	Presenting only the reasons or data (10% less sugar) in the argument that support the conclusion (soda is now healthier – when in fact, there are still 39 grams of sugar in it).
15	Equivocation	Using a word (fine) in two different ways (penalty or something is okay) to make an argument more unclear or ambiguous.
16	Appeal to emotion	Using emotionally charged words or explanations (foreigners into the country) that appeal to emotions such as fear (take our jobs) rather than facts.

17	**Gambler's**	Assuming that something is likely or less likely to happen (rain) based on the frequency of past events (sunny for eight days).
18	**Logical paradox**	Assuming an idea is valid when it is contradictory (Sorry, I don't speak English – but you just did!)
19	**Unwarranted assumptions**	A truth or condition is believed to exist (phone is broken) when in fact it does not (it may just need charging).
20	**Genetic**	Assuming something is true (prepositions rule) because of its origin or source (my teacher). In other words, my teacher said it so it must be true.
21	**Common belief**	Because everyone believes something to be true (most of my classmates believe the exam is on Tuesday), it must be true (the exam is on Tuesday).
22	**Slippery slope**	The assumption that a small action (eating one cookie now) will lead to bigger negative actions (ten cookies – gaining weight).
23	**Ignorance**	Assuming something is true (ghosts) as no one has proved it to be false.
24	**Naturalistic**	Assuming that if something is natural (humans eating meat) it must be good, cannot be wrong, is acceptable (and so we ought to do it).

B. Logical Fallacies: Faulty Conclusions

Introduction

The next 24 activities introduce students to eight logical fallacies related to faulty conclusions (see Table 1.1, Part I). For each logical fallacy, there are three activities that cater for different learner proficiency levels:

Level 1	Elementary to pre-elementary (A2–B1)
Level 2	Intermediate to advanced (B1–B2)
Level 3	High-intermediate to advanced (C1–C2)

94 From Implications to Application

The level of each activity can be found easily in Table 2.6 by referring to the shading of each column (Level 1, Level 2, Level 3). Please note that levels are only an estimated guide. It may be possible to adapt a Level 3 activity for lower-level students. Similarly, there may be something of value for advanced students within a Level 1 activity. Remember, you do not need to do every activity with your students. Please feel free to pick and choose from the 24 activities and adapt them where necessary to your individual teaching context and learners.

TABLE 2.6 Logical Fallacies: Faulty Conclusions: Activity Titles and Aims

Activity/Fallacy:	Title:	Aim:
Activity 22 Non sequitur 1	Does it follow?	To identify whether statements logically follow one another or not. To identify non sequiturs.
Activity 23 Non sequitur 2	Spot the non sequitur	To identify non sequiturs in everyday conversation.
Activity 24 Non sequitur 3	Non sequiturs in politics	To be able to identify non sequiturs in politics and the news.
Activity 25 Probability 1	How probable?	To make statements about the future, to assess probability. To support probability with reasons and evidence.
Activity 26 Probability 2	Drawing the conclusion	To be aware of how the probability fallacy may be used in everyday conversation to draw someone to a particular invalid conclusion.
Activity 27 Probability 3	Fearmongering with probability	To be aware of how fearmongering may be used with the probability fallacy in everyday conversation.
Activity 28 Begging the question 1	Which is the better reason?	To learn about and be able to identify statements that beg the question.
Activity 29 Begging the question 2	Don't beg the question!	To identify statements that beg the question, to give better reasons to support arguments. To avoid begging the question when making arguments
Activity 30 Begging the question 3	To beg or raise the question	To clarify the usage of begging the question and raising the question. To identify arguments that beg the question
Activity 31 Post hoc 1	Does A cause B?	To learn about cause and effect. To determine whether event A is a cause of event B or not.
Activity 32 Post hoc 2	Fallacious connections	To understand the post hoc fallacy. To identify the post hoc fallacy in everyday conversations
Activity 33 Post hoc 3	Correlation not causation	To understand correlation and causation. To be aware that correlation does not imply causation. To determine likely causes for events.
Activity 34 Hasty generalization 1	All students in this class …	To use quantifiers to make statements about classmates. To be aware of generalizations made from insufficient proof or sample size. To correct generalizations.

(Continued)

TABLE 2.6 Continued

Activity/Fallacy:	Title:	Aim:
Activity 35 Hasty generalization 2	Don't be hasty!	To understand and identify hasty generalizations. To determine ways to avoid making hasty generalizations
Activity 36 Hasty generalization 3	Everyday generalizations	To understand and identify everyday hasty generalizations that people may make or experience. To share examples of everyday hasty generalizations. To discuss ways to avoid hasty generalizations.
Activity 37 Single cause 1	Many causes	To learn about cause and effect; to be aware of the single cause fallacy. To determine many causes for one effect.
Activity 38 Single cause 2	A popular restaurant	To talk about popular restaurants; to learn about and understand the single cause fallacy. To consider multiple causes for one event.
Activity 39 Single cause 3	How many causes?	To understand the single cause fallacy. To determine multiple causes for complex events.
Activity 40 False equivocation 1	Comparing apples to oranges	To identify similarities and differences between 2 items. To understand that items are seldom equal. To learn indirectly about false equivalence
Activity 41 False equivocation 2	They're not the same	To understand and be aware of false equivalences. To explain why the examples are indeed false equivalences. To research or come up with further false equivalence examples
Activity 42 False equivocation 3	Wronger than wrong	To understand and be aware of false equivalences. To understand Asimov's axiom of 'wronger than wrong.' To research further examples of false equivalences. To discuss ways to respond to false equivalences
Activity 43 Sunk cost 1	What should they do?	To make decisions on whether to stop or continue an activity based on future benefit or past investment. To understand the sunk cost fallacy
Activity 44 Sunk cost 2	Is it a good decision?	To understand the sunk cost fallacy. To examine how making decisions by focusing on past investments of money, time, or effort is often irrelevant.
Activity 45 Sunk cost 3	What would you do?	To ask hypothetical questions about decision-making behavior. To understand the sunk cost fallacy. To share experiences of the sunk cost fallacy

Non Sequitur

Activity 22: Does It Follow?

Introduction

	This activity helps learners to identify whether statements follow logically from one another or not. It also indirectly introduces the non sequitur logical fallacy to learners.
Aim	To identify whether statements logically follow one another or not; to identify non sequiturs
Level	Elementary to Pre-intermediate
Time	25–50 minutes
Materials	Paper, scissors
Preparation	Sentences for Step 1

Fallacy: Non Sequitur	
Definition	A statement that does not logically follow a previous statement; a conclusion that does not follow from the reasons.
Example	Antonio got a high score in his TOEFL test. He must have many friends.

Procedure

1. On the board, write example sentences or sentence stems and second sentences or clauses that are an appropriate level for your students. Make sure one second sentence, conclusion, or clause follows logically and the other does not follow logically. For example:

   John always gets a high score in his math test.
   A) He is good with words.
   B) He is good with numbers.

   I was late for class, so
   A) the teacher was angry with me.
   B) the teacher gave me A plus.

   I bought an umbrella because
   A) it was raining.
   B) it was Tuesday.

2. Elicit from students which of the two sentences follows logically and why.
3. [Option] At this stage, you may wish to explain to students what a non sequitur is (see definition and example) and that they are often used in everyday conversations and arguments for comedy, to confuse people, or because people have made a mistake in their argument.

From Implications to Application

4. Put students into groups of six. Have each student take one piece of paper and draw eight boxes on the paper. Have students number the boxes on the left '1' and the boxes on the right '2.' For example:

1.	2.
1.	2.
1.	2.
1.	2.

5. Ask students to write four statements in each of the boxes numbered with a '1.' Have students write a second sentence, a conclusion, or a clause that logically follows each of the four statements in each of the boxes numbered with a '2.' For example:

1. It is raining today, so	2. I should stay home.
1. The supermarket near the station has cheap food.	2. I should go shopping there.
1. As I have a date next week,	2. I should get a haircut.
1. The library has many good books and is a quiet place to study.	2. I should do my homework there.

[Option] You may wish to have students only work on the second sentences, conclusions, or clauses. In that case, prepare four statements that are an appropriate level for your class, dictate the sentences to your students, and have them write each sentence in the boxes on the left. They then complete the boxes on the right with their own ideas.

6. Have each student use scissors to cut their paper into eight separate strips (it may be possible to rip the paper if students do not have scissors). Each student places their statement 1s and 2s into separate piles. One student in the group collects all of the 1s, shuffles them, and places them face down on the left-hand side of the table (6 students in a group = 24 1s). Another student in the group collects all of the 2s, shuffles them, and places them face down on the right-hand side of the table (6 students in a group = 24 2s).

7. Student 1 in the group turns over one piece of paper from the left-hand side of the table and one piece of paper from the right-hand side of the table. The other students in the group ask, 'Does it follow?' If the answer is yes, Student 1 collects the two pieces of paper and takes another turn. If the answer is no, Student 1 returns the paper face down and Student 2 takes the next turn. For example:

| 1. It is raining today, so | 2. I should get a haircut. |

does not logically follow. It is a non sequitur.

| 1. It is raining today, so | 2. I should stay home. |

logically follows.

8. Repeat the game until all statements have been matched. Students count their paper. The winners are those with the most pieces of paper.
9. [Option] After the game is completed, have students put all 1s and 2s into two piles. Have them switch their sentences with a different group. Make sure all groups have new sentences and repeat the game.
10. Have students reflect on the activity and discuss what they have learned about identifying statements that do or do not logically follow one another.

Activity 23: Spot the Non Sequitur

Introduction

This activity introduces the non sequitur fallacy to learners. Learners analyze example sentences, identify a non sequitur in an everyday conversation, and then work together to make their own dialogs and listen out for each other's non sequiturs.	
Aim	To identify non sequiturs in everyday conversation
Level	Intermediate to Advanced
Time	30–40 minutes
Materials	Worksheet
Preparation	Copies of worksheets for every student. Example sentences for Step 2

Fallacy: Non Sequitur	
Definition	A statement that does not logically follow a previous statement; a conclusion that does not follow from the reasons.
Example	Antonio got a high score in his TOEFL test. He must have many friends.

Procedure

1. On the board, write 'Non Sequitur' and explain to students what a non sequitur is (see definition and example) and that they are often used in everyday conversations and arguments for comedy, to confuse people, or because people have made a mistake in their arguments.

2. Write four example sentences with non sequiturs. For example:
   A) He does a part-time job every evening. He must be rich.
   B) If I am Mexican, I am South American. I am not Mexican. Therefore, I am not South American.
   C) Susan is great at making pasta. She should be on the soccer team.
   D) Cakes are healthy, so I'm going to eat one every day.
3. Put students into pairs. Have them discuss why each sentence is an example of a non sequitur. Possible answers:
   A) The conclusion 'rich' does not follow the premise of doing a part-time job in the evening.
   B) It infers the opposite is true from the original statement and is an illogical argument.
   C) The conclusion of 'being on the soccer team' has no relation to being 'great at making pasta.'
   D] We know that cakes are high in calories and not considered a healthy food. As the statement is incorrect, it leads to a faulty conclusion of 'eating one every day.'

   Elicit answers from each pair.
4. Point students to the example dialog on the worksheet. Have pairs work together to identify the non sequitur. Elicit answers from pairs.

   Answer: <u>He's really tall, so he'll make a very good leader</u>.
5. Have pairs work together to write a dialog on a topic of their own choosing. Instruct pairs that the dialog must contain one non sequitur.
6. Have students join another pair to form a group of four. Have each pair perform their dialog for the other two students. Instruct listeners to listen carefully (Receive – Critical Thinking Cycle), decide what the non sequitur was in the dialog (Reason – Critical Thinking Cycle), and restate the argument by politely pointing out the non sequitur (Respond – Critical Thinking Cycle).
7. [Option 1] Pairs join a new pair to form a new group of four and repeat Step 6.
8. [Option 2] Call on pairs to perform their dialogs in front of the class. Class members listen, identify the non sequitur, and politely point it out to the speakers.
9. Have students reflect on the activity and discuss what they have learned about identifying non sequiturs in everyday conversations.

WORKSHEET

Underline the non sequitur in the following dialog:

A: Hey, how are you doing?
B: Pretty good, thanks. How about you?
A: Not so good actually.
B: Oh why? What's wrong?
A: Well, we have that project due next month, don't we?
B: Yes, my group met yesterday. We made some good progress.
A: Well, my group met yesterday, too, but we couldn't decide on a project leader.
B: Oh really? Well, Tim is in your group, isn't he?
A: Yes, he is. Why?
B: Choose him. He's really tall, so he'll make a very good leader.
A: Yes, and he's very good at communicating and making quick decisions.
B: Very important qualities of leadership. It looks like you have your leader then.

Work with a partner. Choose a topic and make your own dialog.
Include one non sequitur.

A:	
B:	
A:	
B:	
A:	
B:	
A:	
B:	
A:	
B:	
A:	
B:	

Get ready to perform your dialog. See if your classmates can spot your non sequitur!

Activity 24: Non Sequiturs in Politics

Introduction

The final activity focusing on the fallacy of non sequitur looks at examples from the world of politics and the news. Learners analyze examples and discuss why they are non sequiturs. Learners then search for more examples of non sequiturs in current news.	
Aim	To be able to identify non sequiturs in politics and the news
Level	High-intermediate to Advanced
Time	50–60 minutes
Materials	None
Preparation	Examples of non sequiturs in politics for Step 5

Fallacy: Non Sequitur	
Definition	A statement that does not logically follow a previous statement; a conclusion that does not follow from the reasons.
Example	Antonio got a high score in his TOEFL test. He must have many friends.

Procedure

1. Write on the board, 'Politics,' and elicit from students related words.
2. On the board, write 'Non Sequitur' and explain to students what a non sequitur is (see definition and example) and that they are often used in everyday conversations and arguments for comedy, to confuse people, or because people have made a mistake in their arguments.
3. Put students into groups of four and have them discuss non sequiturs in politics. Possible questions could be:

   A) What do you think of politics and politicians?
   B) Why do you think politicians may use non sequiturs?
   C) If you were a journalist and a politician replied with a non sequitur, what would you do?

4. Elicit answers from each group.
5. Put some examples on the board of non sequiturs that have been used in politics. Have groups discuss why each example is a non sequitur. Some examples are:

a	*Journalist:*	What is your policy on immigration?
	Politician:	I'm way ahead in the polls.
b	*Senator:*	If you consider defunding Obamacare, I'll consider voting for your missile strike on [Country].

c	Journalist:	[Name of politician] said they would rather you stop tweeting as it is a distraction.
	Politician:	[Name of politician] is a wonderful man.
d	Journalist:	I want to quote you when you said your dream was to have open borders. Is that your dream?
	Politician:	Well, I was talking about energy. But you are clearly quoting something that appeared in Wikileaks. Many private email accounts have been hacked by foreign countries and the information was then given to Wikileaks to put online.
e	Journalist:	Could you respond to the claims that you won't speak to governors unless they are favorable to you?
	Politician:	You're fake news!

6. Elicit answers from each group. Possible answers:

   A) The politician's response does not answer the question. The non sequitur is likely used to avoid answering the question and bring the focus back onto the politician's achievement of being ahead in the polls.
   B) The consequence of supporting the missile attack does not follow logically the condition of defunding medical care in the States. There is no relation between missile attacks and medical care.
   C) The politician's response does not follow from the statement made by the journalist. The journalist is indirectly requesting a response about the criticism from a colleague. The politician uses a non sequitur to avoid answering and deny the implicit request.
   D) The politician avoids answering the question by introducing a new topic of a country hacking private accounts (see red herring fallacy). It is a non sequitur as the politician gives the response as if it follows logically on from the premise of the quotation. However, the actions of Wikileaks are an independent issue to the quotation itself.
   E) Once again, to avoid answering the question, the politician responds with an ad hominem attack on the journalist (see ad hominem fallacy). The assertion that the journalist and their new organization lacks integrity can also be considered a non sequitur as the response does not follow the question being asked.

7. Have students work individually to search online for further examples of non sequiturs used in politics or the news. Students may wish to search for examples in English or in their mother tongue and then translate them into English. Have students in each group take turns to share their examples and explain why they are non sequiturs.

8. [Option] Have students work in new groups to share and explain their examples.

9. Have students reflect on the activity and discuss what they have learned about the use of non sequiturs in politics and the news.
10. Set students a homework task to pay attention to politics and news over the following week and to make a note of any non sequiturs they hear or read. Students can then report their findings in the next lesson.

Probability Fallacy

Activity 25: How Probable?

Introduction

This activity introduces learners to probability and supporting claims through reasons and evidence. It does not teach the probability fallacy directly, however it encourages students to think critically about claims made regarding probable future events.	
Aim	To make statements about the future, to assess probability, to support probability with reasons and evidence
Level	Elementary to Pre-intermediate
Time	50–60 minutes
Materials	None
Preparation	Sentences for Step 2

Fallacy: Probability	
Definition	A conclusion that something will definitely happen because it is possible.
Example	There are many earthquakes in Japan. We shouldn't go there on vacation as there may be an earthquake when we are there.

Procedure

1. Pre-teach the word 'Probable.' Write on the board

   100% – will definitely happen
   75% – will probably happen
   50% – may happen
   25% – will probably not happen
   0% – will definitely not happen

2. Give students three statements about the future. After each statement, ask students to write down how probable they think each statement is and why they think that. Example sentences could be:

- It is going to snow tomorrow.
- You will have a test at the end of this lesson.
- [Name of student] will become a famous rock star.

3. Designate five probability areas in the classroom (a 100% space, a 75% space, a 50% space, a 25% space, and a 0% space). Ask students to stand up.
4. Read out the first statement again. Have students move to the space in the classroom that matches how probable they think the statement is. E.g., if a student feels it will definitely snow tomorrow, they move to the 100% space.
5. Have students share the reasons for their answers together. (Please note: It is possible that one student will be standing alone in a probability area – that is okay! They can think again about their answer and get ready to share.)
6. Next, elicit from each area the reasons for their answers. You may also ask students what evidence would support their claim. For example:

Teacher: Okay, this group thinks it will definitely snow tomorrow. Why?
Students: We saw the weather report this morning. They said it will snow.
Teacher: Can you trust this weather report?
Students: Yes, they are usually right.
Teacher: Okay, so there is strong evidence that it will snow tomorrow.

7. Repeat Steps 4 to 6 with the second and third statements from Step 2.
8. Have students write three statements about the future on a piece of paper or in their notebooks.
9. Put students into groups of three or four. Student 1 in each group reads out their first statement and group members answer how probable they think the statement is and why. Then, student 2 reads out their first statement and so on.
10. [Option] Have students think about their reasons or evidence to support their claims. Have them evaluate whether they are strong or weak claims.
11. [Option] Put students into new groups and repeat Step 9.
12. Have students reflect on the activity and discuss what they have learned about the future, probability, and providing evidence to support claims that something will or will not happen.

Activity 26: Drawing the Conclusion

Introduction

This activity enables learners to be aware of how the probability fallacy may be used in everyday conversation to draw someone to a particular invalid conclusion about what will happen. Learners also consider the reasons why people may use the fallacy and the evidence that should be provided to support claims of probability.

Aim	To be aware of how the probability fallacy may be used in everyday conversation to draw someone to a particular invalid conclusion
Level	Intermediate to Advanced
Time	30–40 minutes
Materials	Worksheet
Preparation	Copies of worksheet for each student

Fallacy: Probability	
Definition	A conclusion that something will definitely happen because it is possible.
Example	There are many earthquakes in Japan. We shouldn't go there on vacation as there may be an earthquake when we are there.

Procedure

1. On the board, write:

    Probability fallacy:

    Reason: X is possible.
    Conclusion: X will happen or is likely to happen.

    Using this pattern, elicit examples from students. For example: Reason: snow is possible tomorrow. Conclusion: It will snow tomorrow. For each example, explain that the conclusion is not valid – just because something is possible does not mean it is likely to happen.

2. Write the following example conversation on the board:

    A) I'm going to buy a new computer soon.
    B) What type are you going to get?
    A) I'm going to get a(n) [Elicit brand of computer from students]
    B) Oh! A(n) [Brand]? It might break.

    Elicit from students what the implied conclusion by Speaker B is in the conversation; that is, Speaker B wants Speaker A to draw or come to the conclusion that the computer will break if Speaker A buys Brand X.

3. Explain that the conclusion is not valid as just because something might happen doesn't mean it is likely to happen.

4. Put students into groups of three or five. Have them discuss the reasons why Speaker B is using the probability fallacy to draw Speaker A to the conclusion.

Possible answers:

- Speaker B wants to lower Speaker A's expectations
- Speaker B wants Speaker A to be cautious and think more about the purchase
- Speaker B wants Speaker A to change their behavior
- Speaker B wants to create doubt in Speaker A
- Speaker B is jealous of Speaker A
- Speaker B has a negative opinion of or experience with Brand X
- Speaker B wants to destroy Speaker A's good mood

5. Elicit answers from groups.
6. Have students think about reasons Speaker B could give to increase the probability of the conclusion or strengthen its validity. For example – 'It might break. I heard from several news sources that Brand X is recalling its computer due to a defect.'
7. Give the worksheet to students and have them work through the task.
   Possible answers:

   1) Speaker B wants Speaker A to conclude that the taxi will not show up. It is not a valid conclusion. To strengthen the validity, Speaker B could provide evidence such as many negative customer reviews.
   2) Speaker B wants Speaker A to conclude it will rain. It is not a valid conclusion. Speaker B could show several weather reports to strengthen the validity of the conclusion.
   3) Speaker B wants Speaker A to conclude that Speaker B will win the lottery. It is not a valid conclusion. As winning the probability of winning the lottery is very low, one evidence to strengthen the validity is if the lottery had been drawn and Speaker B already had the results.
   4) Speaker B wants Speaker A to conclude that Speaker A will be robbed, attacked, or be in great danger. It is not a valid conclusion. Speaker B would need to show strong statistical evidence related to the number of attacks on travelers in each European country to strengthen the validity of the conclusion.
   5) Speaker B wants Speaker A to conclude the plane will crash. This is not a valid conclusion. Speaker B would need to show strong statistical evidence related to the poor safety record of the airline to strengthen the validity of the conclusion.

8. Elicit answers from each group.
9. [Option 1] Have students go back through Conversations 1 to 5 on the worksheet and consider why Speaker B may have used the probability fallacy to draw Speaker A to each conclusion.

10. [Option 2] Have students think of their own example conversations and share them in new groups. Group members need to determine the conclusion Speaker B wants Speaker A to draw in each example.
11. [Option 3] Have students think of and share real examples of when somebody used the probability fallacy with them and what action they took as a consequence.
12. Have students reflect on the activity and discuss what they have learned about the use of the probability fallacy to lead people to an invalid conclusion.

WORKSHEET

Read the following short conversations. For each conversation, think about:

- What conclusion does Speaker B want Speaker A to draw?
- Do you think it is a valid conclusion? Why or why not?
- What reasons or evidence could Speaker B give to increase the probability?

Conversation 1:

A: I booked a taxi to take me to the airport tomorrow.
B: It might not show up.

Answers:

Conversation 2:

A: Hey! Good to see. I'm looking forward to this walk around the river.
B: Oh, you didn't bring an umbrella?

Answers:

Conversation 3:

A: Why are you so happy today?
B: I bought a lottery ticket. I'm thinking about what I will buy with the winnings.

Answers:

Conversation 4:

A: I'm going to travel to Europe after I graduate.
B: Really? You might be robbed, attacked, or worse.

Answers:

Conversation 5:

A: I'm flying home tomorrow.
B: Which airline?
A: [Name of airline]
B: Oh! They have a really bad safety record.

Answers:

Activity 27: Fearmongering with Probability

Introduction

> Fearmongering is the action of making people afraid or alarmed about a particular issue. This final activity focusing on the probability fallacy introduces students to fearmongering techniques they may encounter in everyday conversation and how they can be used to manipulate people and lead them to invalid conclusions.

Aim	To be aware of how fearmongering may be used with the probability fallacy in everyday conversation
Level	High-intermediate to Advanced
Time	50–60 minutes
Materials	None
Preparation	Examples of fearmongering for Step 3

Fallacy: Probability	
Definition	A conclusion that something will definitely happen because it is possible.
Example	There are many earthquakes in Japan. We shouldn't go there on vacation as there may be an earthquake when we are there.

Procedure

1. On the board, write:

    'Probability fallacy:

    Reason: X is possible.

    Conclusion: X will happen or is likely to happen.'

    Using this pattern, elicit examples from students. For example: Reason: snow is possible tomorrow. Conclusion: It will snow tomorrow. For each example, explain that the conclusion is not valid – just because something is possible does not mean it is likely to happen.

2. Write on the board, 'Fearmongering' and elicit the meaning from students or explain it. For example, 'Fearmongering is the action of trying to make someone afraid of something when it is not necessary to do so.' Explain that people may use the probability fallacy for the purpose of fearmongering.

3. Give students an example of fearmongering. For example, write on the board:

    A: I check my bank online every day.
    B: Really? Online? Be careful! You might be hacked.

4. Ask students the following questions:

    A) What conclusion does Speaker B want Speaker A to draw?
    B) How probable do you think it is?
    C) Is the conclusion valid?
    D) Why do you think Speaker B said this? What is Speaker B's hidden agenda?

Possible answers:

A) Premise: You might be hacked online. Conclusion: You will be hacked online and lose your money
B) Answers will vary. One answer could be – It is slightly possible but not certain to happen.
C) No, it isn't. It doesn't follow that because something is possible, it will happen.
D) Answers will vary. Possible answers – Speaker B may wish to warn Speaker A indirectly about online banking; Speaker B may have fallen prey to an online scam; Speaker B may have seen a news article about hacking; Speaker B may want Speaker A to worry or feel bad and ruin Speaker A's day; Speaker B may a pessimistic person who wishes to force this pessimism on others.

5. Have students write a list of actions that they do every day or future actions they wish to do. For example:

- I take the train to school.
- I want to visit New York.
- I'm going to get an ice cream after this class.
- I always vote in the election by mail.
- I'm going to John's party on Saturday.

6. Put students into pairs. Assign them roles of Speaker A and Speaker B. Speaker A reads one of the actions from their list. Speaker B fearmongers by using a probability fallacy to draw a conclusion from Speaker A and change Speaker A's behavior. For example:

A) I take the train to school every day.
B) Really? There are so many people on the train in rush hour. You might catch a virus and get sick.
A) I want to go to New York next summer.
B) New York? There's a lot of crime in New York. You might get mugged or even worse, you might get shot.

7. Next, have pairs discuss the probability fallacies used by Speaker B:

- Were they convincing?
- Did they make you feel afraid?
- Did they make you think about changing your behavior?
- Why or why not?

8. Repeat Steps 6 and 7 but have pairs switch roles. Speaker B reads their actions and Speaker A fearmongers.
9. [Option 1] Put students into new pairs and repeat Steps 6 to 8.

10. [Option 2] Elicit example conversations from students and discuss them as a class.
11. [Option 3] Have students think of and share real examples of when somebody used the probability fallacy to fearmonger with them and what action(s) they took as a consequence.
12. Have students reflect on the activity and discuss what they have learned about the use of the probability fallacy to fearmonger and lead people to invalid conclusions.
13. Set students a homework task to pay attention to fearmongering in their everyday conversations and/or in the news over the following week and to make a note of any probability fallacies they read or hear. Students can then report their findings in the next lesson.

Begging the Question

Activity 28: Which Is the Better Reason?

Introduction

In this activity, learners read eight statements with two possible reasons and decide which is the better reason and why. Through discussions and answers, learners are able to identify statements that beg the question and learn to look out for this fallacy.	
Aim	To learn about and be able to identify statements that beg the question
Level	Elementary to Pre-intermediate
Time	30–40 minutes
Materials	Worksheet
Preparation	Copies of the worksheet for each student

Fallacy: Begging the Question	
Definition	The reason or premise in the argument already assumes that the conclusion is true.
Example	This is the best pizza in the world as no one makes a better pizza than this restaurant.

Procedure

1. On the left-hand side of the board write, 'We are going to work in groups today...' In the middle of the board, write because ...' Then, elicit reasons from students and write them on the right-hand side of the board. Have students choose which they feel is the best reason and why.

2. Put students into groups of three or four. Give each student a copy of the worksheet. Have students work through the eight statements on the worksheet to decide which reason (a or b) is the best and why.
3. Elicit answers from each group and ask them why they chose 'a' or 'b'.
4. Go through the answers and explain to students the begging the question fallacy. The answers are:

1	a	Reason b begs the question. It just restates or assumes the conclusion 'left the party.' It does not offer a reason.
2	b	Reason a begs the question. It just restates or assumes the conclusion 'everyone wants the new phone.' We can assume that everyone wants one because it is popular.
3	b	Reason a begs the question. It just restates or assumes the conclusion 'good for you.' It does not offer a reason.
4	a	Reason b begs the question. It just restates or assumes the conclusion 'dangerous' by offering the opposite. It does not offer a reason.
5	b	Reason a begs the question. It just restates or assumes the conclusion 'should study.' It does not offer a reason. It is a circular argument – I should study because I have to, therefore I should because I have to.
6	b	Reason a begs the question. It just restates or assumes the conclusion 'having friends is best.' It does not offer a reason.
7	b	Reason a begs the question. It just restates or assumes the conclusion 'women write better' by offering the opposite. It does not offer a reason.
8	a	Reason b begs the question. The claim 'UFOs are real' is supported by the premise, 'I have seen a UFO' which itself assumes that the claim 'UFOs are real' is true. Reason a is not a great reason either. However, it offers some evidence that many pilots have reported seeing UFOs in the sky. Remember, UFO does not necessarily imply alien but rather an unidentified flying object.

5. Have students work individually to write their own examples using 'because' with two subordinate clauses, one that begs the question and one that does not.
6. Put students in new groups and repeat Steps 2 and 3 with student examples.
7. Have students reflect on the activity and discuss what they have learned about identifying arguments that beg the question or already assume the conclusion is true.

WORKSHEET

Read the following eight statements.
For each one, decide which is the better reason, 'a' or 'b' and why.

1. Everyone left the party early because a) it was already midnight.
   b) they went home.

Circle 'a' or 'b' and give reasons for your choice:

2. Everyone wants the new smartphone because a) it is very popular.
   b) it is lighter.

Circle 'a' or 'b' and give reasons for your choice:

3. Fruit and vegetables are good for you because a) they are healthy.
   b) they have vitamins.

Circle 'a' or 'b' and give reasons for your choice:

4. Driving fast is dangerous because a) you can lose control of the car.
   b) it is not safe.

Circle 'a' or 'b' and give reasons for your choice:

5. I should study hard for the test because a) I have to study for it.
   b) I want a good grade.

Circle 'a' or 'b' and give reasons for your choice:

6. Having friends is the best because
   a) it is great to have good friends.
   b) they can teach you many things.

Circle 'a' or 'b' and give reasons for your choice:

7. Women write better because
   a) men do not write as well.
   b) they are better at grammar.

Circle 'a' or 'b' and give reasons for your choice:

8. UFOs are real because
   a) many pilots have seen them.
   b) I have seen a UFO.

Circle 'a' or 'b' and give reasons for your choice:

Activity 29: Don't Beg the Question!

Introduction

In this activity, learners analyze statements that beg the question and discuss giving better reasons to support arguments. It is hoped that by being aware of the fallacy, learners may avoid begging the question when making their own arguments.

Aim	To identify statements that beg the question, to give better reasons to support arguments, to avoid begging the question when making arguments
Level	Intermediate to Advanced
Time	40–50 minutes
Materials	Worksheet
Preparation	Copies of worksheet for each student

Fallacy: Begging the Question	
Definition	The reason or premise in the argument already assumes that the conclusion is true.
Example	This is the best pizza in the world as no one makes a better pizza than this restaurant.

Procedure

1. Write on the board:

    Young boy: Can I stay up late tonight?
    Parents: No, you can't. Go to bed.
    Young boy: Why?
    Parents: Because we said so.

    Elicit from students, what the conclusion is (Answer: Conclusion: The young boy cannot stay up late). Next, elicit from students what the reason is (Answer: Reason: The parents said the young boy cannot stay up late). Write on the board:

    Reason: The parents said the young boy cannot stay up late
    Conclusion: Therefore, the young boy cannot stay up late.

    Finally, elicit from students what the problem is with this argument (Answer: It begs the question. The reason does not support the conclusion. Instead, the reason restates or assumes that the conclusion is true.)

2. Explain the begging the question fallacy to students: The reason or premise in the argument already assumes that the conclusion is true.
3. Put students into groups of three or four. Have them discuss the example on the board. Ask them, 'Instead of begging the question, what better reason could be given by the parents?'
4. Elicit ideas from each group. Possible answers are:

    - You'll get overtired if you stay up late.
    - You have an important test tomorrow and sleep will help your concentration
    - Sleep will help you grow strong.
    - Sleep can help keep you strong.

5. Keep students in their groups and give a copy of the worksheet to everyone. Have students work through the five example conversations and think of better reasons that avoid begging the question.
6. Elicit answers from each group. [Option] Put students into new groups to share their answers together.

Possible answers:

1. Because we clean it on weekends.
2. Because many people have confirmed that this happened.
3. Because she has always helped me and given me advice.
4. Well, it's a question of faith. It is something you just have to believe. But many religions do teach that the soul is immortal.
5. They should absolutely be held responsible because they polluted the water.

7. [Option 1] Have students work individually to think of or find their own examples of begging the question online. Have them share their examples in groups and discuss how to change the examples so they are not begging the question.
8. [Option 2] Elicit a list of topics from students (e.g., money). In groups, have students make arguments about the topic and support them with reasons that do not beg the question (e.g., it's important to save money for the future, because when you retire you will have no salary).
9. [Option 3] Elicit a list of topics from students (e.g., money). Give students time to prepare two arguments – one that begs the question and one that does not. In groups, students share their arguments. Group members listen to the two arguments and say which one begs the question and which one does not (e.g., Student 1 - It's important to save money for the future, because money will be vital. Student 2 – That begs the question!)
10. [Option 4] Refer back to Activity 2: Supporting Opinions. Repeat the activity but focus on students avoiding begging the question.
11. Have students reflect on the activity and discuss what they have learned about how to avoid begging the question.

WORKSHEET

Read the following five short conversations. Change the last line of each conversation, so that it does not beg the question.

Conversation 1:

Caretaker: Sorry, nobody is allowed to use this room on weekends.
Visitor: Why not?
Caretaker: Because people are allowed to use the room on weekdays.

Your idea:

> Caretaker:

Conversation 2:

Friend A: This book is telling the truth.
Friend B: How do you know?
Friend A: Because it says so on the first page.

Your idea:

Friend A:

Conversation 3:

Friend A: My mother is my hero.
Friend B: Why?
Friend A: Because she has always acted heroically in her life.

Your idea:

Friend A:

Conversation 4:

Friend A: The soul is immortal.
Friend B: How do you know?
Friend A: Because it lives forever.

Your idea:

Friend A:

Conversation 5:

Reporter: Do you think the company should be held responsible for what they did?
Politician: They should absolutely be held responsible because they are responsible.

Your idea:

Politician:

Activity 30: To Beg or Raise the Question

Introduction

This final activity focusing on the begging the question fallacy helps learners to clarify the differences in the usage of the terms begging the question and raising the question and to identify arguments that either beg or raise the question.

Aim	To clarify the usage of begging the question and raising the question, to identify arguments that beg the question
Level	High-intermediate to Advanced
Time	30–40 minutes
Materials	Worksheet
Preparation	Copies of worksheet for each student

Fallacy: Begging the Question	
Definition	The reason or premise in the argument already assumes that the conclusion is true.
Example	This is the best pizza in the world as no one makes a better pizza than this restaurant.

Procedure

1. Elicit from students the name of a person that is always in the news. Divide the board into three sections, left, middle, and right. On the left-hand side of the board, write:

    A: Why is [NAME] always in the news?
    B: I guess they want more people to watch the news program.
    A: Yeah – which _____ the question. Why are people so interested in [NAME]?

   In the middle of the board, write two words:

   begs
   raises

   On the right-hand side of the board, write:

    A: Why is [NAME] always in the news?
    B: Well, they're very newsworthy because they're everywhere. They're in magazines, on the news, in commercials. You name it.
    A: That _____ the question. They're newsworthy because they're newsworthy?

2. Put students into groups of three or four. Have them look at the example conversations on the board. Ask students to match the words in the middle to the spaces in each of the conversations and give reasons for their choices.
3. Give the answers to students. Explain that the left-hand conversation is 'raises.' This means to invite or elicit a further question in response. The question in this example is why people are so interested in finding out information about the famous person. Explain that the right-hand conversation is 'begs.' The premise in the argument that the famous person is everywhere assumes that the conclusion of being newsworthy is true. The argument is the person is newsworthy because they are newsworthy. Explain that a common mistake in English is for people to say 'beg the question' when they mean 'raise the question.'
4. Keep students in their groups and give a copy of the worksheet to everyone. Have students work through the 5 example conversations and decide if each one is begging or raising the question.
5. Elicit answers from each group and ask them why they chose 'beg' or 'raise.'
6. Go through the answers. The answers are:

1	begs	The reason restates or assumes the conclusion to be true – the room should be cleaned because it needs to be cleaned.
2	raises	The situation of Susan being good at job but being stuck in her current position invites the question of why she stays and does not look for a new job.
3	begs	The reason restates or assumes the conclusion to be true. Conclusion – cigarettes kill/Premise – they are toxic.
4	raises	The situation of Greg being a straight A student invites the question for Teacher B of whether Greg can be classified as 'the best student I've ever taught.'
5	begs	By stating her premise or reason (the experience of having met her husband) as a result of chance, Friend 2 has already assumed the conclusion that fate is real.

7. Elicit from students the difference between begging the question and raising the question.
8. Have students work individually to think of or find their own examples of begging or raising the question online. Have them write the examples as a short conversation on a piece of paper.
9. Put students in new groups and have them show or read out each conversation and ask whether it is an example of begging or raising the question.
10. Have students reflect on the activity and discuss what they have learned about the difference between begging the question and raising the question and identifying arguments that beg the question.

WORKSHEET

Read the following five short conversations. For each one, decide if it begs or raises the question. Give reasons for your answer.

Conversation 1:

Mother: Clean up your messy room.
Son: Why?
Mother: Because it needs to be cleaned

Does this beg or raise the question? Why?

Answer:

Conversation 2:

Colleague 1: Susan is intelligent, hard-working, and a great communicator. The customers love her.
Colleague 2: But she's been passed over for manager three times. Why does she stay?

Does this beg or raise the question? Why?

Answer:

Conversation 3:

Friend 1: Why did you quit smoking?
Friend 2: Well cigarettes can kill you, right? After all, they're toxic.

Does this beg or raise the question? Why?

Answer:

Conversation 4:

Teacher 1: Greg has done really well this semester. He's scored As in all of his assignments and worked really well in class.

Teacher 2: Yes, he's done really well in my class, too. He may be the best student I've ever taught.

Does this beg or raise the question? Why?

Answer:

Conversation 5:

Friend 1: Do you believe in fate?

Friend 2: Yes, fate is real because I met my husband by chance.

Does this beg or raise the question? Why?

Answer:

Post Hoc Fallacy

Activity 31: Does A Cause B?

Introduction

As a first step to understanding the post hoc fallacy, this activity introduces students to cause and effect. Learners can determine whether event A is a cause of event B or not through a series of example tasks and then make their own true or false cause-and-effect examples.

Aim	To learn about cause and effect, to determine whether event A is a cause of event B or not
Level	Elementary to Pre-intermediate
Time	50–60 minutes
Materials	None
Preparation	[Option] You may wish to provide alternative examples for Steps 2 and 4

Fallacy: Post Hoc	
Definition	Concluding that an earlier unrelated event causes a second event to happen.
Example	My child went out playing in the snow. She got a cold. Playing in the snow causes people to catch colds.

Procedure

1. On the left-hand side of the board write, '<u>CAUSES</u>.' On the right-hand side of the board, write '<u>EFFECTS</u>.' Under causes write, 'I press the light switch.' Go over to the light switch. Elicit from students what the effect will be – 'the lights go off.' Under causes write, 'I drop the chalk.' Pick up the chalk and elicit from students what the effect will be – 'it breaks.' Elicit 2 or 3 more examples of cause and effect from students.
2. Put students into groups of 3 or 4. Next, write on the board:

It is a hot and sunny day ...	... so my ice cream melts.
	... so I feel happy.
	... so I wear sunglasses.
	... so I gain weight.

Have students discuss which effect does not belong on the list and why.
3. Elicit the answer and their reasons from each group. Answer: ... so I gain weight. The first event does not cause the second event to happen.
4. Write a new example on the board:

Every time I wash my friend's car ...	I am tired.
	the car is clean.
	it starts to rain.
	my friend is happy.

Have students discuss which effect does not belong on the list and why.
5. Elicit the answer and their reasons from each group. Answer: It starts to rain. Although people may falsely claim that it does, the first event does not cause the second event to happen.
6. Have students work individually to write two or three of their own examples in their notebooks or on paper. For each example, have students write one cause and four possible effects. One of the four possible effects should be 'false.' The first event does not cause the effect to happen.

7. Have each group member take turns to read out their examples. Listeners listen to each cause and four effects and decide which one does not belong on the list and why. The group member confirms whether the other students in the group are correct or not by saying, 'Yes, that's right' or 'I'm afraid that's not correct.' Have groups continue until they have worked through all of their examples.
8. [Option 1] Once groups have finished, put students into new groups and repeat Step 7.
9. [Option 2] Once groups have finished, call on individuals to share their examples with the whole class and have students from different groups answer which effect does not belong and why.
10. [Option 3] Have students think about and share experiences in their lives in which they have mistaken at first event being the cause of a second event.★
11. Have students reflect on the activity and discuss what they have learned about identifying or mistaking cause and effect.

★Note
Depending on proficiency level, students may wish to carry out Step 10 (Option 3) in their native language.

Activity 32: Fallacious Connections
Introduction

This activity provides learners with examples of how the post hoc fallacy works. Learners identify the events and conclusions in five example conversations and explain why the speaker's conclusions are fallacious.	
Aim	To understand the post hoc fallacy; to identify the post hoc fallacy in everyday conversations
Level	Intermediate to Advanced
Time	40–50 minutes
Materials	Worksheet
Preparation	Copies of worksheet for each student

Fallacy: Post Hoc	
Definition	Concluding that an earlier unrelated event causes a second event to happen.
Example	My child went out playing in the snow. She got a cold. Playing in the snow causes people to catch colds.

Procedure

1. Write on the board:

   > Event 1 happens
   > Event 2 happens after Event 1
   > Conclusion: Event 1 causes Event 2

   > Event 1: It rained heavily all day and night.
   > Event 2: The river flooded.
   > Therefore, the heavy rain (Event 1) caused the river to flood (Event 2).

   Confirm with students that this is indeed logical; that Event 1 causes Event 2. Have students provide one or two more examples of cause and effect using this pattern.

2. Explain to students that one logical fallacy that people can make frequently is the post hoc fallacy. It is concluding that Event 1 causes Event 2 when this may not be true. Write an example on the board:

   > Event 1: The rooster crows in the morning
   > Event 2: The sun rises.
   > Therefore, the rooster (Event 1) causes the sun to rise (Event 2).

   Confirm with students that this is indeed illogical or a fallacy; that Event 1 does not cause Event 2. [Option] At this point in the lesson, you may wish to have students provide one or two more examples of the post hoc fallacy cause and effect using this pattern.

3. Put students into groups of three or four. Give each student a copy of the worksheet. Have them work together to analyze the examples and explain why they are fallacious.

4. Elicit answers from each group. Possible answers are:

Example 1

Event 1	Keeping the wallet, not handing it in
Event 2	Bad luck happens
Conclusion	Keeping the wallet causes the bad luck.

> This may be fallacious because the bad events that happened are most likely a coincidence and have no direct relation to keeping the money (although morally, the person should have handed in the money).

Example 2

Event 1	Buying/wearing the aftershave
Event 2	Becoming more attractive
Conclusion	The aftershave makes people more attractive.

This may be fallacious because there is no direct relation between aftershave and attraction. The company just wants to sell the product.

Example 3

Event 1	The football team lost
Event 2	Prom is canceled
Conclusion	The football team losing caused the prom to be canceled.

This may be fallacious because there is no direct relation to the loss of the team and the prom being canceled. The football team may have lost to a better side. The prom may be canceled due to flooding of the building. The person is making a fallacious connection between two unrelated events.

Example 4

Event 1	Doing a rain dance
Event 2	It rains
Conclusion	The rain dance causes it to rain.

This may be fallacious because it is most likely a coincidence. The person would have to repeat this action again and again to make it more convincing. It should be noted that some cultures strongly believe in the ability to cause it to rain by ritual dance.

Example 5

Event 1	The building of 5G towers
Event 2	The coronavirus
Conclusion	The building of 5G towers causes the coronavirus pandemic.

This may be fallacious because there is no scientific basis to suggest a relation between 5G and coronavirus. Instead, this may be considered a fallacious conspiracy theory.

5. [Option 1] Have students think of times in their lives they have mistakenly believed X caused Y and what the real cause may have been. Have students share their examples in groups. For example:

   'When I was young, I always believed that if I took my lucky toy bear to an exam, I would pass. I believed that bringing the toy bear caused me to pass the exam. However, studying hard was probably the real cause. This is an example of the fallacy.'

6. [Option 2] Have students search on the Internet for other examples of the post hoc fallacy and share them in groups. For example:

   'I found a good one. It is the car washing causes rain fallacy. People often say that it always rains after they wash their car. But this is a fallacy, right? The car washing does not cause the rain.'

7. For both Option 1 and Option 2, have groups share some examples with the whole class.
8. Have students reflect on the activity and discuss what they have learned about the post hoc fallacy.

WORKSHEET

Read the following examples. For each example, determine what is Event 1, Event 2, and the Conclusion. Give reasons why the conclusion may be fallacious.

Example 1:

Last week, I found a wallet on the street. I think somebody had dropped it by accident. So, I decided to keep the money and not hand it in to the police. After that, a lot of bad things started to happen to me. First, my girlfriend got sick. Then, I got in trouble with my manager at work. Finally, I crashed my car into a wall. It's going to cost me a lot of money to get it repaired. You know what? I should have handed that wallet I found to the police.

Event 1	
Event 2	
Conclusion	

This is fallacious because

From Implications to Application   **127**

Example 2:

Wow! I just saw this great ad on TV. This guy buys this new aftershave. He puts it on in the morning and then everyone is suddenly attracted to him. People on the train are smiling and smelling the air around him. He walks into school and his classmates turn around in class and notice him. One woman even asks to sit next to him. I'm going to buy this aftershave right away.

Event 1	
Event 2	
Conclusion	

This is fallacious because

Example 3:

The school football team lost last week, and now they've canceled prom! What am I going to do?

Event 1	
Event 2	
Conclusion	

This is fallacious because

Example 4:

I planted some vegetables in my garden, and I really needed it to rain. We had had nothing but sun for weeks. So, I read on the Internet about rain dances. I decided to give it a go. I went into the garden, danced around, and did a special rain prayer. You'll never guess what happened! It rained that afternoon.

Event 1	
Event 2	
Conclusion	

This is fallacious because

Example 5:

After they started building those 5G cell towers, people got sick with the coronavirus. Instead of giving everyone a vaccine, they should take those towers down.

Event 1	
Event 2	
Conclusion	

This is fallacious because

Activity 33: Correlation not Causation

Introduction

	This final activity focusing on the post hoc fallacy helps learners to understand that correlation does not always imply causation. Learners are introduced to two graphs to show correlation and causation and correlation without causation. Learners then use their imaginations to commit the post hoc fallacy with their classmates.
Aim	To understand correlation and causation; to be aware that correlation does not imply causation; to determine likely causes for events
Level	High-intermediate to Advanced
Time	80–90 minutes
Materials	None
Preparation	Example events for Step 6

Fallacy: Post Hoc	
Definition	Concluding that an earlier unrelated event causes a second event to happen.
Example	My child went out playing in the snow. She got a cold. Playing in the snow causes people to catch colds.

Procedure

1. Draw the following line graph on the board:

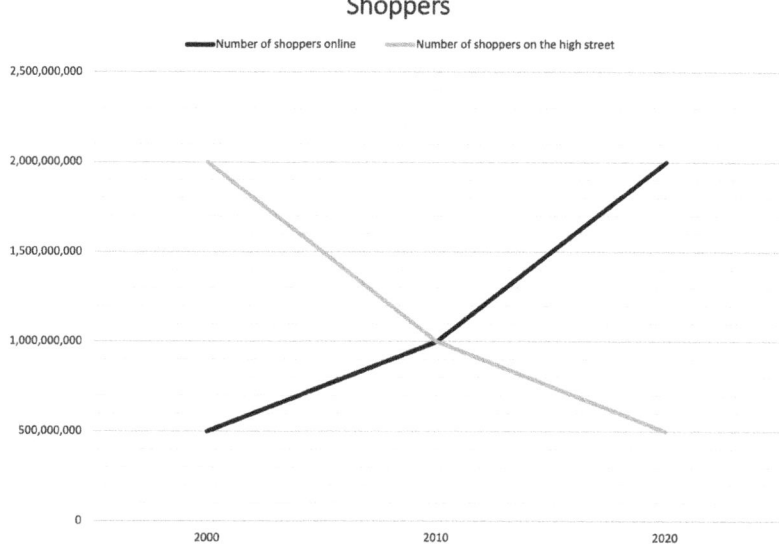

2. Have students look at the graph. On the board, write:

   Event 1:
   Event 2:
   Conclusion:

   Elicit from students:

Event 1:	An increase in the number of shoppers online
Event 2:	A decrease in the number of shoppers on the high street
Conclusion:	An increase in the number of shoppers online causes a decrease in the number of shoppers on the high street.

   Confirm with students that this is indeed logical; that Event 1 is most likely one of the causes of Event 2. You may want to point out that causation is not always that simple and this could be a chain reaction of Event 1 causing Event 2 which in turn causes more of Event 1 which in turn causes more of Event 2 and so on.

3. Draw a second line graph on the board:

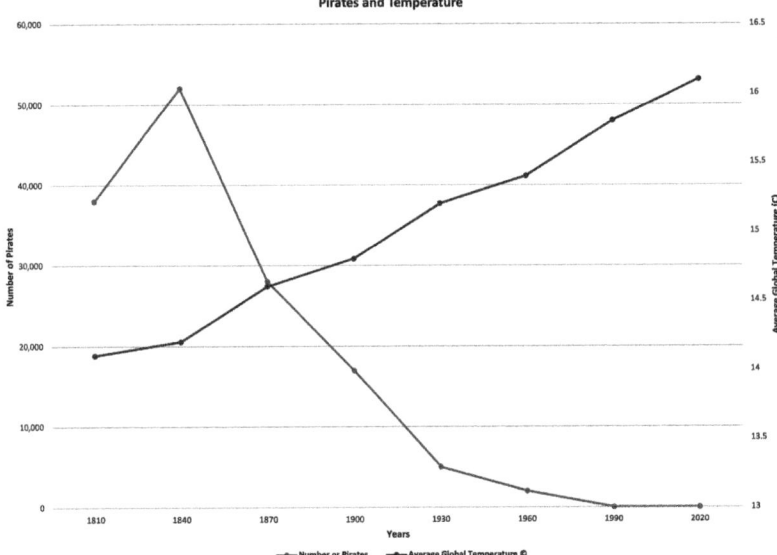

4. Have students look at the graph. On the board, write:

   Event 1:
   Event 2:
   Conclusion:

   Elicit from students:

Event 1:	An increase in global temperatures
Event 2:	A decrease in pirates
Conclusion:	An increase in global temperature causes a decrease in the number of pirates OR a decrease in the number of pirates causes an increase in global temperatures.

   Ask students to consider whether this is logical or not. Tell students (with a smile on your face) that we have found a simple way to stop global warming. We need to increase the number of pirates! Confirm with students that this conclusion is indeed illogical or a fallacy; that Event 1 does not cause Event 2 or vice versa.
5. Explain that the two events, 'global warming' and 'pirates,' have correlation; that Event 1 and Event 2 happen concurrently and thus, there is a relationship between them. Explain, however, that we cannot assume that there is causation; correlation does not imply causation – when we mistakenly infer causation, we may be guilty of committing the post hoc fallacy.

6. Put students into pairs. Have them use their imaginations and work together to research online (or make up the data!!) and create a graph based on two events that may correlate but have absolutely no clear causal relationship. For example:

    - The decline in album sales in a country and the increase in air travel
    - The increase of coffee shops and the increase in smartphone usage
    - The increase in vaccinations and the increase of autism in children

7. Have pairs prepare a short talk to convince class members that one event caused the other to happen. For example:

    > 'Of course, with the sudden increase in coffee shops in the city, the number of people sitting alone at tables with nothing to do also increased. As these coffee shops offered free Wi-Fi the natural progression was for the customer to go out and buy a smartphone to take advantage of the Wi-Fi.'

8. Have each pair come up to the front of the class, draw their graph on the board, and present their talk to their classmates. Have classmates listen carefully, take notes, and evaluate each talk out of five based on how convincing they felt it was. For example:

5	Very convincing
4	Convincing
3	Somewhat convincing
2	Slightly convincing
1	Not convincing

9. After each talk, elicit scores from classmates and reasons for their particular scores and award the highest score with the 'Most convincing Post Hoc fallacy award!'
10. Choose some of the events that students have mentioned in their talks and list them on the board. Put students into groups. Have them discuss what they think to be the most likely causes for these events. For example:

    > 'Well, I think the popularity of online streaming services like Spotify is one of the causes of the decrease in album sales.'

    > 'Yes, I agree. In fact, I used to buy CDs all the time, but now I subscribe to Apple Music and just listen to them online.'

11. Elicit some of the likely causes for each event from groups.
12. [Option 1] Have students think of times in their lives they have mistakenly assumed causation from correlation. Have students share their examples in groups. For example:

'Once, I did my essay the night before the deadline. I stayed up all night to get it done. I handed it in and got an amazing score. So, I believed there was a causal link to doing my homework the night before and getting a better grade. This was a fallacy!'

13. [Option 2] Have students search on the Internet for other examples of correlation not meaning correlation. Have them share their examples in groups.
14. Have students reflect on the activity and discuss what they have learned about the Post Hoc fallacy, the differences between correlation and causation, and being aware that correlation may not mean causation.

Hasty Generalization

Activity 34: All Students in This Class ...

Introduction

In this activity, learners use quantifiers to make statements about their classmates. Learners are made aware of generalizing from a small sample size and how to use evidence to support statements rather than making hasty generalizations.	
Aim	To use quantifiers to make statements about classmates; to be aware of generalizations made from insufficient proof or sample size; to correct generalizations
Level	Elementary to Pre-intermediate
Time	70–80 minutes
Materials	None
Preparation	[Option] A list of questions for Step 3/[Option] A list of hasty generalizations for Step 12

Fallacy: Hasty generalization	
Definition	Coming to a conclusion based on insufficient proof.
Example	My grandpa ate fries every day and lived to 103. French fries must help you live longer.

Procedure

1. Tell students that today they are going to find out about and make some statements about their classmates. Write on the board or pre-teach:

All students	100%
Most students	–
Many students	–

Half of the students	50%
A few students	–
No students	0%

2. Make some statements about the students in the class to illustrate the quantifiers and check agreement with the group. For example:

   'All students are taking this class.' 'Is that right?'
   'Many students in this class have a notebook in front of them.' 'Do you agree?'
   'About half of the students in this class are male.' 'Am I right?'
   'A few students in this class are not here today.' 'Is that correct?'
   'No students in this class are famous yet!' 'Do you agree?'

3. Put students into groups of four. Tell students that they are going to ask questions to find out about each other. Have students come up with their own two yes/no questions or provide students with a list of questions to choose from. For example:

   'Are you good at tennis?'
   'Do you have an older brother?'
   'Do you like horror movies?'
   'Do you have a part-time job?'
   'Can you cook?'
   'Have you ever been to Paris?'

4. Have students take turns to ask their two questions to each member of the group and write down their answers. Students should also answer their own questions and include their answers in their notes. For example:

Questions:	Number of students:
Are you good at tennis?	2
Do you have an older brother?	0

5. Have students use the quantifiers from Step 1 to write two sentences based on the results of their questions. For example:

   'Half of the students are good at tennis.'
   'No students have older brothers.'

6. Elicit some sentences from each group and write five or six examples on the board.

7. Above the five or six examples, write, 'In this class….' Read through all of the sentences starting with the phrase, 'In this class…' Ask students, 'Is this right?'

8. Elicit from students that each sentence was based on information from a group of four students and not the whole class. Introduce and explain the word, 'generalization.'
9. Tell (or elicit from) students that a person would need to check with everybody in the class before they can state that the five or six example sentences are true. Otherwise, it is a generalization.
10. Nominate a student to come to the front of the class. The student turns the statement into a question and asks the class to raise their hands if the answer is yes. For example:

    'Are you good at tennis? Put your hands up if the answer is yes.'

    Have the student count the number of hands raised and correct the statement on the board accordingly. For example:

    '1, 2, 3, 4, 5. There are 5 out of 35 students. So, we can say that in this class, A FEW students are good at tennis.'

11. Have the student nominate a new student to come to the front of the class. Repeat Steps 10 and 11 with all of the example sentences on the board.
12. [Option 1] Have students think of times in their lives they have made generalizations or reached conclusions based on limited or insufficient information. Have students share their examples in groups.* For example:

    'I went to the new supermarket in town. It was really crowded. So, I believed it was always crowded. I never went back.'

13. [Option 2] Introduce other examples of hasty generalizations to students. Have them discuss what is wrong with each example and how they could make each statement more believable, true, or valid. For example:

    - Three out of four students have a smartphone. (You only asked four students.)
    - Old people cannot use computers. (Your grandparents cannot use a computer.)
    - All men hate cooking. (You have three male friends who dislike cooking.)

14. Have students reflect on the activity and discuss what they have learned about making generalizations from insufficient evidence or information.

*Note
Depending on proficiency level, students may wish to carry out Step 12 (Option 2) in their native language.

Activity 35: Don't Be Hasty!

Introduction

In this activity, learners are introduced to the hasty generalization fallacy through an example about dentists. Learners work through a series of further examples to determine whether they are hasty generalizations or not and discuss ways to avoid making hasty generalizations in their lives.	
Aim	To understand and identify hasty generalizations; to determine ways to avoid making hasty generalizations
Level	Intermediate to Advanced
Time	40–50 minutes
Materials	Worksheet
Preparation	Copies of worksheet for each student

Fallacy: Hasty Generalization	
Definition	Coming to a conclusion based on insufficient proof.
Example	My grandpa ate fries every day and lived to 103. French fries must help you live longer.

Procedure

1. Pre-teach 'hasty.' Ask students to give example situations in their lives in which they have been hasty. For example:

    'I bought a computer because it was in a Black Friday sale. The computer wasn't good. I made a hasty decision.'

2. Give students an example of a hasty generalization. Have them listen and take notes. For example:

    'I met a dentist the other day. He was very rude to me. My dentist is also really rude. You know, dentists are just rude people.'

3. Put students in pairs or groups to discuss what is wrong with the conclusion.
4. Elicit from students that the conclusion is hasty. The conclusion has been reached after meeting one or two dentists only. There is not enough evidence to support the conclusion that all dentists are rude! Explain to students that this is an example of a hasty generalization.
5. [Option] To explain further, write on the board:

Sample A	is taken from	Population B
(2 dentists)		(All dentists)

Sample A	is a very small part of	Population B
(2 people)		(All dentists)

Conclusion is taken from Sample A and applied to Population B
(All people in Population B…)

6. Give each student a copy of the worksheet. Have them work together in their pairs or groups to decide whether the six examples are hasty generalizations or not.
7. Elicit answers from each group. Answers are:

    Example 1: Yes – there is only a sample of one.

    Example 2: Yes – the sample is larger but there is insufficient evidence to determine that 'all' dentists are rich. There may be dentists who make a lower salary. There may be many dentists paying off huge student loans.

    Example 3: No – as the quantifier 'some' is used it is not a generalization. 'Some' implies the existence of counterevidence; 'some' are not kind and informative.

    Example 4: Yes – the sample is only of a few times of taking the medicine. The cause of the upset stomach may not be the medicine prescribed by the dentist (refer students to Post Hoc fallacy).

    Example 5: No – it is a fact. In most, if not all countries, it is a legal requirement for dentists to study and obtain qualifications to get a license to practice.

    Example 6: Yes – there is only a sample of one.

8. Have students work in their pairs or groups to look again at Examples 1, 2, 4, and 6. Have them discuss the evidence they would need to help prove each conclusion OR how they could rephrase the conclusion to make it less of a generalization. For example:

    Example 1: Give a large sample of male and female dentists of all ages from around the world an intelligence test

    Example 2: The conclusion needs to be rephrased to 'some' or 'a few' or even change the term 'rich' to 'better off as compared to people in [X] occupation.'

Example 4: The patient would need to take the medicine over a longer period of time to verify the causal link or be tested by experts to confirm an allergic reaction to the medicine.

Example 6: Get a large sample of handwriting from male and female dentists of all ages from around the world to check for legibility.

9. Elicit a list of occupations on the board.
10. Have students choose one of the occupations and write three statements about the occupation. Some of the statements should be hasty generalizations.
11. Put students into new groups of three or four. Have each student read out their statements. Group members listen to the statements and decide which are hasty generalizations and which are not.
12. [Option 1] Have groups look at the statements that were hasty generalizations and think of the evidence they would need to prove it or how the statement could be rephrased to avoid a hasty generalization.
13. [Option 2] Have students think of times in their lives they have made generalizations or reached conclusions about occupations based on limited or insufficient information. Have students share their examples in groups.*
For example:

> 'My teacher always looked stressed. I don't want to be a teacher because it's such a stressful job.'

14. Have students reflect on the activity and discuss what they have learned about making and avoiding hasty generalizations.

WORKSHEET

Read the following examples. For each example, decide whether the conclusion is a hasty generalization or not and why.

Example 1:

All dentists are really intelligent. My mother is a dentist and she's really smart.

A hasty generalization?   YES/NO

Why?

Example 2:

All dentists are rich. I did research on 3,000 dentists. They all make over $100,000 a year.

A hasty generalization?　　　　　YES/NO

> Why?

Example 3:

Some dentists are really kind and informative. My dentist always takes time to explain everything to me carefully.

A hasty generalization?　　　　　YES/NO

> Why?

Example 4:

My dentist gave me some medicine for my toothache. I took it a few times and got an upset stomach. I took some aspirin and felt fine. I've decided not to take the medicine the dentist gave me.

A hasty generalization?　　　　　YES/NO

> Why?

Example 5:

You need to be qualified to be a dentist.

A hasty generalization?　　　　　YES/NO

Why?

Example 6:

Dentists have terrible handwriting. I can never read the prescription my dentist gives to me. I'm surprised they know what medicine to give me at the pharmacy.

A hasty generalization?   YES/NO

Why?

Activity 36: Everyday Generalizations
Introduction

In this final activity of focusing on the hasty generalization fallacy, learners discuss the kinds of hasty generalizations that people may make every day, why the conclusions are faulty, and how to avoid making hasty generalizations.	
Aim	To understand and identify everyday hasty generalizations that people may make or experience; to share examples of everyday hasty generalizations; to discuss ways to avoid hasty generalizations
Level	High-intermediate to Advanced
Time	60–70 minutes
Materials	None
Preparation	Example hasty generalizations for Step 5

Fallacy: Hasty generalization	
Definition	Coming to a conclusion based on insufficient proof.
Example	My grandpa ate fries every day and lived to 103. French fries must help you live longer.

Procedure

1. Write 'generalization' on the board. Ask students to give a definition of the term and an example of a generalization. Write a list on the board. For example:

    'All British people love tea.'
    'Toyota Lexus drivers are rich.'

2. Put students into pairs or small groups. Have them discuss each generalization and what may be wrong with the belief or conclusion. Elicit ideas from each pair or group.
3. Explain about the hasty generalization fallacy. Write on the board:

    Sample A is taken from Population B

    Sample A may be a small part or not representative of Population B

    Conclusion is taken from Sample A and applied to Population B

    Explain that we tend to make hasty generalizations that may be inaccurate in everyday life.
4. Give students examples of some everyday hasty generalizations that people make or experience. For example:

    - Racial stereotyping: Asians are good at math.
    - Social media: My friends on social media are living fantastic lives.
    - News media: [Name of news organization] is fake news.
    - Anecdotal evidence: The service in that restaurant was awful. I'm never going back.
    - Advertising: America's favorite breakfast cereal!
    - Politics: According to polls, [Politician] is projected to win by a landslide.

5. Have pairs or group discuss each example and what may be wrong with the belief or conclusion. Possible answers are:

    - 'Asians are good at math' – is a generalization based on a popular narrative in some countries. Although it may appear as a compliment, it is racist. First, it may not be true for all people within the ethnic group. Second, it is a means of framing or dehumanizing a social group.
    - 'My friends on social media are living fantastic lives' – we can see one or two photos posted by our friends and jump to the conclusion that they are living very content lives. This hasty generalization based on a small sample size can lead people to feel that they are missing out on fun elements within their own lives. However, we cannot know if our friends are truly happy from their social media feed.

- '[Name of news organization] is fake news' – it is possible that a news organization has misreported news on occasion. However, it is a hasty generalization to conclude that the organization always provides false information.
- 'The service in that restaurant was awful' – this is a common hasty generalization for us all. We cannot reach a valid conclusion based on one or two visits to a restaurant.
- 'America's favorite breakfast cereal' – unless the manufacturer has surveyed all Americans, this is a false claim.
- 'According to polls, [Politician] is projected to win by a landslide' – often polls are not representative of the total population. For example, polls conducted by phones may target older voters only. As we have seen in recent elections, polls are often hasty generalizations.

6. Give students time to think about hasty generalizations they have made or experienced in their lives. Have students also think about how hasty generalizations can be avoided. Have students make notes in their notebooks.
7. Put students into new pairs or groups. Have them share their own experiences of hasty generalizations. Have them discuss how hasty generalizations can be avoided.
8. [Option] Put students into new pairs or groups and repeat Step 7.
9. Have pairs of groups share some example and ideas with the whole class.
10. Have students reflect on the activity and discuss what they have learned about hasty generalizations in everyday life and how to avoid making them.

Single Cause Fallacy

Activity 37: Many Causes

Introduction

In this activity, learners are first introduced to cause and effect. Then, learners are made aware of the single cause fallacy. Learners then determine many causes for different effects and share their answers with their classmates. It is hoped that learners conclude that effects may have multiple causes.	
Aim	To learn about cause and effect; to be aware of the single cause fallacy; to determine many causes for one effect
Level	Elementary to Pre-intermediate
Time	45–60 minutes
Materials	A cup for Step 1
Preparation	[Option] A list of effects for Step #8

Fallacy: Single Cause	
Definition	Coming to a conclusion that there is only one cause for an event.
Example	Ever since I got this new computer, I have been getting better scores in my tests.

Procedure

1. On the left-hand side of the board write, '**CAUSES**.' On the right-hand side of the board, write '**EFFECTS**.' Under causes write, 'I press the light switch.' Go over to the light switch. Elicit from students what the effect will be – 'the lights go off.' Under causes write, 'I drop the cup.' Pick up a cup and elicit from students what the effect will be – 'it breaks.' Gesture 'feeling hot.' Under effects write, 'I feel hot.' Draw the Sun on the board and elicit the cause. Under causes write, 'It is sunny today.'
2. [Option] Elicit two or three cause-and-effect examples from students.
3. Go through the examples of cause and effect on the board. Ask students, 'How many causes?' Elicit from students that there may be one single cause.
4. Dictate the following sentence to students: 'Ever since I started classes with [Your name], my English has gotten better.' Have students write the sentence in their notebooks. Elicit from students what the cause and effect is in this example:

    Cause: You, the teacher
    Effect: English is better

    Put students into pairs or groups. Have them discuss if there is anything wrong with this statement or conclusion.
5. Elicit ideas from each pair or group. Explain that the problem with the statement or conclusion is that there is only one cause. There are probably many reasons why students English has improved.
6. Have each student turn to a new page in their notebooks. Have them draw a circle in the middle of the page. In the middle of the circle, have students write, 'My English has gotten better.' Have them work together in their pairs or groups to create a mind map of many different reasons (causes) for their English having improved (effect). For example:

7. Put students into new groups. Have each student in the group share their mind maps together. For example:

   'There are many reasons my English has gotten better. First, my teacher is great, and I really like her lessons. Second, I play games on my phone in English. Third, I read many easy books in English. Fourth, I practice with my classmates on WhatsApp. We text each other in English. Finally, I watch videos on YouTube. There are some great videos for English learners.'

8. Elicit new effects from students or provide them with a list to choose from. For example:

   - I was late for class.
   - I am really happy.
   - I cannot go out this weekend.
   - I need to find a part-time job.
   - I crashed my car.
   - [Name] got many new friends.
   - My sister/brother isn't talking to me.

9. Repeat Steps 6 and 7 with the new effects.
10. Have students reflect on the activity and discuss what they have learned about causes and effects. In their reflections, it is hoped that students conclude that effects may have multiple causes and that it can be a mistake to think that events happen due to a single cause.

Activity 38: A Popular Restaurant

Introduction

In this activity, learners discuss popular restaurants, share stories about a fictitious popular restaurant, and determine a cause and effect related to its popularity. Learners then consider multiple causes for the popularity of restaurants rather than just one single cause.	
Aim	To talk about popular restaurants; to learn about and understand the single cause fallacy; to consider multiple causes for one event
Level	Intermediate to Advanced
Time	50–80 minutes
Materials	Task Cards 1 to 4
Prepration	Copies of Task Cards 1 to 4 for each group

Fallacy: Single Cause	
Definition	Coming to a conclusion that there is only one cause for an event.
Example	Ever since I got this new computer, I have been getting better scores in my tests.

Procedure

1. Have students make a list of four or five popular restaurants they know.
2. Put students into groups of three or four. Have them share their list of popular restaurants and give reasons for their choices. For example:

    'One popular restaurant is Parivaar. It's an Indian restaurant. It's always busy in the week and at weekends. I think it is because they have excellent naan bread and a good choice of curries.'

3. Pre-teach 'cause' and 'effect.'
4. Have students assign themselves a number in their groups (Student 1 to 3 or 4). Have each Student come to the front and collect their task cards (see Student task cards). For example, call Student 1s from each group to come and collect Task Card 1, call Student 2s to collect Task Card 2 and so on. Instruct students to return to their groups, read their task cards, and then place their cards face down on the table.

5. [Option] Put all Student 1s, Student 2s, Student 3s, Student 4s together in the four corners of the classroom. Have them check together that they understand their task cards and the story they will tell in their groups.
6. Have Student 1s read out their task cards and then ask the cause-and-effect questions to their group members. Have Student 1s write down the answers given by the other students.
7. Repeat Step 6 with Student 2s, 3s (and 4s for groups of four).
8. Elicit from groups their answers about cause and effect for each of the task cards. Probable answers are:

Task card:	Cause:	Effect:
1	new items on the menu	an increase in customers
2	advertising online	an increase in customers
3	the closure of a competitor	an increase in customers
4	featured on a TV show	an increase in customers

9. Point out to or elicit from students that although we may sometimes mistakenly believe that an event has one single cause, there can be in fact many different factors at play (new items on the menu, advertising online, the closure of a competitor, featured on a TV show) that cause the event (an increase in customers) to happen.
10. Have students return to their lists of four or five popular restaurants (Step 1). Have them work individually to think of the many possible causes for the popularity of each restaurant.
11. Put students into new groups. Have them share their answers.
12. [Option] Have students think of times in their lives that they have believed there was a single cause for an event that had many causes. For example:

> 'I believed I failed my driving test because my instructor was terrible. In fact, there were many reasons. I was very nervous on the day and made many mistakes. I hadn't practiced driving enough. Also, I knew nothing about clutch control.'

13. Have students reflect on the activity and discuss what they have learned about the single cause fallacy.

Student Task Cards

Student 1:
First, listen to my story: Did you hear about Pippa's? The restaurant's been open for about a year. It does okay, and it's in a good location. However, some days are really quiet. Anyway, last month the owner changed what's on the menu. After a couple of weeks, there was a huge increase in the number of customers going there. In fact, I had to wait over an hour for a seat!

Now, answer my questions:
1. What was the effect?
2. What was the cause?

Student 2:

First, listen to my story:
Have you ever been to Pippa's? It's great. I went there for the first time a couple of weeks ago. The reason I went there was because I saw many ads for it online, so I thought I'd check it out. I had to wait for a long time to get in the restaurant. While I was waiting, I spoke to someone in front of me. They were a regular customer. They said it used to be really quiet, but these days it's gotten really popular. Anyway, the food is amazing. You should try it.

Now, answer my questions:
1. What was the effect?
2. What was the cause?

Student 3:

First, listen to my story:
I used to go to this great restaurant downtown. It was always busy, but it was worth the wait. Anyway, a month ago, the restaurant closed. The owner decided to retire and had nobody to pass the business onto. So, a couple of weeks ago, I decided to check out this restaurant across the street called 'Pippa's.' It opened a year ago, but I'd never been. It always seemed quiet. Well, I couldn't believe it! The day I went there was a long line of customers and I had to wait a long time to get a seat. When I sat down, the waiter apologized and said recently they'd gotten busier and busier. Anyway, the food was excellent, and I'll definitely go again.

Now, answer my questions:
1. What was the effect?
2. What was the cause?

Student 4:

First, listen to my story:
I love watching TV shows where famous celebrities check out restaurants in the local area. A couple of weeks ago, I watched this show where a comedian visited different places in her neighborhood. One of the places was a restaurant called 'Pippa's.' It was a very quiet place. However, the owner seemed very friendly, and the food looked great. So, I decided that I would have to go and try it out. Well, I guess the TV show must have helped their business. The day I went there was a long line of customers and I couldn't get in. I'll have to try again in a few weeks or so.

Now, answer my questions:
1. What was the effect?
2. What was the cause?

Activity 39: How Many Causes?

Introduction

In this final activity focusing on the single cause fallacy, learners are made aware of the single cause fallacy and discuss multiple causes for different complex events.	
Aim	To understand the single cause fallacy; to determine multiple causes for complex events
Level	High-intermediate to Advanced
Time	60–80 minutes
Materials	None
Preparation	Example effects or events for Step 1

Fallacy: Single Cause	
Definition	Coming to a conclusion that there is only one cause for an event.
Example	Ever since I got this new computer, I have been getting better scores in my tests.

Procedure

1. Write on the board 'EFFECT is caused by CAUSE,' and then write four or five example sentence stems that include complex events with multiple causes. For example:

   - Wildfires are caused by …
   - Drug addiction is caused by …
   - Climate change is caused by …
   - A decrease in crime in an area is caused by …
   - School shootings are caused by …

2. [Option] After writing one or two examples on the board, elicit the remaining example sentence stems from the students.
3. Put students into groups of three or four. Have students discuss each topic and complete the sentence stems with a plausible cause. For example:

   'Wildfires are caused by poor forest management.'
   'Drug addiction is caused by low self-esteem.'
   'Climate change is caused by the burning of fossil fuels.'
   'A decrease in crime in an area is caused by an increase in policing.'
   'School shootings are caused by exposure to violence in video games.'

4. Elicit answers from each group and complete the sentence stems on the board with ideas from the students.

5. Pre-teach the word 'fallacy' if you have not done so already. Ask students to discuss in groups what is wrong with each conclusion on the board. Ask students if they can determine the logical fallacy.
6. Elicit answers from students and then explain more about the single cause fallacy to the group. Explain that it is easy for us to attribute one single cause for a phenomenon but by doing so, we may oversimplify it. The danger here is that we may ignore, minimize, or not determine other contributing factors.
7. Put students into new groups of three or four. Assign each group a number. Have each group choose a topic from the board to research. Tell them that they will research or come up with multiple causes for their chosen phenomenon and that the winning group is the one that can identify the most causes. Explain that the causes must be plausible!
8. Set a suitable time limit. Have groups research their topic online, discuss, and note down multiple causes for their particular phenomenon.
9. Have students choose a spokesperson for their group. Have one of the spokespeople come up to the front of the class, say their group number and then present their phenomenon and list of possible causes to the class. Have class members listen carefully and take notes. Assign the group an initial score based on how many causes they mentioned (e.g. Group 1: six causes = six points).
10. After the spokesperson has presented, give class members time to politely challenge any causes that they think are unlikely or unbelievable. Deduct a point from the group for every successful challenge (e.g. one successful challenge – Group 1 now has five points).
11. Repeat Steps 9 and 10 with each group.
12. After each spokesperson has presented, check the scores, and announce the winners.
13. Have students reflect on the activity and discuss what they have learned about the single cause fallacy and determining multiple causes for events.

False Equivalence

Activity 40: Comparing Apples to Oranges

Introduction

In this activity, learners identify the similarities and differences between two items such as apples and oranges to understand that things are seldom equal. The aim of the activity is to introduce students indirectly to the false equivalence fallacy.	
Aim	To identify similarities and differences between two items; to understand that items are seldom equal; to learn indirectly about false equivalence

From Implications to Application 149

Level	Elementary to Pre-intermediate
Time	50–60 minutes
Materials	None
Preparation	None

Fallacy: False Equivalence	
Definition	Coming to a conclusion that something is the same because they share similar characteristics.
Example	They both need looking after. There's no difference in having a dog or a cat.

Procedure

1. On the board, draw two overlapping circles. Write 'Apples' over the left-hand circle and write 'Oranges' over the right-hand circle.
2. Elicit from students some of the similarities between Apples and Oranges and write them in the overlapping section of the two circles. For example:

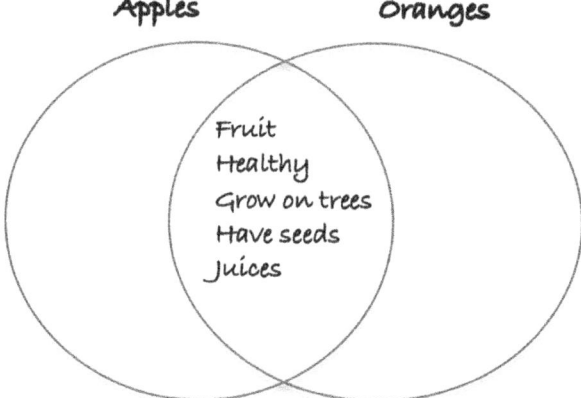

3. Have students open their notebooks and copy the diagram. Then, dictate the following to students:

   'Apple and oranges are both fruit. They're both healthy to eat. They both grow on trees. They both have seeds inside of them. Also, they can both be turned into a juice. They're the same, right?'

   Have them write the dictation under the diagram.
4. Ask students the question again – 'They're the same, right?' Elicit from students 'No, they're not the same.' Elicit some differences between apples and oranges and write them in the corresponding sections of the circles. For example:

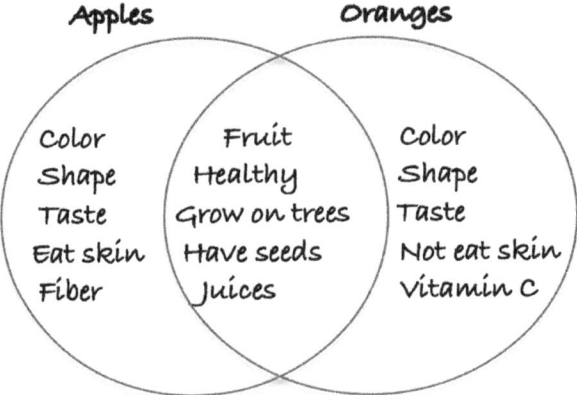

5. Have students write down the differences. Then, dictate the following to students:

   'No, they're not the same. Apples are red or green. Oranges are orange. They have different shapes. They have different tastes. You can eat the skin of the apple. You can't eat the skin of the orange. Apples have more fiber. Oranges have more vitamin C.'

   Have them write under the first dictation.
6. Put students into pairs. Have them choose two items to compare. For example:

   - Two cities
   - Two countries
   - Two people
   - Two pets
   - Two hobbies

7. Have each student draw two overlapping circles in their notebooks and label their circles with the two items they have chosen. Have pairs work together to write the similarities between the two items within the overlapping section of the two circles.
8. Make groups of four by putting pairs together. Pair 1 explains the similarities between their 2 items and claim, 'They're the same, right?' Pair 2 listens, takes notes, and then says, 'No, they're not the same.' Pair 2 then has to think of some differences between the two items. Pair 1 listens and writes the differences in the corresponding sections of the circles in their diagram.
9. Next, Pair 2 explains the similarities between their two items and claim, 'They're the same right?' Pair 2 listens, takes notes, and then says, 'No, they're not the same.' Pair 1 has to think of some differences between the 2 items. Pair 2 listens and writes the differences in the corresponding sections of the circles in their diagram.

10. [Option 1] Elicit some examples from each group.
11. [Option 2] Call on pairs to come up to the front, write their diagrams on the board, and explain to the class the similarities and differences between them.
12. [Option 3] Make groups of four with new pairs and have each pair explain the similarities and differences between their two items to each other.
13. Have students reflect on the activity and discuss what they have learned about the similarity and differences between items. You may also wish to teach students about the false equivalence fallacy at this point or just emphasize that it is a mistake to consider two things equal because they share similar characteristics.

Activity 41: They're Not the Same
Introduction

\multicolumn{2}{l}{In this activity, learners are made aware of the false equivalence fallacy. They analyze five examples to determine the conclusions the speaker wishes the listener to draw and why each example is a false equivalence. Learners also research or come up with their own false equivalence examples.}
Aim	To understand and be aware of false equivalences; to explain why the examples are indeed false equivalences; to research or come up with further false equivalence examples
Level	Intermediate to Advanced
Time	60–70 minutes
Materials	Worksheet
Prepration	Copies of worksheet for each student

Fallacy: False Equivalence	
Definition	Coming to a conclusion that something is the same because they share similar characteristics.
Example	They both need looking after. There's no difference in having a dog or a cat.

Procedure

1. Explain that today students will look at a common logical fallacy called 'False equivalence.' On the board, write:

    'A and B both share C
    Therefore, A and B are equal.'

Next, choose two students in your class and write:

'[Name of student 1] and [Name of student 2] are both in my class. Therefore, [Name of student 1] and [Name of student 2] are the same.'

2. Ask students, 'Are they the same?' Elicit that although they share the same class and have that in common with one another that they are indeed different.
3. Put students into pairs or groups. Give them each a copy of the worksheet and have them work together through Task 1.

Possible answers:

Comment 1: The speaker wants you to draw the conclusion that eating animals and eating plants is the same as animals and plants are both living things. However, this is a false equivalence on many levels. One difference is the level of pain and suffering that plants and animals experience in the 'killing' for food.

Comment 2: The speaker wants you to draw the conclusion that both have committed illegal acts and are therefore not suitable candidates for President. However, this is a false equivalence as the severity of the crimes are different (although this may be subjective depending on country).

Comment 3: The speaker wants you to draw the conclusion that waiting in line for a hamburger and waiting in line to vote are the same thing, therefore mail-in balloting should be stopped. This is a false equivalence. For one, waiting in line for a hamburger is a luxury. Voting is a constitutional right.

Comment 4: The speaker wants you to draw the conclusion that as there are some scientists who do not believe that climate change is caused by humans that we can reasonably question the assertion. The speaker implies that it is 50/50. However, this is a false equivalence in terms of the balance of phenomenon being compared. Around 97% of scientists believe that climate change is caused by humans and around 3% believe that climate change is a hoax. In other words, there is very strong evidence to suggest that climate change is real.

Comment 5: The speaker wants us to draw the conclusion that we cannot ban guns as cars are equally as risky. This is a false equivalence. For one, guns are made as weapons to kill. Cars are made as vehicles for people to get from A to B.

From Implications to Application **153**

4. Elicit answers from each group.
5. Have students work individually to complete Task 2 on the worksheet. Have students research or think of their own false equivalence examples. Refer students back to Comments 1 to 5. Have students write their examples in a similar style in the space provided on the worksheet.
6. Put students into new groups of four. Have them share their comments and then discuss the conclusion that the speaker wishes people to draw and why the comments are indeed false equivalencies.
7. [Option] Have students think of times in their lives they have committed or experienced the false equivalence fallacy.
8. Have students reflect on the activity and discuss what they have learned about the false equivalence fallacy.

WORKSHEET

Task 1: Read the following five comments. For each comment, think about:

- What conclusion does the speaker want you to draw?
- Why are they not the same?

Comment 1:

My friend is a vegetarian because she disagrees with killing animals for food, but vegetables are also living things, right?

Answers:

Comment 2:

I'm not going to vote for either candidate for President. I mean, they're both criminals. One was taken to court for fraud and had to pay his victims millions of dollars in compensation. The other was caught in possession with drugs when he was a college student.

Answers:

Comment 3:

They should stop all mail-in balloting. You know if people can wait in a long line for a hamburger or pastry, they can sure as well wait in line to vote.

Answers:

Comment 4:

You know there are scientists who believe climate change is not caused by humans, so we don't really know, right?

Answers:

Comment 5:

I can't believe some people want to ban guns. I mean, what about cars? They kill people, too, don't they? You don't see people arguing that we should ban cars, right?

Answers:

Task 2: Research or think of your own false equivalence example. Write your example as a comment below:

Comment 6:

_____

_____

_____

_____

Get ready to share and discuss your example with your classmates.

Activity 42: Wronger than Wrong

Introduction

In this final activity of focusing on the false equivalence fallacy, learners are made aware of the fallacy, introduced to Asimov's (1988) axiom of 'wronger than wrong,' and research further examples of false equivalences. Learners then discuss fair and respectful ways to respond to false equivalences.	
Aim	To understand and be aware of false equivalences; to understand Asimov's axiom of 'wronger than wrong;' to research further examples of false equivalences; to discuss ways to respond to false equivalences
Level	High-intermediate to Advanced
Time	60–70 minutes
Materials	Worksheet
Preparation	Copies of the worksheet for each student

Fallacy: False Equivalence	
Definition	Coming to a conclusion that something is the same because they share similar characteristics.
Example	They both need looking after. There's no difference in having a dog or a cat.

Procedure

1. Explain that today students will look at a common logical fallacy called 'False equivalence.' On the board, write:

   'A and B both share C
   Therefore, A and B are equal.'

2. Give students an example. Write the following on the board or dictate it:

   'Hey, you can't criticize the company for polluting the river with waste. Didn't you throw a plastic bottle into the river last week?'

3. Have students answer the following questions about the comment:
   - What is the A, B, and C in this comment?
   - What conclusion does the speaker want you to draw?
   - Why is it a false equivalence?

   The answers are:

   A – the company
   B – you

C – polluting the river
The conclusion – you are equally as bad as the company
They are not equivalent as the company's action is much worse than your action in terms of the degree of damage to the river.

4. Draw or show a picture of the Earth and ask students to describe the picture.
5. Ask students, 'Is it correct to say the Earth is flat?' Elicit that the statement is wrong. Ask students, 'Is it correct to say that the Earth is a perfect sphere?' Elicit that the statement is also wrong.
6. Ask students 'Which statement do you think is more incorrect? (You may wish to introduce the term 'wronger' – See Step 8) Elicit answers from students.
7. Put students into groups of three or four. Give each student a copy of the worksheet. Have them work through Task 1 together.
8. Elicit answers from students. The possible answer is:

    Something that is slightly wrong does not equate to something that is very wrong. This is a false equivalence. If you do this, you are 'wronger than wrong!' (Asimov, 1988).

9. Have students research online and work through Task 2 together.
10. Elicit false equivalence examples from students. Answers may vary. Possible answers are:

    - Some people consider vaccines to be unsafe
    - If liquor stores can stay open during a pandemic, churches should be open
    - Politician A lied but so did Politician B
    - Climate change is real or a hoax
    - Black Lives Matter vs. All Lives Matter

11. Choose a few examples from Step 9 to discuss as a whole class. For each example, discuss:

    - What conclusion does the speaker want us to draw?
    - Why is it a false equivalence?

    For example:

    - It is wrong to say vaccinations are safe for everyone
    - However, it is very wrong to say vaccinations are not safe for everyone
    - The conclusion – anti-vaxxers want people to think that having a vaccination has a risk.
    - This is not equivalent as scientific evidence suggests the risk to health of a having a vaccination is low and outweighs that of not having a vaccination.

12. Have students work through Task 3 together.
13. Elicit answers from students. Answers will vary. Possible answers are
    - Show that the things being compared are not equal
    - Explain the differences between the things being compared as equal
    - Provide evidence and counterexamples
    - Ask for the opponent to provide more evidence to validate their claim
14. Have students reflect on the activity and discuss what they have learned about identifying and responding to false equivalences.

WORKSHEET

Task 1: Read the following quotation from the writer, Isaac Asimov (1988, pp. 288–289). What do you think Asimov means?

> John, when people thought the Earth was flat, they were wrong. When people thought the Earth was spherical, they were wrong. But if *you* think that thinking the Earth is spherical is *just as wrong* as thinking the Earth is flat, then your view is wronger than both of them put together.

We think this quotation means ...

Task 2: Research online and find two examples of a false equivalence. Look for examples in which two wrongs are argued as being equal. Write your examples below:

Example 1:

Example 2:

Task 3: Discuss ways in which we can respond fairly and respectfully to false equivalences:

How to respond to false equivalences:
1.
2.
3.

Get ready to share your ideas with your classmates.

Sunk Cost Fallacy

Activity 43: What Should They Do?

Introduction

In this activity, learners are indirectly introduced to the sunk cost fallacy. Learners listen to different stories or situations and make decisions on whether the person should stop or continue an activity based on future benefit or past investment.	
Aim	To make decisions on whether to stop or continue an activity based on future benefit or past investment; to understand the sunk cost fallacy
Level	Elementary to Pre-intermediate
Time	50–80 minutes
Materials	Story ideas
Preparation	None

Fallacy: Sunk Cost	
Definition	Deciding to continue a plan of action even though continuing may not be the best thing to do.
Example	I'm bored of this book, but I've read the first two chapters so I may as well keep reading to the end.

Procedure

1. Pre-teach the words, 'time,' 'money,' and 'effort.' Elicit from the students activities that people spend time doing, spend money on, or put effort into doing. For example:

   Time: watching a movie, taking this class, reading a book
   Money: a gym membership, a nice lunch at a restaurant, a new car
   Effort: studying a language, doing a project, cooking a meal

2. Draw a stick figure on the board and ask students to give the stick figure a name e.g., Jane. Ask students to choose one of the activities from Step 1 e.g., watching a movie. Explain to students that you will tell them a story about the person (stick figure) and the activity they have chosen. [Option] Rather than coming up with a story on the spot, let students name the character in the story but use the example stories provided (see Step 3 and Story Ideas).

3. Tell students a story about the person using the activity that students have chosen in Step 2. [Option] Use the example stories provided (see below and Story Ideas at the end of the activity). Have students take notes on your story. Make sure your story involves the character thinking about whether to quit the activity or not based on a future benefit versus past investment of time, money, and effort. For example:

   'This is [Jane]. It is evening. [Jane] wants to relax. [She] decides to choose a movie to watch on Netflix. [She] checks how long the movie is. It's a very long movie. The movie is over three hours long. [She] starts to watch the movie. After one hour of watching the movie, [Jane] is really bored. The movie is really boring. [She] is not interested in it. [She] thinks to herself, 'I can stop the movie now. I can choose a better movie to watch.' [She] also thinks, 'But, I have spent 60 minutes already watching this movie. Maybe, I should continue. If I stop now, I wasted 60 minutes of my time.'

4. [Option] If necessary, repeat your story again for students.
5. Have students analyze the story. Ask them the following questions:

   A) What are the two choices?
   B) Why should [Jane] decide on Choice 1?
   C) Why should [Jane] decide on Choice 2?

   Elicit answers and write them on the board. For example:

   A) Stop watching the movie/Continue watching the movie.
   B) She can watch a better movie.
   C) She has spent 60 minutes watching the movie already

6. Have students stand up. Ask students, 'What should [Jane] do?' Have students move to the front of the classroom if they think the character should choose Option 1 of the story. Have students move to the back of the classroom if they think the character should choose Option 2 of the story. Count the number of students at the front and back of the classroom and declare which option has the most votes.
7. Have students return to their seats. Put them in groups of three or four. Have them discuss which option they choose and why.
8. Elicit answers from groups.
9. Repeat Steps 2 to 8 with different stories (see Story Ideas).
10. Teach students about the sunk cost fallacy. Explain that we can often decide to continue an action when it is not the best thing to do. We do this because we have already spent time, money, and effort on it. Refer back to students' decisions based on the story scenarios you used in the class.
11. Have students reflect on the activity and discuss what they have learned about making decisions on whether to continue to stop doing certain activities.

Story Ideas

Story 1:
[Margarita] picks up a book from the library. [She] starts to read the book. [She] really likes the first chapter. However, from the second and third chapter, the book starts to get very difficult [her]. [She] cannot understand the story. [She] gets halfway through the book, but [she] is not enjoying it. [She] thinks to herself, 'I can stop reading this book and take it back to the library. I can spend my time doing something I enjoy.' [She] also thinks to herself, 'But, there are only 150 pages left. Maybe, I should keep reading until the end to find out what happens. Maybe, the book will get better.'

Option 1: Take the book back to the library
Option 2: Keep reading the book

What should [she] do?

Story 2:
[Raphael] wants to exercise. [He] pays for a gym membership. [He] decides to pay for a one-year membership. [He] goes for the first month and really enjoys it. In the second month, [he] has an accident. [He] hurts his leg. [He] thinks about quitting the gym. However, [he] knows that [he] has paid for one year. [He] knows that the gym will not give [his] money back. [He] thinks to himself, 'I know I have hurt my leg, but I can keep going to the gym. I don't want to waste my money. I have 10 months of my membership left.' He also thinks

to himself, 'I should quit the gym. I need to rest until my leg is better, Also, I don't want to have another accident.'

Option 1: Keep going to the gym
Option 2: Quit the gym

What should [he] do?

Story 3:
[Ahmad] is making dinner for [his girlfriend]. [He] went shopping earlier and bought the food. Now, [he] is cooking a special dinner. [He] cuts the meat. [He] cuts the vegetables. [He] adds the spices. [He] makes the rice. About an hour later, [he] tastes the food. It tastes really spicy. [He] thinks to himself, 'I have put a lot of effort into making this dinner. I know it tastes spicy, but I don't want to waste it. Maybe, [my girlfriend] and I can eat it.' [He] also thinks to himself, 'But, it tastes bad. Maybe, I should throw it away and order some take-out food.'

Option 1: Eat the food
Option 2: Throw the food away and order some take-out

What should [he] do?

Activity 44: Is It a Good Decision?
Introduction

In this activity, learners are introduced to different 'sunk cost' situations and determine whether the decision being made is good or bad. Through discussing the examples, learners are made aware of the irrelevance of making decisions by focusing on past investments of money, time, or effort.	
Aim	To understand the sunk cost fallacy; to examine how making decisions by focusing on past investments of money, time, or effort is often irrelevant
Level	Intermediate to Advanced
Time	60–70 minutes
Materials	None
Preparation	None

Fallacy: Sunk Cost	
Definition	Deciding to continue a plan of action even though continuing may not be the best thing to do.
Example	I'm bored of this book, but I've read the first two chapters so I may as well keep reading to the end.

Procedure

1. Pre-teach 'fallacy' if you have not done so already. Explain that today students will look at a common logical fallacy called 'Sunk Cost.' Have students predict what the fallacy may be from its name. For example:

   'Cost? Is it related to money?'

2. Ask students, 'Have you ever been to a restaurant, been really full, but kept on eating because you've paid for the food?' Elicit responses.
3. On the board, write:

   'I am really full. I want to stop eating BUT:

REASON 1:	I have paid money for the food.
REASON 2:	The restaurant will not refund me on the food.★
CONCLUSION:	I will keep eating the food even if it makes me sick.'

   Put students into pairs or small groups. Have them discuss, 'Is it a good decision?'

★Note
You may wish to add the restaurant does not do doggy bags either.

4. Elicit responses from pairs or groups. Answers will vary.
5. Ask students what they think the sunk cost fallacy is. Explain that it is continuing a course of action even though doing so is not the best thing to do. Elicit from students or explain that in Step 3 the sunk cost fallacy is related to money. The person has spent the money on the food so feels that they must continue with the action otherwise it would be a waste of money. The fallacy is the money has already been spent so it is irrelevant to the decision.
6. On the board, write:

   'I am not happy in my relationship BUT:

REASON 1:	I have been with my partner for ten years.
REASON 2:	It would be a waste of time if I end the relationship.
CONCLUSION:	I will stay together with my partner even if I'm unhappy.'

   Put students into pairs or small groups. Have them discuss, 'Is it a good decision?'

7. Elicit responses from pairs or groups. Answers will vary.
8. Elicit from students or explain that in Step 6 the sunk cost fallacy is related to time. The person has invested ten years in the relationship so feels that they must continue with the action otherwise it would be a waste of time. The fallacy is the time has already gone, the person can never get the time back, so the time is irrelevant to the decision.
9. On the board, write:

   'I want to quit studying Spanish and take up a new challenge BUT:

REASON 1:	I have put a lot of effort into getting to my current level.
REASON 2:	It would be a waste of effort if I stop studying Spanish.
CONCLUSION:	I will keep studying it even if it means I cannot start my new challenge.'

   Put students into pairs or small groups. Have them discuss, 'Is it a good decision?'
10. Elicit responses from pairs or groups. Answers will vary.
11. Elicit from students or explain that in Step 9 the sunk cost fallacy is related to effort. The person has put effort into getting to a certain level of Spanish proficiency, so feels that they must continue with the action otherwise it would be a waste of effort. The fallacy is the effort has already been put in, the person can never get the effort back, so the effort is irrelevant to the decision.
12. Put students into new pairs. Using the same pattern as the examples in Step 3 (money), Step 6 (time), and Step 9 (effort), have students make their own examples related to money, time, or effort:

    ```
    _____ BUT
    REASON 1: _____
    REASON 2: _____
    CONCLUSION: _____
    IS IT A GOOD DECISION?
    ```

13. Put two pairs together to form groups. Have them share their examples and for each one, discuss, 'Is it a good decision?'

14. Elicit some example situations and answers from pairs.
15. Have students reflect on the activity and discuss what they have learned about the sunk cost fallacy and whether it is good or bad to make decisions by focusing on past investments of money, time, and/or effort.

Activity 45: What Would You Do?

Introduction

In this final activity focusing on the sunk cost fallacy, learners ask each other hypothetical questions to determine their decision-making behavior and how it relates to the sunk cost fallacy. Learners are encouraged to share experiences in which they have committed the fallacy.

Aim	To ask hypothetical questions about decision-making behavior; to understand the sunk cost fallacy; to share experiences of the sunk cost fallacy
Level	High-intermediate to Advanced
Time	60–80 minutes
Materials	Interview cards
Preparation	Copies of the interview cards for each group or each student

Fallacy: Sunk Cost	
Definition	Deciding to continue a plan of action even though continuing may not be the best thing to do.
Example	I'm bored of this book, but I've read the first two chapters so I may as well keep reading to the end.

Procedure

1. Put students into groups of three or four. Tell students that today they are going to do some research with their classmates. Assign each group with a number (e.g., 1 to 8). Give each group a different interview card (see Interview Cards 1 to 8). Have group members write down the information on their interview card in their notebooks. Alternatively, make enough copies of the interview card for each group member.
2. Give groups time to read their interview cards, check comprehension together, and clarify any vocabulary items they do not know.
3. Explain that students will walk around the classroom and interview students from other groups using their scenario and interview question. Students write down the answers they collect from other group members in their notebooks. Remind students to check that the person has not been interviewed by another member of their group by asking at the beginning,

'Have you been interviewed by anyone from group X?' If the answer is, 'yes,' they should move on to a different classmate.
4. Once a group has interviewed all the members of the other groups, have them return to their seats and share the responses they have collected.
5. Have students think about the responses and what the results may indicate about the decision-making behavior of their classmates.
6. Have each group elect a spokesperson. Have each spokesperson present their results and say what this may indicate about the decision-making behavior of their classmates.
7. Elicit from students or explain the sunk cost fallacy. For example:

> We have a tendency to continue a course of action because of a past investment of money, time, and effort even when it may not be beneficial for us to do so. The 'sunk cost' has already been invested, cannot be returned, and is therefore irrelevant to the current decision we are making.

8. Briefly explain the background to each situation on the interview cards and how it relates to the sunk cost fallacy:

Group 1	An experiment conducted by two psychologists, Arkes and Blumer (1985) showed that 54% of participants choose Ski Trip A due to the greater investment they had made in the ticket.
Group 2	A second experiment by Arkes and Blumer showed that people who had paid for the season ticket at a regular price missed fewer games as their initial investment was higher than those who had paid the special price.
Group 3	An experiment by the psychologist Coleman showed that participants who signed up for Course A were more likely to take that course and not switch to Course B even though it had a higher pass rate. Once again, due to the greater investment, participants felt more reluctant to give up Course A.
Group 4	An experiment by the psychologist Strough showed that younger people were more likely to keep watching the movie until the end as they had paid for it.
Group 5	Another study showed that people who had paid for a tennis club membership were more likely to play tennis against their doctor's suggestion to rest as they did not want to waste the money they had invested.
Group 6	This is a real example in which the British and French governments continued to fund the Concorde project even though it was a commercial failure. As they had invested time, money, and political effort into the venture, they felt it necessary to continue despite the financial losses.

Group 7	A study showed that coaches in the NBA tended to give more play time to the players who had been selected higher in the drafts even when they performed badly. The past investment again irrationally influenced the decision to play the player.
Group 8	Free simulation games often use 'sunk cost' psychology to keep their players playing the game and thus making money for the company. Players feel they must keep playing due to past investment of time, effort (and often money), otherwise they will lose their current status in the game.

9. Ask students to think about a time they have committed the sunk cost fallacy. Give students time to make notes about their sunk cost experience.
10. Put students into new groups. Have them share their personal experiences of the sunk cost fallacy.
11. Have students reflect on the activity and discuss what they have learned about the sunk cost fallacy. [Option] Have students discuss whether they may change their behavior as a result of the activity.

Interview Cards

GROUP 1
Have you been interviewed by anyone from Group 1?
I want you to imagine that you have spent $300 on a ski trip. Let's call this Ski Trip A. Later, you book a second ski trip for $100. Let's call this Ski Trip B. Then, you realize you have booked the ski trips for the same weekend. Both trips are nonrefundable. You've read reviews about Ski Trips A and B and most skiers say that Ski Trip B is more enjoyable. Which trip would you go on and why?

GROUP 2
Have you been interviewed by anyone from Group 2?
I want you to imagine that you have bought a season ticket to see your favorite sports team. You got a great price. Over a season, the ticket saves you about 20% off the ticket price per game. There are about 80 games in one season. How many games do you think you would you go to and why? Now imagine that you bought the season ticket, but you had to pay the regular price. Over a season, the ticket saves you about 2% off the ticket price per game. How many games do you think you would go to and why?

GROUP 3
Have you been interviewed by anyone from Group 3?
I want you to imagine that you are signing up for an important college course. You need to pass this course to get a certain job. You find a course that has a 75% pass rate. Let's call this Course A. There is a special discounted rate only for today. So, you sign up and pay a nonrefundable fee of $1,000. The next day, your friend tells you about an identical course that has a 90% pass rate, and it is free. Let's call this Course B. Your friend has signed you up for this course. Which course would you take and why?

GROUP 4
Have you been interviewed by anyone from Group 4?
I want you to imagine that you paid to watch a movie on pay TV. The movie costs $20. You are really excited as you have heard some great things about the movie. You start watching the movie, but ten minutes later you are really bored. How long would you keep watching the movie for and why? Now imagine the same situation but you didn't have to pay to watch the movie. How long would you keep watching for and why?

GROUP 5
Have you been interviewed by anyone from Group 5?
I want you to imagine that you play tennis regularly. One day, your arm feels quite sore. It feels quite painful when you play. You go to the doctor. She suggests that you rest your arm over the next six months, and it will get better. How many times would you play tennis over the next six months and why? Now imagine that you had paid $2,000 for an annual membership to a tennis club. The payment is nonrefundable. Your membership will expire in six months. How many times would you play tennis over the next six months and why?

GROUP 6
Have you been interviewed by anyone from Group 6?
I want you to imagine that you work for the government. You have a joint project with another country to develop a supersonic plane that will fly between your two countries and the USA. The project has already cost the taxpayers of your country millions of dollars and gone over budget. However, the plane is ready. After several years of operation, the project is still losing money and requires additional funds to keep the plane flying. Would you keep the project going or pull the plug?

GROUP 7
Have you been interviewed by anyone from Group 7?
I want you to imagine that you are the manager of a soccer team. You bought a new center forward for $80 million. He started off well in his first few games and scored some goals. However, for the last ten games, he has played poorly, given the ball away, and been a liability for the team. Would you continue to play the center forward or put him on the substitute's bench and why?

GROUP 8
Have you been interviewed by anyone from Group 8?
I want you to imagine that you have downloaded a simulation game on your smartphone. You must build and manage a farm. The game is free to play. However, you must keep returning to the game to plant seeds, grow crops, harvest them, and raise livestock. If you don't return regularly, you won't receive your game rewards, your crops and animals will die, and your farm will be ruined. You've been playing the game regularly for a year. You've been doing really well on it. However, recently you have gotten busy at work. Would you continue to play the game and why?

C. Logical Fallacies: Questionable Reasons

Introduction

The next 24 activities introduce students to eight logical fallacies related to questionable reasons (see Table 1.1, Part I of this book). For each logical fallacy, there are three activities that cater for different learner proficiency levels:

Level 1	Elementary to pre-elementary (A2–B1)
Level 2	Intermediate to advanced (B1–B2)
Level 3	High-intermediate to advanced (C1–C2)

The level of each activity can be found easily in Table 2.7 by referring to the shading of each column (Level 1, Level 2, Level 3). Please note that levels are only an estimated guide. It may be possible to adapt a Level 3 activity for lower-level students. Similarly, there may be something of value for advanced students within a Level 1 activity. Remember, you do not need to do every activity with your students. Please feel free to pick and choose from the 24 activities and adapt them where necessary to your individual teaching context and learners.

TABLE 2.7 Logical Fallacies: Questionable Reasons: Activity Titles and Aims

Activity/Fallacy:	Title:	Aim:
Activity 46 Ad hominem 1	Don't attack me!	To be aware of strategies used in an argument to attack the person. To learn about disagreeing by addressing the argument and providing a reason.
Activity 47 Ad hominem 2	Attack the argument!	To understand the ad hominem fallacy. To listen to and identify ad hominem attacks versus statements that address the argument.
Activity 48 Ad hominem 3	Guilt by association	To understand the ad hominem fallacy and guilt by association. To think of examples that illustrate guilt by association; to research examples online and/or share real-life examples of guilt-by-association attacks.
Activity 49 Red herring 1	Avoiding the question	To identify when someone is answering or avoiding a question. To learn about the red herring fallacy indirectly.
Activity 50 Red herring 2	Don't distract me!	To understand the red herring fallacy; to understand how people can distract or divert attention away from the argument. To role-play red herring conversations.
Activity 51 Red herring 3	Red herrings in politics	To understand red herrings used in politics; to research examples of red herrings. To listen for and identify red herrings or real answers
Activity 52 Circular reasoning 1	Don't go round in circles	To understand and identify circular reasoning. To make arguments that provide a reason rather than assume the conclusion.
Activity 53 Circular reasoning 2	You gotta do what you gotta do!	To understand circular reasoning; to listen for and identify circular reasoning in daily conversations. To avoid circular reasoning and make better arguments in daily conversations.
Activity 54 Circular reasoning 3	Is circular reasoning begging the question?	To understand the subtle differences between circular reasoning and begging the question. To research and share examples of circular reasoning and begging the question.
Activity 55 Straw man 1	Don't exaggerate!	To understand exaggerations. To identify how somebody can exaggerate in order to change or distort from the original argument to make it easier to attack to reach new conclusions.
Activity 56 Straw man 2	Family arguments	To understand straw man arguments. To identify how an argument can be changed or distorted from the original topic to make it easier to attack to reach new conclusions.
Activity 57 Straw man 3	Countering a straw man argument	To understand the straw man fallacy and research examples online. To discuss ways to counter a straw man argument. To practice countering straw man arguments via short role-plays.

(Continued)

TABLE 2.7 Continued

Activity/Fallacy:	Title:	Aim:
Activity 58 Either/or 1	The third option	To understand the either/or fallacy indirectly. To challenge questions in which only two options are presented. To offer alternative options to questions in which only two options are presented.
Activity 59 Either/or 2	Either A or B but what about C?	To understand the purpose of either/or statements; to respond to either/or statements with alternative options.
Activity 60 Either/or 3	It's not so black and white!	To understand the either/or fallacy. To understand arguments that force a person to choose either black or white. To state alternative choices for black-and-white arguments.
Activity 61 Stacking the deck 1	Half the picture	To understand the stacking the deck fallacy indirectly. To present/listen to both sides of an argument before making a decision.
Activity 62 Stacking the deck 2	The full picture	To understand the importance of obtaining all the evidence before reaching a conclusion. To understand the 'stacking the deck' fallacy.
Activity 63 Stacking the deck 3	Fair play or stacking the deck?	To understand the stacking the deck fallacy, to identify ways that stacking the deck can be used when arguing. To determine ways to avoid stacking the deck.
Activity 64 Equivocation 1	Homonyms	To understand homonyms. To identify how using a word in a different way can result in making an argument unclear or reaching a faulty conclusion.
Activity 65 Equivocation 2	Changing the meaning	To understand equivocation. To understand how language can be used in an argument to be ambiguous and mislead or confuse the listener.
Activity 66 Equivocation 3	Equivocation in politics	To understand the use of equivocation in politics. To analyze quotations for equivocation. To research for further examples of equivocation.
Activity 67 Appeal to emotion 1	How does it make you feel?	To learn positive and negative emotion words. To understand how advertising may appeal to certain emotions.
Activity 68 Appeal to emotion 2	Be afraid, be very afraid	To understand how the appeal to fear fallacy works, to support arguments with evidence. To come up with further examples of appeal to emotion arguments.
Activity 69 Appeal to emotion 3	So many emotions	To understand how the appeal to emotion fallacy may be used to persuade or manipulate. To identify different appeal to emotion arguments. To discuss how to respond to appeal to emotion arguments.

Ad Hominem

Activity 46: Don't Attack Me!

Introduction

In this activity, learners are made aware of strategies that may be used in an argument to attack the person. By looking at example conversations and choosing the best response for each one, learners can learn to disagree by addressing the argument and providing a reason rather than attacking the person. The activity provides an indirect means of teaching learners about the ad hominem fallacy.

Aim	To be aware of strategies used in an argument to attack the person; to learn how to disagree by addressing the argument and be providing a reason
Level	Elementary to Pre-intermediate
Time	60–80 minutes
Materials	Worksheet
Preparation	Copies of the worksheet for each student

Fallacy: Ad Hominem	
Definition	Attacking a person or people instead of dealing with the facts of the argument.
Example	This idea for recycling is just a bunch of crazy liberals trying to tell us what to do.

Procedure

1. Write on the board, 'I don't think the teacher should _____.' Elicit some ideas from the students and write them on the board. For example:

    'I don't think the teacher should give us homework today.'

2. Pre-teach 'agree' and 'disagree.' Ask students how they could disagree with this statement/argument. Elicit some ideas. For example:

    'Really? I think homework will help us get ready for the final test.'

3. Put students into pairs. Give each student a copy of the worksheet. Have pairs work through Task 1 together. Have students check their dictionaries or ask the teacher to explain unknown vocabulary. At this stage, students should just answer the multiple-choice questions by considering which is the best response (a to d).

4. Elicit answers from each pair. Then, give the answers to students (Task 2):
   1. c
   2. b
   3. d
   4. c
5. Put pairs together to make groups. Have students work through Task 3 together. For each conversation, students should consider why the three incorrect responses are not a good way to respond to Student 1's statement/argument.
6. Elicit ideas from each group.
7. Go through the answers with students:

Conversation 1:	Choices a, b, and d attack the person and do not address the argument. Choice c provides a reason why Student 2 disagrees.
Conversation 2:	Choices a, c, and d attack the person by showing how Student 1 benefits from the situation and does not address the argument. Choice b provides a reason why Student 2 disagrees.
Conversation 3:	Choices a, b, and c attack the person by focusing on their past arguments or actions rather than the current argument. Choice d provides a reason why Student 2 disagrees.
Conversation 4:	Choices a, b, and d attack the person by giving negative information about Student 1 before Student 1 can provide their reason. This 'poisons the well' and does not address the argument. Choice c provides a reason why Student 2 disagrees.

8. Have pairs work together to make their own example dialogs ('I don't think the teacher should …') in which they attack the person instead of addressing the argument. Put pairs into groups of four. Have pairs present their dialogs to each other and then discuss how to change Student 2's response so that it provides a reason for disagreeing with Student 1.
9. Have students reflect on the activity and discuss what they have learned about how to disagree with each other without attacking the person.

WORKSHEET

Task 1: Look at the following conversations. For each one, choose the best response:

Conversation 1:

Student 1: I don't think the teacher should give us so much homework.
Student 2: _____

  a) Really? Well, I think you're an idiot!
  b) Really? Well, I think you're just lazy!
  c) Really? Well, I think you can get more practice by doing it!
  d) Really? Well, I think you don't know what you're talking about!

Conversation 2:

Student 1: I don't think the teacher should include the quiz scores in the final grade.
Student 2: _____

  a) Is that because you got 2/25 in the last quiz?
  b) But the quizzes are a useful way to show that we understand the lessons, aren't they?
  c) But then you'll get a higher final grade than Susan, won't you?
  d) Weren't you late for class and missed all of the quizzes?

Conversation 3:

Student 1: I don't think the teacher should speak so fast.
Student 2: _____

  a) You never complained about Mr. Gonzalez. He spoke really fast.
  b) Huh? Last week, you said the teacher spoke too slowly.
  c) When I first met you, you spoke really fast too. I couldn't understand you.
  d) I see what you're saying, but it's a good challenge for our listening practice.

Conversation 4:

Student 1: I don't think the teacher should make us buy the coursebook.

Student 2: _____

Student 1: Well, it's really expensive.

a) Why not? We know that you'll copy it from me anyway.
b) Why not? We know that you're really rich.
c) Why not? We'll use it in class and for homework.
d) Why not? You're always complaining about money.

Task 2: Check your answers with your teacher.

Task 3: Look again at each conversation and best response. For each conversation, discuss what you think is wrong with the other three responses. Get ready to share your ideas with your class.

Activity 47: Attack the Argument!

Introduction

In this activity, learners discuss a series of statements to determine whether they attack the argument or the person. Learners are introduced to different ad hominem attacks. They then play a game in which they listen to arguments to identify if they attack the argument or attack the person.

Aim	To understand the ad hominem fallacy; to listen to and identify ad hominem attacks versus statements that address the argument
Level	Intermediate to Advanced
Time	60–70 minutes
Materials	Attack cards
Preparation	Copy a set of 12 attack cards for each group (see Step 9)

Fallacy: Ad Hominem	
Definition	Attacking a person or people instead of dealing with the facts of the argument.
Example	This idea for recycling is just a bunch of crazy liberals trying to tell us what to do.

Procedure

1. Write on the board:

    1] 'People should not eat meat.'
    2] 'People should eat meat.'

2. Put students into groups of three or four. Have students list ways that they can disagree with one or both statements. Elicit ideas from each group. For example:

> 'I disagree with Statement 1. Meat is an important source of protein'

> 'I disagree with Statement 2. It's not necessary for us to eat meat. People can get protein from many non-animal sources.'

3. Explain to students that these statements address or 'attack' the argument.
4. Next, write on the board:

> *Person 1:* 'Mary thinks we should not eat meat.'
>
> *Person 2:* 'I disagree with her. Meat can be an important source of protein.'
>
> *Person 3:* 'She would say that. Mary's just a crazy liberal.'
>
> *Person 4:* 'Yeah, but Mary owns a vegetarian café. Of course, she doesn't want people to eat meat.'
>
> *Person 5:* 'Yeah, but she's wrong. I mean Mary eats meat. I saw her in a steak restaurant yesterday.'

Have students discuss what are the differences between the responses of Persons 2 to 5.

5. Elicit responses from students.
6. Explain that Person 2 addresses or 'attacks' Mary's argument. However, Persons 3 to 5 attack Mary not the argument. Explain that Person 3 uses an 'ad hominem abusive' attack to try to discredit Mary. However, it does not address her argument. Explain that Person 4 uses an 'ad hominem circumstantial' attack to create doubt and imply that Mary's argument is false due to her circumstances – her business. In other words, the implication is the only reason she put forward the argument is to promote her business. Once again this does not attack the argument. Finally, explain that Person 5 uses an 'ad hominem Tu quoque (You too)' to focus on a past action of Mary that is inconsistent with her argument. In other words, because Mary eats meat, it is hypocritical to argue that people should not eat meat. However, this attacks Mary rather than the argument itself.
7. [Option] Have students find more examples of ad hominem attacks on the Internet and share them with their classmates.
8. Put students into groups of three. Give each group of three a set of 12 attack cards (6 Attack the Person cards and 6 Attack the Argument cards

— see Attack Cards*). Have students shuffle the cards and put them face down on the table.
9. Student 2 takes a card from the pile, reads it, and keeps it hidden. Student 3 takes the next card from the pile, reads it, and keeps it hidden. Student 1 thinks of an argument that somebody has put forward (this may be from the news or can also be from imagination). For example, Student 1 could say:

> 'The president wants to reduce the number of immigrants coming into the country.'

> OR

> '[Imaginary name] thinks that the food in the college canteen should be cheaper.'

Student 2 then responds. If Student 2 has an 'Attack the Person' card, Student 2 uses an ad hominem attack to discredit the argument. If Student 2 has an 'Attack the Argument' card, Student 2 gives a valid reason for disagreeing with the argument. Student 3 then responds. Student 1 listens to both responses and guesses which cards Students 2 and 3 have. Then Students 2 and 3 reveal their cards to Student 1. For example:

Student 2:	'But didn't the president marry an immigrant?'
Student 3:	'But it has been shown that immigrants contribute to the economy of the country.'
Student 1:	'Okay, I think [Student 2] has an 'Attack the Person' card. I think [Student 3] has an 'Attack the Argument' card. Am I right?'

Students 2 and 3 reveal their cards.

10. Repeat Step 9 but this time Students 3 and 1 take a card from the pile and Student 2 thinks of an argument.
11. Repeat Step 9 but this time Students 1 and 2 take a card from the pile and Student 2 thinks of an argument.
12. Repeat Steps 9 to 11.
13. [Option] Put students into new groups of three to repeat Steps 9 to 11.
14. Have students reflect on the activity and discuss what they have learned about the ad hominem fallacy and how the argument should be attacked rather than the person.

*Note
Photocopy twice and cut out to make a set of 12 attack cards (6 Attack the Person and 6 Attack the Argument).

Attack Cards

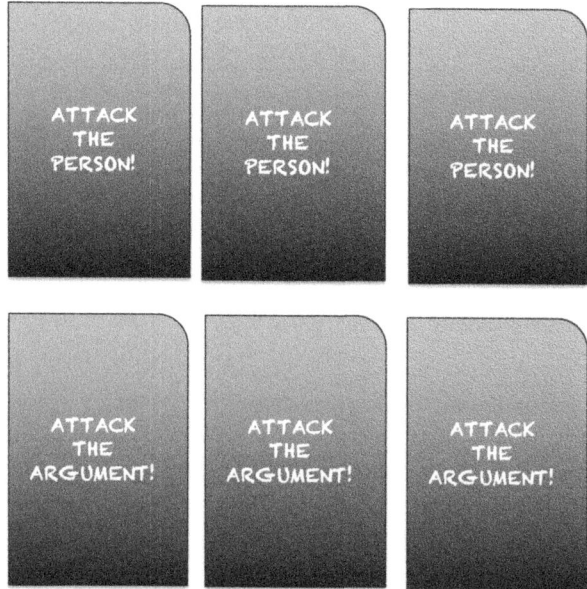

Activity 48: Guilt by Association

Introduction

	In the final activity focusing on the ad hominem fallacy, learners are introduced to the guilt by association as a type of ad hominem attack. Learners examine and discuss examples of guilt by association that can be used to attack someone rather than the argument itself and then think of their own guilt-by-association examples or experiences.
Aim	To understand the ad hominem fallacy; to understand guilt by association; to think of examples that illustrate guilt by association; to research examples online and/or share real-life examples of guilt-by-association attacks
Level	High-intermediate to Advanced
Time	50–60 minutes
Materials	None
Preparation	[Option] Research or think of examples of guilt by association prior to the class for Steps 10 and 12/13

178 From Implications to Application

Fallacy: Ad Hominem	
Definition	Attacking a person or people instead of dealing with the facts of the argument.
Example	This idea for recycling is just a bunch of crazy liberals trying to tell us what to do.

Procedure

1. On the board, write:

   'Do not compare yourself to others. If you do so you are insulting yourself.'

   Ask students what the quotation means, how they feel about this quotation, and whether they agree with it. Elicit responses from students.
2. Ask students to guess which famous person said this quotation. Elicit some responses and then give students the answer – this is a quote by Hitler.
3. Ask students how they feel about this quotation now and whether they still agree with it. Elicit responses from students.
4. If students now disagree with the quotation (as well as they might) ask them why they have changed their minds. The answer will probably be the source as Hitler. Explain to students that by discrediting the argument due to its source they have committed the ad hominem fallacy of attacking the person rather than addressing the argument. The fact that Hitler said the quotation may be irrelevant to the soundness or unsoundness of the argument.
5. Put students into groups of three or four. Explain that today students will look at one type of ad hominem attack; guilt by association. Write on the board:

   Mary: 'I think all young people should do art. Art can help young people to be more creative and studies have shown art helps to relax them. For example, schools with art programs have reported fewer behavioral problems and suspensions amongst students.'
6. Tell students to imagine they disagree with Mary. Have groups think of ways they could respond to Mary's argument. Elicit responses from students. Make sure students' address the argument.
7. Now, write on the board:

   Tom: 'Yeah, Mary, but Hitler was an artist when he was a young person and looked what happened to him.'
8. Ask each group to discuss Tom's response. How does Tom try to discredit Mary's argument? Elicit responses from each group. Possible answers:

As people may quickly reject the argument that art helped Hitler to become a better person, Tom implies that Mary's argument should be rejected, too. Tom associates Mary and her argument with a person considered historically to be bad/evil so that it is easier to knock down her argument. However, this is fallacious. Hitler's experience as an artist does not address the argument at hand.

9. Explain to students that the guilt-by-association form of this argument is as follows:

   Person 1 states that X is true.

   Person 2 also states that X is true, but Person 2 is morally flawed in some way.

   Therefore, Person 1 is also morally flawed and should not be trusted.

10. Using the logical form, have groups work together to come up with an example of the guilt-by-association fallacy. For example:

    Ted argues that the government should do a better job of controlling the number of immigrants entering the country.

    Nigel also argues that the government should do a better job of controlling the number of immigrants entering the country but is the leader of a white supremacy group and is known to have extreme racist views.

    Therefore, Ted must also be a racist and should not be trusted.

11. Put two groups together. Have them share their examples.
12. [Option 1] Have groups research on the Internet to find further examples of guilt by association. Have groups share their examples with their classmates.
13. [Option 2] Have groups think of and share real-life experiences of using or being the victim of the guilt-by-association attack or have students think of and share examples they have seen in the news, politics, or on social media. For example:

    'As my friend is a [political party], I find it difficult to believe anything he says. Usually, I just reply to his arguments by saying, "Well, you're a [political party]!" – that's an example of the guilt-by-association fallacy.'

14. Have students reflect on the activity and discuss what they have learned about the ad hominem fallacy and guilt by association. [Option] As we may all be guilty of ad hominem attacks from time to time, have students discuss whether they will change their behavior as a result of the activity.

Red Herring

Activity 49: Avoiding the Question

Introduction:

In this activity, learners can learn to identify when someone answers or avoids answering a question. Learners also practice responding to answer or avoid the question. The activity indirectly teaches learners to be aware of the red herring fallacy.	
Aim	To identify when someone is answering or avoiding a question; to learn about the red herring fallacy indirectly
Level	Elementary to Pre-intermediate
Time	70–80 minutes
Materials	Worksheet
Preparation	Copies of the worksheet for each student

Fallacy: Red Herring	
Definition	Avoiding the real topic by replacing it with an unrelated topic.
Example	Daughter: I want an ice cream. Mother: Oh, look at that cute cat over there.

Procedure

1. Pre-teach the verb, 'avoid.'
2. Have students make a list of things they avoid. Elicit some examples from students. For example:

    'I avoid crowded places.'
    'I avoid doing my homework.'
    'I avoid watching scary movies.'

3. Explain to students that there is a new horror movie showing at the movie theater. It's called *Zombies in Tokyo*. Everybody is talking about this movie. However, the movie is very scary. Many people have left the movie theater in the middle of the movie. Have students imagine they have a young son or a daughter or brother or sister who wants to see the movie. They ask (and write this on the board):

    'Can I go and see *Zombies in Tokyo* at the movie theater tomorrow night with my friends?'

4. Put students into pairs. Tell students to think of two or three responses to the question to not give permission to go to the movie.
5. Elicit responses from pairs and put some of them on the board.

6. Explain to students that sometimes we may avoid a question by introducing something that is not related, not connected, or irrelevant.
7. Give each student a copy of the worksheet. Have pairs work through Task 1 together.
8. Elicit answers from each pair. Then, give the answers to students (Task 2):
   1. A – this provides a reason that is related to the question.
   2. B – this avoids the question by shifting the focus on the responder. It does not provide a reason.
   3. A – this provides a reason that is related to the question.
   4. B – this avoids the question by shifting the topic to an alternative movie choice. It does not provide a reason.
   5. B – this avoids the question by changing the topic to focus on the friend. It does not provide a reason.
9. Have pairs look at the responses written on the board during Step 5. Have them discuss whether the responses answer or avoid the question.
10. Have pairs work through Task 3 together.
11. Put students into new pairs. Have Student 1 read Question 1 (Task 3). Student 2 chooses a response to give Student 1 (either 'answer' or 'avoid'). Student 1 listens to the response and then decides if Student 2 was answering or avoiding the question. Student 2 clarifies – 'I was answering the question' or 'I was avoiding the question.' Repeat with Question 2 and 3 and then have students switch roles.
12. [Option 1] Put students into new pairs and repeat Step 11.
13. [Option 2] Elicit some examples from pairs and put them on the board for students to copy down in their notebooks.
14. Have students reflect on the activity and discuss what they have learned about answering and avoiding the question.

WORKSHEET

QUESTION: 'Can I go and see *Zombies in Tokyo* at the movie theater tomorrow night with my friend?'

Task 1: Look at the following responses.

Do they answer the question or avoid the question?

Response 1:

'No, I'm sorry. I hear it's a very scary movie. Many people have left the movie theater in the middle of the movie feeling sick. They had nightmares for days after. I'm afraid you are too young to see the movie.'

A) This answers the question.
B) This avoids the question.

Response 2:

'No, you can't. When I was your age, I never watched scary movies.'

A) This answers the question.
B) This avoids the question.

Response 3:

'No, you can't. The movie is rated 18 and you're only 12. You won't get in.'

A) This answers the question.
B) This avoids the question.

Response 4:

'Why don't you watch a different movie instead?'

A) This answers the question.
B) This avoids the question.

Response 5:

'I hear your friend passed her English test last week. That's great news!'

A) This answers the question.
B) This avoids the question.

Task 2: Check your answers with your teacher.

Task 3: Read the following questions. For each question, write a response that answers the question and a response that avoids the question.

Question 1:	Teacher: Why didn't you hand in your homework on time?
Answer:	
Avoid:	

Question 2:	Mother: Why did you buy so much junk food?
Answer:	
Avoid:	

Question 3:	Boy/girlfriend: Why are you breaking up with me?
Answer:	
Avoid:	

Activity 50: Don't Distract Me!

Introduction

In this activity, learners are introduced to red herring responses to be aware of how people can distract or divert attention away from the argument. Learners make a list of situations and role-play red herring conversations.

Aim	To understand the red herring fallacy; to understand how people can distract or divert attention away from the argument; to role-play red herring conversations
Level	Intermediate to Advanced
Time	60–70 minutes
Materials	Worksheet
Preparation	Copy of the worksheet for each student

Fallacy: Red Herring	
Definition	Avoiding the real topic by replacing it with an unrelated topic.
Example	Daughter: I want an ice cream. Mother: Oh, look at that cute cat over there.

Procedure

1. Tell students to imagine they have run up an expensive bill on their smartphones. Their parents or partners are very angry with them. Write on the board:

    'I can't believe how much your phone bill is in [Month]. Just look at it!'

2. Put students into groups of three or four. Have students think of how they would respond to the speaker in this situation. Have them write down three or four responses.
3. Elicit responses from students. Write some of them on the board. Show how their responses address the problem. For example:

Problem:	Your phone bill is high.
Response:	I'm sorry. I sent many text messages to my friends. I thought they were free, but I was charged for them.
Reason 1:	I sent many text messages to my friends.
Reason 2:	The text messages weren't free.
Conclusion:	My phone bill was high.

4. Give each student a copy of the worksheet. Have groups work through Task 1.
5. Elicit answers from each group. Answers: Students should notice that each response attempts to divert attention away from the problem by changing the topic. For example:

1	Completely changes the topic to shift focus on schoolwork
2	Shifts the focus onto the complainer without addressing the problem
3	Changes the topic to talk about the design of the phone
4	Changes the topic to talk about the electricity bill
5	Completely changes the topic to shift focus to dinner

6. Explain about red herrings to students. A red herring is a fallacy that is used often by people to distract from the original topic, argument, or question by replacing it with an unrelated topic.
7. Have students work through Task 2 on the worksheet individually.
8. Elicit some of the situations and arguments students have written down in Task 2.
9. Put students into pairs. Refer students to the example conversation in Task 3 (Worksheet). Have them role-play similar conversations using the situations and arguments they wrote in Task 2. First, students assign each other roles. For example, 'I will be the employee and you be the boss.' Then, they role-play the conversation. Student 1 gives the argument. Student 2 must try to use a red herring to distract from the argument. Have students choose a new situation and argument and switch roles. Repeat until students have role-played all situations and arguments.
10. [Option 1] Call on pairs to come to the front and role-play one of their situations. Have the class listen carefully for how students try to distract each other from the original argument.
11. [Option 2] Put students into new pairs and repeat Step 9.

12. Have students reflect on the activity and discuss what they have learned about the red herring fallacy and how people may try to distract them from their original arguments or questions.

WORKSHEET

Argument: 'I can't believe how much your phone bill is. Just look at it!'

Task 1: Read the five responses to the argument.

What do you notice about each response?

1	Yeah, recently my classes at school have been difficult, but I got a great score in math the other day.
2	How about your phone bill? It's always huge!
3	Yeah, but my phone is really cool. Everybody loves the new purple design.
4	Yeah, the electricity bill was high this month, too.
5	Wow! Something smells good. What's for dinner?

Share your answers with the class.

Task 2: Make a list of five situations and arguments below. For example:

- Employee to boss: 'I think you should give me a raise!'
- Teacher to student: 'I can't believe you copied your homework assignment!'
- Voter to politician: 'We need more revenue to support programs in the local community!'

1	
2	
3	
4	
5	

Get ready to role-play your arguments with a partner.

Task 3: Use the situations and arguments you wrote down in Task 2. Role-play them with a partner. For each situation, Student 2 distracts Student 1 from the original argument! For example:

> Student 1: Okay, I'll be the employee. You be the boss!
> Student 2: Okay. Let's begin.
> Student 1: Thanks for meeting with me today. As you know I've been working very hard recently. I'd like you to give me a raise.
> Student 2: Well, we've all been working hard and the new product we're selling is doing well. In fact, we're going to expand the business.
> Student 1: I see, but how about my raise?
> Student 2: We're all working hard and I'm working hard, too. In fact, I haven't had a vacation in years.
> Student 1: Yes, we're all busy these days. However, I think we all deserve a raise.
> Student 2: Sorry, that's my phone. I got to take this call.

Activity 51: Red Herrings in Politics

Introduction

In this final activity focusing on the red herring fallacy, learners analyze real examples of red herrings in politics to avoid answering the question. Learners then examine the red herring fallacy and then role-play a press conference with a politician. They listen to identify red herrings or real answers made by the politician.

Aim	To understand red herrings used in politics; to research examples of red herrings; to listen for and identify red herrings or real answers
Level	High-intermediate to Advanced
Time	50–60 minutes
Materials	Dice for Step 7
Preparation	[Option] Search online for some current red herring examples in politics to supplement Step 3

Fallacy: Red Herring	
Definition	Avoiding the real topic by replacing it with an unrelated topic.
Example	Daughter: I want an ice cream. Mother: Oh, look at that cute cat over there.

Procedure

1. On the board, write:

   Journalist: 'Would you like comment on the tape that's been released in which you describe sexually assaulting women?'

   Politician: 'Well, that was locker-room talk. I'm not proud of it. And, I've said sorry to my family. But, you know what, we have a world where terrorists are killing people …'

   Put students into pairs or groups. Have them discuss the politician's response to the question by the journalist. Elicit some responses. [Option] Check online for and use an alternative example than the one provided. Look for an example in which a politician commits a red herring fallacy by introducing an irrelevant topic to the point at hand to divert attention away from the original issue (there are many!).

2. On the bord, write 'Red Herring' and explain to students that introducing topics that are irrelevant to the topics being discussed to distract from the main issue or avoid answering the questions is a common strategy used in politics. Write on board:

   'Person 1 introduces/asks a question about Argument X

   Person 2 presents/answers about Argument Y

   Therefore, Argument X is avoided.

3. Have pairs or groups search online for red herring examples in politics (there are many!). Have them share examples with the class. For example:

   Journalist: 'What would you do to help people in this country get access to healthcare?'

   Politician: 'That's a good question. There have been some good developments in healthcare over the last few months like the recent bill to lower the cost of medication. It's just like our foreign policies. We've made some great progress there, too!'

4. Have pairs or groups make a list of four or five current issues facing their country (e.g., unemployment, immigration, crime, climate change, healthcare, poverty, racism, LGBT rights, and education).
5. Elicit some issues from each pair or group and write them on the board.
6. Tell students to imagine they are journalists. They are going to attend a press conference in which they can ask questions to a politician about these issues. Give students some time to write three or four questions in their notebooks.

7. Put students into large groups. Give each group one die. Have each group decide their roles; one student is a politician for the ruling party and the other students are journalists. Explain that the journalists will ask questions to the politician. The student who is the politician secretly rolls the die. If the die shows an even number (2,4,6), the politician will answer the question. If the die shows an odd number (1, 3, 5), the politician will use a red herring to avoid answering the question. One of the journalists asks a question. The politician answers according to the role of the die. The journalists listen to the answer and have to say whether the answer was a red herring or not. For example:

Politician: [Rolls die and rolls a 4].
Journalist 1: Hi, this is [Name] from [Media outlet]. Recently, universities in this country have fallen in the global ranking. Could I ask you how your party plans to improve this situation?
Politician: That's a good question. We are aware of the ranking situation and are planning to invest money into higher education. We are also looking at ways that universities can recruit more educators to increase the number of staff to student ratio.
Journalists: We think you answered the question.
Politician: Yes, correct. [Rolls die and rolls a 3].
Journalist 2: Hi, [Name] from [Media outlet] here. In the election, your party said you were going to get tough on crime. And yet, a recent study has shown crime is getting worse in the inner cities. Can you comment on this?
Politician: Thank you. Yes, we are aware of the numbers. However, these numbers are lower than when the other party was in power. In fact, since coming to power, we've increased the number of police officers by 10%. Also, we've started several prison reform initiatives ...
Journalists: We think you avoided the question. There were several red herrings in your answer.
Politician: Yes, you got it. [Rolls die again].

8. Repeat Step 7 with the politician answering three or four more questions from the journalists. Then, have groups choose a new politician to answer questions in their group. The new politician is given the die and students repeat Step 7.
9. [Option] If Step 7 is challenging for your class, modify it. Have students choose one of their questions from Step 6 to ask each student who will take on the role of the politician. Have students share their questions in their

groups ahead of time. Give students time to think how they would answer or avoid each question in the role of the politician before starting Step 7.
10. Have students reflect on the activity and discuss what they have learned about the red herring fallacy in politics. [Option] Have students watch the news over the coming week and look out for red herring answers by politicians. Have students note them down and share them in the next class.

Circular Reasoning

Activity 52: Don't Go Round in Circles

Introduction

In this activity, learners are introduced to the circular reasoning fallacy. Learners analyze a series of circular arguments to discuss what is wrong with them and determine better ways to support each argument.	
Aim	To understand and identify circular reasoning; to make arguments that provide a reason rather than assume the conclusion
Level	Elementary to Pre-intermediate
Time	60–70 minutes
Materials	Worksheet
Preparation	Copies of the worksheet for each student

Fallacy: Circular Reasoning	
Definition	Similar to begging the question, the reason or premise assumes what it is attempting to prove in the conclusion.
Example	Everybody loves Susan because she is popular.

Procedure

1. Pre-teach the word, 'circular'
2. On the board, draw:

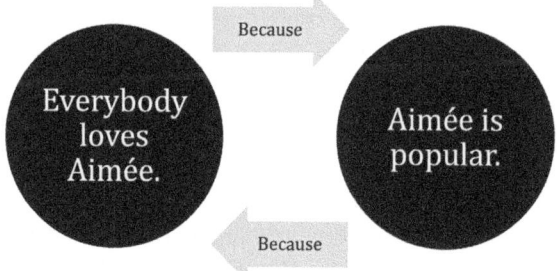

3. Ask students, 'Why does everybody loves Aimée?' Elicit the reason and write:

   Reason: She is popular
   Conclusion: Everybody loves her

4. Ask students, 'Why is she popular?' Elicit the reason and write:

   Reason: Everybody loves her
   Conclusion: She is popular

5. Put students in pairs or small groups. Ask students, 'What is the problem with the statement?' Have them discuss and then elicit some ideas. The answer is that the argument is circular. The conclusion (Everybody loves her) is true because of the reason (She is popular). However, the reason (She is popular) is only true, because of the conclusion (Everybody loves her). Thus, the reason does not help to support or prove the conclusion. Instead, it returns to the beginning of the argument without providing any useful information.

6. Elicit a better argument from students for Aimée being loved. For example:

   'Because she is kind.'

7. Give students a copy of the worksheet. Have pairs or small groups work through Task 1 (Worksheet).
8. Elicit answers from pairs or small groups. Answers are:

   1) They cannot win because I'm not voting for the politician.
   2) He told me he never told lies. It's true because Andy never tells lies.
   3) It is better than other cities because my city is the best place to live.
   4) I have to go because I can't stay.

9. Have pairs or small groups work through Task 2 (Worksheet).
10. Elicit answers from pairs or small groups. Possible answers are:

    1) The argument is circular. If you don't vote, the politician have no chance of winning.
    2) The argument is circular. Andy saying he never lies does not prove he does not lie. What if what he told you was a lie?
    3) The argument is circular. If the city is the best, it would be better because it is the best.
    4) The argument is circular. The reason returns to the conclusion which returns to the reason and so on.

11. Have pairs or small groups work through Task 3 (Worksheet).
12. Put pairs or small groups together to form new groups. Have students share their 'better' arguments together (Task 4 – Worksheet). Possible answers are:

1) I'm not voting for the politician because I disagree with her ideas.
2) I believe Andy never lies because his friends always talk about how honest he is.
3) My city is the best place to live because it is safe, has some beautiful parks, and there are many things to do.
4) I can't stay because my parents told me to be back home by 10pm.

13. [Option] Have students choose some example arguments to share with the whole class.
14. Have students reflect on the activity and discuss what they have learned about circular reasoning and making better arguments.

WORKSHEET

Task 1: Look at the four circular arguments. In each box, complete the missing words of the circular argument.

Argument 1:

I'm not voting for the politician. — Because → They can't win. — Because →

Circular argument:	I'm not voting for the politician because the politician cannot win. They cannot win because, _____.

Argument 2:

Andy never lies. — It's true because → He told me. — It's true because →

| **Circular argument:** | Andy never lies. It's true because he told me. He told me he never told lies. It's true because _____. |

Argument 3:

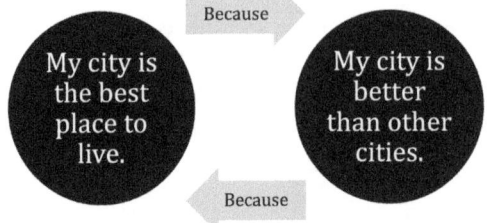

| **Circular argument:** | My city is the best place to live because it is better than other cities. It is better than other cities because _____. |

Argument 4:

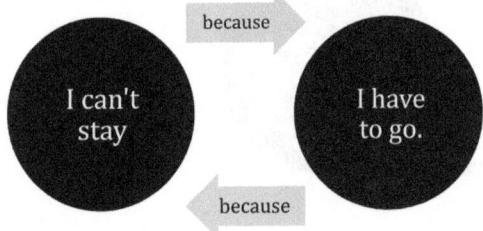

| **Circular argument:** | I can't stay because I have to go. I have to go because _____. |

Task 2: What is wrong with each argument? Discuss.

Task 3: Write better arguments for 1 to 4:

1	I'm not voting for the politician because
2	Andy never lies because
3	My city is the best place to live because
4	I can't stay because

Task 4: Share your better arguments with your classmates!

Activity 53: You Gotta Do What You Gotta Do!

Introduction

	In this activity, learners are introduced to the fallacy of circular reasoning. Learners examine dialogs to identify circular reasoning in everyday conversations and make their own circular reasoning arguments. Learners then discuss how to change circular reasoning into better arguments.
Aim	To understand circular reasoning; to listen for and identify circular reasoning in daily conversations; to avoid circular reasoning and make better arguments in daily conversations
Level	Intermediate to Advanced
Time	70–80 minutes
Materials	Worksheet
Preparation	Copy of the worksheet for each student

Fallacy: Circular Reasoning	
Definition	Similar to begging the question, the reason or premise assumes what it is attempting to prove in the conclusion.
Example	Everybody loves Susan because she is popular.

Procedure

1. On the board, write:

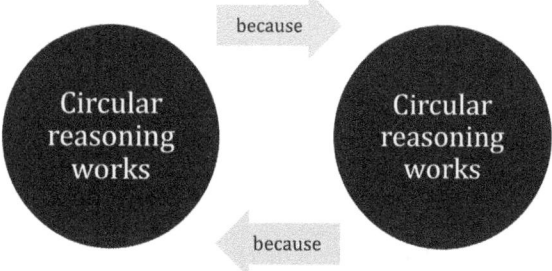

   Put students into small groups. Have them discuss what they think circular reasoning is from the example.
2. Elicit responses and explain to students that circular reasoning is when an argument returns to its beginning without moving forward or proving the conclusion. Write:

   Conclusion B: Circular reasoning works
   Reason A: Circular reasoning works

   A is true because of B and B is true because of A.

3. Give students a copy of the worksheet. Have groups work through Task 1.
4. Elicit answers from groups and go through Task 1 together as a class. Answers are:

1	Well, I guess you've got to do what you've got to do. **Conclusion**: You've got to quit your job **Reason:** You've got to quit your job
2	Well, I mean, learning about fallacies will help you develop your critical reasoning because it will help you think more critically. **Conclusion**: It will help you think more critically **Reason:** It will help you think more critically
3	You must follow the rules because you mustn't break them. The rules are the rules. **Conclusion:** You mustn't break the rules **Reason 1:** You mustn't break the rules **Reason 2:** The rules are the rules
4	Humans get to live because they are human **Conclusion**: Humans get to live **Reason:** They are human **Conclusion 2:** We should eat meat **Reason 2:** A steak is a steak!

5. [Option] Have students work through the four conversations in Task 1 (Worksheet) and change the statements so that they provide better reasons to support each conclusion. For example:

   A: I've decided to quit my job.
   B: Oh really? Why?
   A: I just feel like I've gone as far as I can. I want to try some new challenges.
   B: Well, I guess if that is how you feel, I think you should quit your job. It's important to challenge yourself so that you keep engaged and interested in what you do.
   A: Thanks!

6. Have groups work through Task 2 (Worksheet).
7. Have groups elect two members to perform the dialogs. Have each elected pair come to the front of the class and perform their dialogs. Have other students listen carefully and identify the circular reasoning statements in the dialogs.
8. Have groups swap worksheets. For example, Group 1 worksheet is given to Group 2, Group 2 worksheet is given to Group 3 and so on. Have groups look at the Task 2 dialogs and change the circular reasoning statement in each dialog so that it is a well-formed argument (the premise does not assume what it is attempting to prove in the conclusion.

9. Have each group elect two people to perform the dialogs. Have each elected pair come to the front of the class and perform. Have other students listen carefully for the modified statements in the dialogs. Have them discuss whether they provide better reasons to support each conclusion.
10. Have students reflect on the activity and discuss what they have learned about circular reasoning and making better arguments.

WORKSHEET

Task 1: Read the four dialogs and underline the statements that contain circular reasoning

Conversation 1:

A: I've decided to quit my job.
B: Oh really? Why?
A: I just feel like I've gone as far as I can. I want to try some new challenges.
B: Well, I guess you've got to do what you've got to do.
A: Thanks!

Conversation 2:

A: I've been studying fallacies in my English class recently, but the topic's quite difficult.
B: Yeah, but it's useful, isn't it?
A: How so?
B: Well, I mean, learning about fallacies will help you develop your critical reasoning because it will help you think more critically.
A: Yes, you're right. I didn't think about that.

Conversation 3:

A: I'm thinking of cheating on my English test.
B: No, you mustn't do it.
A: Why not?
B: You must follow the rules of the class.
A: Why?
B: Because you mustn't break them.
A: Why?
B: Because they're the rules and rules are rules. It's as simple as that!
A: Okay then.

Conversation 4:

A: I've decided to give up eating meat and become a vegetarian.
B: Wow, that's a big decision.
A: Yeah, but it's better for the environment and anyway, why do humans get to live and yet animals are killed for their meat?
B: Because they're human?
A: Yeah, but we can all eat vegetables instead.
B: I disagree. After all, a steak is a steak!

Task 2: Make your own dialog. Include a circular reasoning statement in your dialog:

A:	
B:	
A:	
B:	
A:	
B:	
A:	
B:	

Get ready to perform your dialogs for the class!

Activity 54: Is Circular Reasoning Begging the Question?

Introduction

In this final activity focusing on the circular reasoning fallacy, learners are made aware of the subtle differences between circular reasoning and begging the question (see Activities 28 to 30). Learners analyze two example arguments; one that is circular and one that is non-circular to understand the differences. They research and share further examples of circular reasoning and begging the question to discuss the differences between the fallacies.

Aim	To understand the subtle differences between circular reasoning and begging the question; to research and share examples of circular reasoning and begging the question
Level	High-intermediate to Advanced
Time	50–60 minutes
Materials	None
Preparation	None

Fallacy: Circular Reasoning	
Definition	Similar to begging the question, the reason or premise assumes what it is attempting to prove in the conclusion.
Example	Everybody loves Susan because she is popular.
Fallacy: Begging the Question	
Definition	The reason or premise in the argument already assumes that the conclusion is true.
Example	This is the best pizza in the world as no one makes a better pizza than this restaurant.

Procedure

1. On the board, write:

    'Eighteen-year-olds have the right to vote because …'

    Have students think of some reasons to complete the statement and elicit some responses.

2. On the board, complete the statement with:

    '… it is legal for eighteen-year-olds to vote.'

    Put students into pairs. Have them discuss the problem with this argument. Elicit responses from students.

3. On the board, draw:

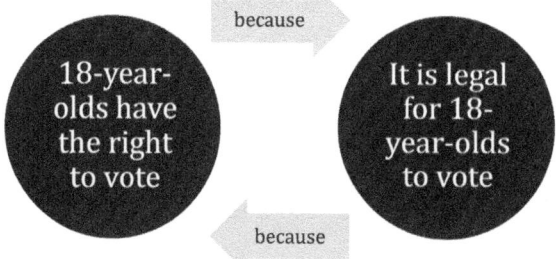

Explain that the argument is circular:

Reason: 18-year-olds can legally vote
Assumption: As it is legal, they have the right to vote
Conclusion: 18-year-olds have the right to vote

The premise (legal to vote) assumes what it is attempting to prove or assert in the conclusion (the right to vote) and by doing so creates a loop without providing additional evidence to assert the conclusion.

4. On the board, complete the statement in Step 1 with:

    '… they are mature.'

    Have pairs discuss the problem with this argument. Elicit responses from students.
5. Explain that the argument 'begs the question' but is not circular. (Refer students back to Activities 28 to 30):

Reason:	18-year-olds are mature
Assumption 1:	People who are mature enough should have the right to vote
Assumption 2:	If you have the right to vote, you must be mature enough
Conclusion:	18-year-olds have the right to vote

    The premise asks us to assume all 18-year-olds are mature to support the conclusion that they have the right to vote. However, the argument is not circular. It is possible to disagree with the premise (18-year-olds are mature) yet accept the conclusion (18-year-olds have the right to vote). It is also possible to agree with the premise and reject the conclusion. Explain that the circular reasoning and begging the question fallacies are very similar but some examples of begging the question may not be circular.
6. Have pairs research on the Internet for examples of begging the question or circular reasoning. Have them analyze the examples and discuss whether they are circular or non-circular. For example:

    '[Name of movie] was the greatest movie ever because it was the number one top grossing movie of all time.'

    This begs the question but is not circular. It is possible to disagree that the movie that made the highest amount of movie can be considered the greatest. Many poor movies make money.

    'The news is fake because it's just not true.'

    This is circular:

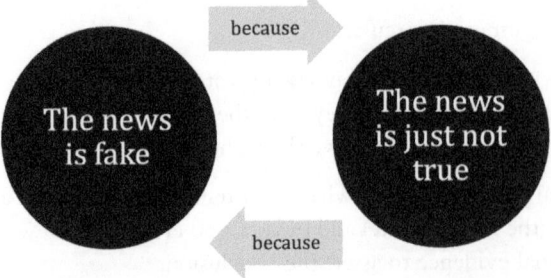

7. Put two pairs together to form a group. Have each pair share their examples.
8. [Option] Switch pairs again to form new groups and share their examples.
9. Elicit some issues from each pair or group and write them on the board.
10. Have students reflect on the activity and discuss what they have learned about circular reasoning and begging the question. [Option] Have students listen out for examples on the news or in real-life conversations over the following week and have them report on their examples in the next class.

Straw Man

Activity 55: Don't Exaggerate!

Introduction

In this activity, as a first step to understanding the straw man fallacy, learners are introduced to exaggerations. Learners identify how somebody may use exaggerations in everyday conversations to change or distort the original argument and make it easier to reach new conclusions.

Aim	To understand exaggerations; to identify how somebody can exaggerate in order to change or distort from the original argument to make it easier to attack to reach new conclusions
Level	Elementary to Pre-intermediate
Time	50–60 minutes
Materials	Worksheet
Preparation	Copies of the worksheet for each student

Fallacy: Straw man	
Definition	B makes an exaggerated version of A's assertion, claim, or statement so that it is easier to attack.
Example	Father: You must be home from the party by 10pm. Son: Why do you hate me?

Procedure

1. Write on the board, 'I've told you a million times not to exaggerate!' Have students look up the meaning of the word, 'exaggerate.' Elicit the meaning of the joke statement from students.
2. Explain that when people disagree with another person they may exaggerate or change the topic of the argument so that it is easier to attack it. Write on the board:

    Student: I think the class should be easier.
    Teacher: I can't give 'A's to every student!

3. Ask students, 'What is the student's argument?' Elicit, 'The class is too difficult. It should be easier.' Ask students, 'Does the teacher disagree?' Elicit, 'Yes.' Ask students, 'What is the teacher's argument?' Elicit that the argument is that the teacher cannot give an A grade to every student in the class. Ask students, 'Did the student ask the teacher to give every student an A?' Elicit, 'No.' Elicit from students that the teacher's response is an exaggeration. Explain that the exaggeration makes it easier to attack the student's opinion. It makes it difficult for the student to complain further. Also, it changes the argument from the level of the class to grading students.
4. [Option] Put students into pairs or small groups to think of a better response by the teacher. For example:

    Teacher: I hear what you're saying, but I need to get you ready for the IELTS test.

5. Give each student a copy of the worksheet. Have pairs or small groups work through the task.
6. Elicit answers from each pair or group. Answers are:

1	d	Exaggerates and changes the topic from staying home to attacking Speaker 1 for never wanting to have fun.
2	c	Exaggerates. Speaker 1 never mentioned hating dogs.
3	a	Exaggerates and changes the topic from the class project to the upcoming school festival.
4	b	Exaggerates. Speaker 2 has many shirts so will have something to wear at the party.

7. Using the worksheet conversations as a guide, have students make their own two-line dialogs. In Line 1, Speaker 1 gives an opinion. In Line 2, Speaker 2 disagrees with it. Students can decide to use a response that exaggerates or not in Line 2.
8. Call on volunteers and have students perform their dialogs in front of the class. Have class members listen to each dialog and decide if Speaker 2's response is an exaggeration or not.
9. Have students reflect on the activity and discuss what they have learned about how people can exaggerate to make it easier to attack the original argument to reach new conclusions.

WORKSHEET

Task: Look at each conversation and choose the response (a to d) that exaggerates the original argument:

Conversation 1:

Speaker 1: I'd rather stay home today.

Speaker 2: a) Oh really? But it's a beautiful day.
b) We should go out and get some fresh air.
c) But we stayed home yesterday.
d) You never want to have any fun.

Conversation 2:

Speaker 1: I'd rather get a cat than a dog.
Speaker 2: a) But dogs are friendlier.
b) Why do you think so?
c) Why do you hate dogs?
d) But cats are selfish.

Conversation 3:

Speaker 1: I think we should work hard on this class project.
Speaker 2: a) So, you don't care about the school festival?
b) I'm too busy with preparations for the school festival.
c) We still have lots of time to finish it.
d) We could but it is only 10% of the final grade.

Conversation 4:

Speaker 1: I don't think you should buy a new shirt. You already have many shirts at home.
Speaker 2: a) But I really like it.
b) But I'll have nothing to wear for the party tomorrow.
c) But it's on sale at the moment.
d) But this one is perfect for the party tomorrow.

Check your answers with your classmates and teacher.

Activity 56: Family Arguments

Introduction

	In this activity, learners examine a series of conversations between a teenager and a parent. Learners identify how each argument can be changed or distorted from the original topic to make it easier to reach new conclusions.
Aim	To understand straw man arguments; to identify how an argument can be changed or distorted from the original topic to make it easier to attack to reach new conclusions
Level	Intermediate to Advanced
Time	50–60 minutes
Materials	Worksheet
Preparation	Copies of the worksheet for each student

Fallacy: Straw Man	
Definition	B makes an exaggerated version of A's assertion, claim, or statement so that it is easier to attack.
Example	Father: You must be home from the party by 10pm. Son: Why do you hate me?

Procedure

1. Pre-teach the word, 'argument.'
2. Put students into small groups. Have them list the types of arguments or fights that may occur between parents and their children (e.g., staying out late at night vs. being back home/messy rooms vs. tidy rooms/too much time on the smartphone vs. not enough time doing homework).
3. Elicit some responses from each pair or group and write them on the board.
4. Give each student a copy of the worksheet. Have groups choose two members to stand up and perform the short dialog (Task 1) worksheet for their group.
5. Ask students the following questions about the dialog:

    A) Where does the teenager want to go?
    B) Does the parent say yes or no to the teenager?
    C) What is the reason?
    D) What is the teenager's argument?
    E) Is it the same topic of the argument?
    F) What do you think the parent's reply will be?

    Possible answers:

    A) The movie theater with friends
    B) No

From Implications to Application   203

  C) It is a school night. The teenager has school the next day.
  D) The parent does not want the teenager to have any friends.
  E) No, it is different. The teenager has changed the argument. By making the parent's reason/refusal to let the teenager go out with his friends sound much worse than it is, it is easier for the teenager to attack the reason/refusal or for the parent to give in and say yes.
  F) The parent may say, 'No, it is good for you to have friends. Okay you can go just this one time.'
6. Have groups work through Task 2 on the worksheet.
7. Elicit answers from each group. Possible answers are:

Conversation 1:
1. To get a dog
2. Dogs are expensive and need walking every day.
3. 1) they will protect the family and 2) the parent does not want to protect the family.
4. 1) Yes – it is a good reason but 2) changes the topic of the argument. The argument of the parent not wanting to protect the family is an exaggeration to make the refusal sound worse.
5. Of course, I want to protect the family. However, we're not getting a dog.
Conversation 2:
1. To get a higher allowance
2. The teenager gets a good enough allowance and gets the same as his or her sister.
3. 1) the sister is younger so should get less money and 2) the sister always gets what she wants.
4. 1) Possibly – if you believe children should get an allowance based on age but 2) changes the topic of the argument to attack the parent of being unfair and favoring the sister. This has nothing to do with the original argument of believing the allowance is fair.
5. No, she doesn't. (A dangerous reply as the topic has now been changed from the original argument.)
Conversation 3:
1. To get the smartphone back
2. The teenager has homework to do.
3. 1) to check messages and 2) attack the parent for making the teenager's life difficult.
4. 1) Yes – it is a good argument if the messages are related to the homework but 2) changes the topic – it is an exaggeration to make the refusal sound worse – you make 'everything' difficult has nothing to do with the original argument of homework and smartphones.
5. I bought you the smartphone! (A dangerous reply as the topic has now changed from the original argument.)

8. [Option 1] Using the worksheet conversations as a guide, have students make their own teenager and parent dialog. Have students perform their dialogs in front of the class. Have class members listen for the straw man argument by the teenager.
9. [Option 2] Introduce the straw man fallacy to students:

    Person A: Makes an argument
    Person B: Presents a changed/exaggerated argument (a straw man) that is easier to attack
    Person B: Attacks Person A's argument.

10. Have students reflect on the activity and discuss what they have learned about how arguments can be changed by people to make them easier to attack to reach new conclusions.

WORKSHEET

Task 1: Choose two people in your group to perform the following dialog:

Example conversation:

Teenager: Can I go and watch a movie with my friends tomorrow night?
Parent: What time does the movie finish?
Teenager: It's the late show, so about 11.30pm.
Parent: No, I'm sorry. It's a school night, so you need to be in bed by 11pm.
Teenager: You don't want me to have friends, do you?

Task 2: Look at the following three dialogs. For each dialog, choose two people to perform it for your group and then answer the questions below.

Conversation 1:

Teenager: Can we get a dog?
Parent: No, I'm sorry. Dogs are expensive to look after, and they need walking every day.
Teenager: But a dog will protect the family.
Parent: The answer is still no.
Teenager: I can't believe you don't want to protect our family.

1. What is the teenager's request?

2. What is the parent's reason for saying no?

3. What are the two arguments of the teenager?

4. Are they the same topic of the argument?

5. What do you think the parent's reply will be?

Conversation 2:

Teenager: Can you increase my allowance?
Parent: No, I'm sorry. You get more than enough. Also, if I increase your allowance, I will need to increase your sister's allowance.
Teenager: But, she's two years younger than me.
Parent: That's not important.
Teenager: It's not fair. She always gets what she wants.

1. What is the teenager's request?

2. What is the parent's reason for saying no?

3. What are the two arguments of the teenager?

4. Are they the same topic of the argument?

5. What do you think the parent's reply will be?

Conversation 3:

Teenager: Can I get my smartphone back?
Parent: No, I'm sorry. You have homework to do. I'll give it back to you after you finish.
Teenager: But, I need to check my messages.
Parent: You can check them after.
Teenager: Why do you always have to make my life difficult?

1. What is the teenager's request?
2. What is the parent's reason for saying no?
3. What are the two arguments of the teenager?
4. Are they the same topic of the argument?
5. What do you think the parent's reply will be?

Activity 57: Countering a Straw Man Argument

Introduction

In this final activity focusing on the straw man fallacy, learners analyze an argument on self-driving cars. Learners research online to find more examples of straw man arguments and discuss ways they can counter these arguments. They then demonstrate strategies for countering via short role-plays.	
Aim	To understand the straw man fallacy; to research examples online; to discuss ways to counter a straw man argument; to practice countering straw man arguments via short role-plays
Level	Intermediate to Advanced
Time	70–80 minutes

Materials	None
Preparation	You may wish to research examples of the straw man fallacy for Steps 6 to 8

Fallacy: Straw Man	
Definition	B makes an exaggerated version of A's assertion, claim, or statement so that it is easier to attack.
Example	Father: You must be home from the party by 10pm. Son: Why do you hate me?

Procedure

1. Put students into pairs or small groups. Ask students to discuss what they think of self-driving cars.
2. Elicit some ideas from pairs or groups.
3. On the board, write:

    Speaker A: I think self-driving cars are the way forward. I mean they are much safer and minimize the potential of mistakes that people often make when driving. Some of these mistakes can be fatal.

    Speaker B: You just value technological advancements over people's jobs. Think about the job losses in the transportation industry. Don't you care about the economy?

4. Elicit from students what Speaker A's position is:

    Speaker A: Self-driving cars are safer.

    Ask students whether they believe Speaker B addressed Speaker A's position or not.

    Elicit that Speaker B did not.

    Have students think about Speaker B's response. Ask students, 'What did Speaker B do?'

    Elicit responses and explain that Speaker B created a 'straw man' response – a distorted, exaggerated version of Speaker A's position. Then, Speaker B proceeded to attack that distorted version of the argument. Explain that this is called the 'Straw man fallacy' and is used quite often by people to distract from the real issue or argument at hand.

5. On the board, write:

    Straw man fallacy

Speaker A:	asserts position X
Speaker B:	(1) creates a 'straw man' or distorted version of position X (Y), (2) attacks position Y, (3) concludes X is false

6. Have pairs or groups research two or three examples of the straw man fallacy online.
7. Put pairs or groups together to form larger groups and share the examples they found online. They may use Step 5 as a means of presenting their examples. For example:

Speaker A:	We should improve public transportation so that more people use it. Single occupancy vehicle use is contributing to climate change. (Position X)
Speaker B:	So, you think people should stop using their cars? (Creates Position Y). That's crazy! (Attacks Position Y) People need to get to work or go grocery shopping. Do they just walk to these places? (Supports Position Y). We can't stop people using their cars. (Concludes X is wrong).

8. Have new groups think of ways to counter a straw man argument. Have them use the examples they shared in Step 7 and determine ways they could respond to Speaker B's use of a straw man argument.
9. Elicit ideas from each group.★ Possible answers are:

    - Point out that their response is a straw man argument and ask them to explain how it is connected to the original argument (For example: 'I hear what you're saying but I am not sure how it is related to my original point. Can you explain in more detail how what you said is connected to my point on improving public transportation?')
    - Ignore the straw man argument and continue to support your original position. (For example: 'Yeah, so I think the government needs to spend more money on improving the buses, trains, and subways in the city.')
    - Accept the straw man argument and defend against it. (For example: 'Yeah, I hear what you're saying, people do need to get to work or go grocery shopping, but some of those people may be encouraged to use public transportation if …')

★Note
Provide any ways that students have not considered and provide examples of each way to counter a straw man argument for students (see possible answers and examples above).

10. Put students into pairs. Give them time to prepare a straw man dialog. Have them choose one straw man example from Step 7. Pairs decide their roles: Speaker A (asserts the position) and Speaker B (gives a straw man argument). They also decide the best way for Speaker A to counter the straw man argument using strategies from Step 9.
11. Call on volunteer pairs to perform their straw man dialogs in front of the class. Have other students listen carefully to the dialogs for Speaker A's argument, Speaker B's straw man response, and Speaker A's counter.
12. Have students reflect on the activity and discuss what they have learned about the straw man fallacy and how to counter it.

Either/Or

Activity 58: The Third Option

Introduction

In the activity, learners ask each other preference questions with two options. Learners then consider the problem of an either/or choice. The learners practice offering alternative options to questions in which only two options are presented. This activity indirectly introduces learners to the either/or fallacy.	
Aim	To understand the either/or fallacy indirectly; to challenge questions in which only two options are presented; to offer alternative options to questions in which only two options are presented
Level	Elementary to Pre-intermediate
Time	40–50 minutes
Materials	Worksheet
Preparation	Copies of the worksheet for each student

Fallacy: Either/Or	
Definition	Only two choices are given in the reasoning when more choices exist.
Example	Either you get married, or you will spend the rest of your life alone.

Procedure

1. Pre-teach, 'Would you rather X or Y?'
2. Give each student a copy of the worksheet. Have them read through Questions 1 to 6 on the worksheet and write their own 'Would you rather …' questions for Questions 7 and 8 (Task 1 – Worksheet).
3. Have students walk around the classroom with their worksheets, ask their questions to their classmates, and write down the replies they receive (Task 2 – Worksheet). Set a time limit for Step 3 and then have students return to their seats.
4. Go through Questions 1 to 8 and elicit some of the responses to the questions.
5. Put students into small groups and ask them if they can think of any problems with Questions 1 to 8 or whether they experienced any problems when answering the questions. Elicit from students that the questions only offer two options, X or Y. [Option] Ask students how many options each question has and then ask them what the problem is with the 'Would you rather' questions.
6. Have students ask you some of the questions (1 to 8) and give a third option for each answer. For example:

    Student 1: Would you rather have a cat or a dog for a pet?
    Teacher: Well, actually, I'd rather not have a pet. I am too busy to look after one.
    Student 2: Would you rather eat Italian food or eat Chinese food?
    Teacher: Well, actually, I'd rather eat Indian food right now.

7. Have students repeat Step 3 but this time they should answer with a third option – 'Well, actually, I'd rather …' (Task 3 – Worksheet).
8. Go through Questions 1 to 8 and elicit some of the third-option responses students gave to the questions.
9. [Option] Have students think of times in their lives in which they were offered only two options, but other options existed. For example:

    'When I was young, my father told me I had to eat all of my vegetables on my plate or I could not leave the table. There was a third option! My mother said I could leave the table!'

10. Have students reflect on the activity and discuss what they have learned about being presented with only two options when other choices exist.

WORKSHEET

Task 1: Read Questions 1 to 6 – 'Would you rather ...?' Make your own 'Would you rather' questions for 7 and 8.

1. Would you rather have a cat or a dog for a pet?
2. Would you rather eat Italian food or eat Chinese food?
3. Would you rather play soccer or play tennis?
4. Would you rather live in America or live in Australia?
5. Would you rather travel in summer or travel in winter?
6. Would you rather be inside or outside on a sunny day?
7. _____ ?
8. _____ ?

Task 2: Ask your classmates the eight questions and make a note of their responses in the spaces provided above.

Task 3: Ask your classmates the eight questions again and make a note of the third-option responses they gave you in the spaces provided below:

1	
2	
3	
4	
5	
6	
7	
8	

Activity 59: Either A or B But What About C?

Introduction

In this activity, learners are introduced to and understand the purpose of the either/or fallacy. Learners are encouraged to respond to either/or statements with an alternative option C.	
Aim	To understand the purpose of either/or statements; to respond to either/or statements with alternative options
Level	Intermediate to Advanced
Time	50–60 minutes

Materials	Worksheet
Preparation	Copies of the worksheet for each student

Fallacy: Either/Or	
Definition	Only two choices are given in the reasoning when more choices exist.
Example	Either you get married, or you will spend the rest of your life alone.

Procedure

1. On the board write, 'You can either come with me to the party or you can stay home and be bored.' Elicit from students the situation in which they may hear this type of argument.
2. On the board write:

    Either A or B
    Not B
    Then A

3. Elicit from students that A is go to the party, B is stay home and be bored; as B (staying home) is less desirable, the preferred response is A (go to the party). Explain that this is the 'either/or fallacy.' Ask students, 'In the example on the board, what is the speaker's intention in using the either/or fallacy?' Elicit the speaker's purpose is to make B seem less desirable and have the listener make what appears to be the right choice – 'Come with me to the party.'
4. Put students into pairs or small groups. Have them look again at the 'either/or' statement in Step 1. Explain that the speaker presents only two options for the listener. However, in reality there are many options for the listener. Have students list other options besides B – staying home and being bored.
5. Elicit ideas from each pair or group. Possible answers are:
    - Stay home and do something exciting
    - Stay home and get some sleep
    - Stay home and save some money
    - Stay home and ask friends over for a rival party
    - Stay home and catch up on homework
    - Stay home and not have to go out in the rain
6. Give a copy of the worksheet to students. In their pairs or groups, have them complete each 'either/or' statement with a less desirable option B.

For example:

2) Either you do your homework, or you will fail this course.
3) You can either drink water and be healthy or drink soda and get sick.
4) You can either pursue your dream job or be miserable the rest of your life.
5) Either you get married, or you spend the rest of your life alone.
6) Either you vote for [NAME] or nothing will change.
7) You are either with us or against us.
8) You either study critical thinking or get tricked with either/or arguments all of the time.

[Option] Have students look again through the list of statements and think of the situation in which they may hear it. For example:

2) Classroom – Teacher to student
3) Dinner time – Parent to child
4) Coffee shop – Friend to friend
5) Home – Parent to child
6) Coffee shop – Friend to friend
7) Union – worker to worker
8) Classroom – Teacher to student

7. Elicit some examples and put them on the board.
8. Tell students they must try to persuade you to choose Option A and you will respond by pointing out a third option. Call on volunteers to stand up, come to the front, and try to convince you to do Option A. Listen and point out Option C. For example:

Student: Either you do your homework, or you will fail this course.
Option C: I might not do my homework and still pass as it is only worth 10% of the final grade. Also, I might win the lottery tomorrow and stop coming to school altogether!

9. Give students some time to read through the worksheet again and think of Option Cs to each of the either/or statements.
10. Put students into new pairs. Have Student 1 use one of the either/or statements from Step 6 to persuade Student 2. Student 2 points out an Option C to Student 1. Have them switch roles and repeat with a new statement. Repeat until all statements have been used.
11. [Option] Have students research online for more either/or examples (NB: When searching online, point out to students that the fallacy is also called 'False Dilemma'). Have students share their examples and think of how they would respond to each either/or statement.
12. Have students reflect on the activity and discuss what they have learned about the either/or fallacy, how it may be used to persuade people, and how listeners can respond to it by pointing out alternative options.

WORKSHEET

Task: Complete each either/or argument with a less desirable Option B:

	Option A:	Option B:
1	You can either come with me to the party	or you can stay home and be bored.
2	Either you do your homework	or
3	You can either drink water and be healthy	or
4	You can either pursue your dream job	or
5	Either you get married	or
6	Either you vote for [NAME]	or
7	You are either with us	or
8	Either you study critical thinking	or

Activity 60: It's Not So Black and White!

Introduction

In this final activity focusing on the either/or fallacy, learners are introduced to arguments that force a person to choose either black or white. Learners analyze either/or arguments and discuss alternative choices. Important: please feel free to modify or change the examples on the worksheet if you feel the topics are not suitable for your learners.

Aim	To understand the either/or fallacy, to understand arguments that force a person to choose either black or white, to state alternative choices for black-and-white arguments
Level	Intermediate to Advanced
Time	60–70 minutes
Materials	Worksheet
Preparation	Copies of the worksheet for each student. [Option] Prepare an appropriate 'either/or' example for your students for Step 2

Fallacy: Either/Or	
Definition	Only two choices are given in the reasoning when more choices exist.
Example	Either you get married, or you will spend the rest of your life alone.

Procedure

1. On the board, write:

    Either A or B
    Not B
    Then A

2. Explain that today we will look at the either/or fallacy, a type of black-or-white thinking in which only two options are seen as possible – you are either good or bad. Give an example to students to help them understand. One example is George Bush's war on terror after 9/11 in which he stated, 'You are either with us, or you are with the terrorists.' Break down the example to show students how the either/or fallacy works:

    You are either with us (A) or you are with the terrorists (B)
    Being with the terrorists (B) is a bad choice
    Then you must be with us (A)

    Often, the listener is presented with only two choices with one being the less desirable choice.

3. Put students into pairs. Have them work through Task 1 on the worksheet.
4. Elicit answers from students. Answers are:

    - (1) Support praying (A) or an atheist (B)
      Being an atheist (B) is seen as a bad choice
      Then you must support praying (A)
    - (2) Vote for the female candidate (A) or you are against women's rights (B)
      Being against women's rights (B) is seen as a bad choice
      Then you must vote for the female candidate (A)
    - (3) You are pro war (A) or you are against the troops (B)
      Being against the troops (B) is seen as a bad choice
      Then you must be pro war (A)
    - (4) You are either for guns (A) or you want anarchy (B)
      Anarchy (B) is seen as a bad choice
      Then you must be for guns (A)
    - (5) We either enforce the death penalty (A) or the murderers will be released one day (B)
      Having murderers on the streets (B) is seen as a bad choice
      Then we must enforce the death penalty (A)
    - (6) We are either against increasing pay for low paid workers (A) or we want the economy to collapse (B)
      Wanting the economy to collapse (B) is seen as a bad choice
      Then we must be against raising the minimum wage (A)

5. Have students work through Task 2 on the worksheet.
6. Elicit answers from students. Possible answers are:

   - The listener may be religious but believe praying should be done in a place of worship, or at home with the family.
   - The listener may believe in women's rights but disagree with the policies of the candidate.
   - The listener may support the idea of a country having armed forces as a form of self-defense; the listener may believe the war is politically motivated.
   - The listener may be against citizens owning guns but believe in law and order. They may believe only the police should carry guns.
   - The listener may believe that people who commit terrible crimes can be rehabilitated into society.
   - The listener may believe that prices will not increase. The budget could come from paying top management smaller bonuses.

7. Have students work through Task 3 on the worksheet.
8. Put students into new pairs. Have them swap their 'either/or' statements from Step 7. Give students time to read through the statements and think of alternative options.
9. Have students turn their statements from Step 7 into dialogs. Student 1 says the either/or statement and Student 2 says, 'It's not so black and white,' and explains alternative options. For example:

   Student 1: Either you are for investing in coal or you want us to be more energy dependent on our enemies.

   Student 2: Sorry, it's not so black and white. We could invest in renewable energy, for example. Then, we would be self-reliant and not need to buy energy from other countries.

   Have students keep switching roles and work through their statements from Step 7.
10. [Option 1] Call on volunteer pairs to perform one of their dialogs in front of the class.
11. [Option 2] Put students into new pairs and repeat Step 9.
12. Have students reflect on the activity and discuss what they have learned about the either/or fallacy and how to counter it.

218 From Implications to Application

> **WORKSHEET**
>
> **Task 1:** On a separate piece of paper, rewrite the following statements as –
>
> > Either A or B
> > Not B
> > Then A
>
> **Statement 1:** Either you support praying in schools, or you're an atheist.
> **Statement 2:** Either you vote for the female candidate, or you don't believe in women's rights.
> **Statement 3:** Either you're for the war, or you're against the troops.
> **Statement 4:** Either you believe in the right to bear arms, or you believe in anarchy.
> **Statement 5:** If we don't have the death penalty, eventually we'll have murderers set free roaming the streets to kill again.
> **Statement 6:** If we pay employees a higher wage, this will significantly increase prices, reduce business, and collapse the economy.
>
> **Task 2:** Look again at Statements 1 to 6. For each argument, it is not so black and white.
>
> What are some alternative choices or ideas? Discuss and make notes on a separate piece of paper.
>
> **Task 3:** Look again at Statements 1 to 6. Think of some controversial topics. Write three or four of your own 'either/or' statements about these topics on a separate piece of paper. Get ready to share your statements.

Stacking the Deck

Activity 61: Half the Picture

Introduction

	In this activity, learners understand the need to present and listen to both sides of an argument before making a decision. The activity indirectly teaches learners the stacking the deck fallacy.
Aim	To understand the stacking the deck fallacy indirectly; to present/listen to both sides of an argument before making a decision
Level	Elementary to Pre-intermediate
Time	50–60 minutes

Materials	Blank paper for Step 3
Preparation	None

Fallacy: Stacking the deck	
Definition	Presenting only the reasons or data in the argument that support the conclusion.
Example	Advert: This soda now has 10% less sugar (the original had 49 grams of sugar).

Procedure

1. Pre-teach, 'for/against'
2. On the board, write,

   The best city to live.
   The best pet to have.
   The best season.
   The best day of the week.

   Elicit from students four or five more 'best' topics to talk about in class and write them on the board.
3. Put students into pairs. Have them choose one of the 'best' topics from the board. For example – The best season. Give each pair a piece of blank paper. Have them write at the top of the paper. 'The best [TOPIC] is [THEIR CHOICE]' For example – 'The best season is summer.' Then, have them draw a line from their title down the middle of the paper. On the left-hand side, have them write 'For' under their title at the top of the paper. Have them work together to list reasons for their argument. For example:

The best season is summer	
FOR • It is hot • We have a vacation from school • We can enjoy barbecues outside • We can go to the beach • We can wear shorts • There are summer festivals	

4. Put pairs together to form groups. Have each pair read out their paper and present their arguments to each other.

5. Ask students to think about the arguments they have listened to in their groups and ask them, 'What is one problem for the listeners trying to decide if they agree or disagree?' As a hint, pick up one of the papers from one pair and show the blank right-hand side of the paper. Ask students, 'What is missing?' Elicit from or explain to students that they have only heard the arguments for and not against. They have only heard the positives, not the negatives, so for the listeners trying to decide if they agree or not, they have only heard half of the picture.
6. Have pairs in each group swap their papers. Pair 1 swaps their paper with Pair 2 and Pair 2 swaps their paper with Pair 1. On the right-hand side, have them write 'Against' under their title at the top of the paper. Have them work together to list reasons against the other pair's argument. For example:

The best season is summer	
FOR	AGAINST
• It is hot • We have a vacation from school • We can enjoy barbecues outside • We can go to the beach • We can wear shorts • There are summer festivals	• It is too hot • We can get sick when we relax • We have a lot of chores to do • I miss my school friends • Many insects bite us • We have to use the air conditioner

7. Have pairs swap their papers back and read the arguments against. Give them time to clarify with each other any arguments they do not understand.
8. Switch pairs so that each original pair from Step 3 joins a new pair to form a new group. Have each pair presents their arguments to each other, however, this time, they present their answers with the reasons against. For example:

> 'We think the best season is summer. Although [Reasons Against], [Reasons For]. Do you agree or disagree with us?'

Pairs listen to the argument and decide if they agree or disagree with the argument and why.
9. [Option] Switch pairs again so that they work with a new pair. Repeat Step 8.
10. Have students reflect on the activity and discuss what they have learned about presenting both sides of an argument to the listener(s).

Activity 62: The Full Picture

Introduction

In this activity, learners are given half the picture of a story and then the full picture and asked if they would change their minds once given the full information. Learners are then introduced to the 'stacking the deck' fallacy and learn the importance of obtaining all the evidence before reaching a conclusion.

Aim	To understand the importance of obtaining all the evidence before reaching a conclusion; to understand the 'stacking the deck' fallacy
Level	Intermediate to Advanced
Time	50–60 minutes
Materials	Half- and full-picture cards
Preparation	Print out/make a set of cards for each group

Fallacy: Stacking the deck	
Definition	Presenting only the reasons or data in the argument that support the conclusion.
Example	Advert: This soda now has 10% less sugar (the original had 49 grams of sugar).

Procedure

1. Put students into small groups. Give each group a copy of 'Card 1' (see Half-Picture and Full-Picture Cards). Have them answer the question at the end of the card and discuss what they will do.
2. Elicit responses from groups.
3. Ask one person from each group to come to the front and collect 'The Full Picture – Card 1.' Explain that the student will share this new information to the group and see if those who wanted to try the soda in Step 1 want to change their minds.
4. Elicit response from groups.
5. Give each group a copy of 'Card 2' (see Half-Picture and Full-Picture Cards). Have them answer the question at the end of the card and discuss what they will do.
6. Elicit responses from groups.
7. Ask one person from each group to come to the front and collect 'The Full Picture – Card 2.' Explain that the student will share this new information

to the group and see if those who didn't want the vaccination in Step 5 want to change their minds
8. Elicit responses from groups.
9. Give each group a copy of 'Card 3' (see Half-Picture and Full-Picture Cards). Have them answer the question at the end of the card and discuss what they will do.
10. Elicit responses from groups.
11. Ask one person from each group to come to the front and collect 'The Full Picture – Card 3.' Explain that the student will share this new information to the group and see if those who wanted to buy the smartphone in Step 9 want to change their minds
12. Elicit responses from groups.
13. Give each group a copy of 'Card 4' (see Half-Picture and Full-Picture Cards). Have them discuss if they agree with the people.
14. Elicit responses from groups.
15. Ask one person from each group to come to the front and collect 'The Full Picture – Card 4.' Explain that the student will share this new information to the group and see if those who wanted to fire the president in Step 13 want to change their minds
16. Elicit responses from groups.
17. On the board, write, 'Stacking the deck.' Explain that if you are playing the cards, stack the deck means to arrange the cards so that you always have the winning hand. Ask students to guess what the 'Stacking the deck fallacy' may be. Elicit responses from groups and explain it is presenting only the arguments or evidence that support your conclusion and ignoring the arguments or evidence that do not support it. This means people make decisions or reach conclusions with only half the picture and not the full picture.
18. [Option 1] Have students research other examples of 'stacking the deck' and present their examples in their groups.
19. [Option 2] Have students think about the four arguments they were presented in Steps 1 to 16 and how having the full picture may have caused them to change their minds about each conclusion. Have them think of their own examples of 'stacking the deck.' Have students make their own 'half-picture' and 'full-picture' cards and then present them to the group following a similar procedure: (1) present the half-picture information; (2) discuss; (3) present the full-picture information; (4) see if group members change their minds once the information is given.
20. Have students reflect on the activity and discuss what they have learned about stacking the deck and getting the full picture before reaching a conclusion.

Half-Picture and Full-Picture Cards

Card 1:
You see a commercial on TV for a can of soda. The commercial says the relaunched soda is refreshing, delicious, and healthy. It has 20% less sugar than the previous soda. Will you try it?

The Full Picture Card 1:
The previous soda contained 68 grams of sugar.

Card 2:
You see a talk show host on TV talking about the dangers of getting vaccinated for a deadly virus. He says that people have suffered blood clots and died. Will you still have the vaccination?

The Full Picture Card 2:
Studies show that only 4 in a million people aged over 55 have suffered serious side-effects. 800 in a million have died due to the virus.

Card 3:
You are in a store and need a new phone. The salesperson is showing you the new brand of smartphones. They are very reasonable, stylish, have a good camera, a folding screen, and come with a lot of storage. Will you buy one?

The Full Picture Card 3:
Many users have complained about the screen. It is easy to scratch. Others have dropped their phones and they break easily. The operating system also does not support some key apps.

> **Card 4:**
> People want the president of a university to be fired. The teachers did not get a pay raise. The students have had to pay a higher tuition. And yet, a new university football stadium has been built. Many people are angry. Do you agree with them?

> **The Full Picture Card 4:**
>
> The funds for the football stadium came from a billionaire alumnus. Due to the work of scholars the president has helped to hire, the school's rankings have dramatically increased.

Activity 63: Fair Play or Stacking the Deck?

Introduction

In this final activity focusing on the stacking the deck fallacy, learners are introduced to the fallacy and examine six examples to determine whether they are fair play or stacking the deck. Learners then determine ways to avoid stacking the deck when arguing.	
Aim	To understand the stacking the deck fallacy, to identify ways that stacking the deck can be used when arguing, to determine ways to avoid stacking the deck
Level	Intermediate to Advanced
Time	40–50 minutes
Materials	Worksheet
Preparation	Copies of the worksheet for each student

Fallacy: Stacking the deck	
Definition	Presenting only the reasons or data in the argument that support the conclusion.
Example	Advert: This soda now has 10% less sugar (the original had 49 grams of sugar).

Procedure

1. On the board, write, 'Stacking the deck.' Explain that if you are playing the cards, stack the deck means to arrange the cards so that you always have the winning hand. Ask students to guess what the 'stacking the deck' fallacy may be. Elicit responses from groups and explain it is presenting only the arguments or evidence that support your conclusion and ignoring or omitting the arguments or evidence that do not support it. This means people make decisions or reach conclusions with only half the picture and not the full picture. Explain presenting both sides of the arguments may allow the listener to reach a fair conclusion.
2. Give students an example:

   'Imagine you want to buy a secondhand car. You go to a car dealership. You talk to a car salesperson. The salesperson shows you a good car. They tell you the car is economical. It has only had one owner. The car looks very nice. It seems to be in good condition. You take it for a test drive. You decide to buy it. However, the salesperson does not explain about the history of the car. It has been in a several accidents due to faulty steering and brakes. It also has a history of breaking down. Has the salesperson stacked the decks?'

3. Elicit responses from students and then explain that selling can be a typical example of stacking the deck. By omitting the history of the car and its problems, the salesperson persuaded the purchaser to reach a conclusion without providing information that may have affected the decision.
4. Put students into pairs or small groups. Give each student a copy of the worksheet. Have them work through the six examples in Task 1 and write their answers on a separate piece of paper.
5. Have students share their answers with the whole class. Possible answers are:*

1	This is stacking the deck. By eating vast quantities of fast food every day and not partaking in any daily exercise, the filmmaker does not represent fairly the effects of fast food on the body as part of a regular diet and as part of the diet of someone who exercises regularly.
2	This is stacking the deck. The spread only contains 13% of hazelnut. Also, a low GI does not equate to being a healthy food option.
3	This is stacking the deck. The YouTuber has been given the product for free by the manufacturer so will be less inclined to give the product a negative review.
4	This is stacking the deck. Switzerland may have a low murder rate but deaths from gun violence are high when compared to other European countries.

| 5 | This is stacking the deck. Although government spending on education may be low, the country may be ranked highly in educational attainment. For example, the country in question was ranked 7 out of 73 in 2020. |
| 6 | This is stacking the deck. To portray climate change as having a balanced argument, the talk show host has given equal weighting to two guests. However, one is a scientific expert in the field of climate change and the other is not. Thus, the talk show host has stacked the deck in favor of climate change denial when the reality is there is a large agreement between scientists that humans are the cause of global warming. |

*NB: Point out to the students that the worksheet activity itself is an example of stacking the deck as it has only presented examples of stacking the deck and is thus one-sided!

6. Have students look back through the six examples and discuss ways that each person could have been more truthful, fairer, and not have stacked the decks.
7. Have students share their ideas with the whole class. Possible answers are:

1	Eat fast food as part of a normal diet (e.g., three times a week). Exercise regularly and check the effects it has on the body.
2	Do not advertise the product as healthy choice but as a treat and have a warning about overeating it.
3	Give a disclaimer at the start of the video that this is not an unbiased review or include the pros and cons of purchasing it.
4	Explain that Switzerland has a high rate in comparison to other countries in Europe but not countries like the US.
5	Provide the information that the country is doing well in actual educational attainment but that the politician would like to see more investment to maintain this level.
6	Explain that the retired CEO holds a minority view and that the world's leading experts almost all agree that humans are the cause of climate change.

8. [Option 1] Have students think of their own examples in which someone may stack the deck. Have them explain their examples to their partner or group members to see whether they agree that it is stacking the deck.
9. [Option 2] Set a homework task for students. Have them listen out or look for examples of stacking the deck in the media, advertising, or in real-life conversations and write them down. Have them share their examples in the following lesson.
10. Have students reflect on the activity and discuss what they have learned about the stacking the deck fallacy and how to avoid it.

WORKSHEET

Task 1: Read the following examples and discuss whether they are examples of stacking the deck or fair play. Give reasons for your answers.

Example 1:
A documentary film maker eats fast food three times a day for 30 days and reports on his weight gain, fatigue, health problems, and high cholesterol. However, he does not do any daily exercise during the experiment.

Example 2:
A famous chocolate spread manufacturer advertises its product as being a healthy choice as it contains hazelnuts and has a low GI (Glycemic Index).

Example 3:
A YouTuber is given a free sample of a new tablet to review on his channel by the manufacturer. He explains many reasons why this is a good tablet for consumers to buy.

Example 4:
A politician argues that guns are safe as many people own guns in Switzerland, and it has one of the lowest murder rates in the world.

Example 5:
A politician criticizes the ruling government for letting the country fall behind the rest of the world in education. She cites a study saying that the country ranks 19th out of 28 developed nations with regards to percentage of GDP spent on education.

Example 6:
A talk show host invites two guests onto the show to talk about climate change. One guest is a well-known climate change scientist who has led two research teams in Antarctica. Her research resulted in the banning of commercial CFCs in the 1990s. Another is a retired CEO of an energy company who writes a blog about the myths of global warming.

Equivocation

Activity 64: Homonyms

Introduction

As a first step to understanding the equivocation fallacy, learners are introduced to homonyms and learn how using a word in a different way can result in making an argument unclear or reaching a faulty conclusion.

Aim	To understand homonyms, to identify how using a word in a different way can result in making an argument unclear or reaching a faulty conclusion
Level	Elementary to Pre-intermediate
Time	50–60 minutes
Materials	Worksheet
Preparation	Copies of the worksheet for each student; example homonyms for Steps 3, 9 and 10

Fallacy: Equivocation	
Definition	Using a word in two different ways to make an argument more unclear or ambiguous.
Example	The sign said, 'fine if I return this book to the library late.' I am late to return the book, so it is fine, right?

Procedure

1. On the board, write:

    Teacher: 'Why did you only write the letter 'A' for your homework?'
    Student: 'Well, you told me to write a letter to someone. Therefore, I wrote the letter, 'A.''

2. Ask students:

    A) What did the teacher want the student to do?
    B) What did the student do?
    C) Is the student correct?

    Elicit the answers:

    A) To write a letter (Dear John …)
    B) Wrote a letter (of the alphabet)
    C) Answers will vary. The student is using language in an unclear/ambiguous way to do an easier homework task.

3. Explain what homonyms are to students. Elicit some examples of homonyms. Make a list on the board.
4. Give each student a copy of the worksheet. Put students into pairs to work through Task 1 (Worksheet).

5. Check answers with students. Answers are:
   1) Headache
   2) Ring
   3) Feet
   4) Fine
   5) Light
6. Have pairs work through Task 2 of the worksheet. Have them make notes on what is wrong with each argument.
7. Put pairs together to form small groups and have them check their answers together.
8. Elicit answers from each group. Possible answers are:

Example 1:
A different meaning of 'fine' is used by the boy to try to get out of paying money for the late return of books in the conclusion.
Example 2:
The meaning of 'feet' in the first two sentences are different so the conclusion is incorrect.
Example 3:
The meaning of 'headache' in the first two sentences are different so the conclusion is incorrect.
Example 4:
A different meaning of 'ring' is used by the boyfriend probably to get out of paying money for expensive jewelry.
Example 5:
A different meaning of 'light' is used by the person giving advice, so the conclusion is incorrect.

9. [Option 1 – Easy] Have groups look at the list of homonyms on the board (Step 3). Have them choose one homonym and make two sentences to show the different meanings of each word. Put two groups together to share their sentences.
10. [Option 2 – More challenging] Have groups look at the list of homonyms on the board (Step 3). Have them write an example situation in which the meaning of the word is changed to reach a faulty conclusion. Put two groups together to share their example situations.
11. Have students reflect on the activity and discuss what they have learned about homonyms and ambiguity in arguments.

WORKSHEET

Task 1: Look at the words in the box. There are two words that are spelled the same and sound the same but have different meanings. Match the words to their meanings:

| Feet | Light | Fine | Headache | Ring |

1) _____	a) a pain you feel in your head. b) something that is difficult to do.
2) _____	a) jewelry worn on the finger. b) British English for call
3) _____	a) the part of the body at the bottom of your legs b) a unit of measurement (1 = 30 centimeters)
4) _____	a) okay b) money that is paid as a punishment
5) _____	a) not dark b) not heavy

Task 2: Look at the five examples. What is wrong with each conclusion?

Example 1:

Sign in library: Fine for late books
Boy to librarian: I am late to return these books. So, it's fine, right?

Example 2:

A centipede has 100 feet. The Eiffel Tower is about 1,000 feet. Therefore, that is 10 centipedes tall.

Example 3:

This homework is a real headache to do. Two or three aspirins can help a headache. Therefore, I should take some aspirins to help me with the homework.

Example 4:

My girlfriend wanted a ring for her birthday. Therefore, I used my smartphone to ring her and wish her a happy birthday!

Example 5:

This big can of paint says light green, therefore it will be light enough for you to carry two cans home.

Activity 65: Changing the Meaning
Introduction

In this activity, learners are introduced to equivocation and analyze five examples of equivocation to understand how language can be used in an argument to be ambiguous and mislead or confuse the listener.	
Aim	To understand equivocation, to understand how language can be used in an argument to be ambiguous and mislead or confuse the listener
Level	Intermediate to Advanced
Time	50–60 minutes
Materials	Worksheet
Preparation	Copies of the worksheet for each student

Fallacy: Equivocation	
Definition	Using a word in two different ways to make an argument more unclear or ambiguous.
Example	The sign said, 'fine if I return this book to the library late.' I am late to return the book, so it is fine, right?

Procedure

1. Tell the story to students of a new worker on the construction site. His supervisor says to him that he needs a 'long stand' to complete his job. He asks the new worker to go over to the other side of the construction site and ask the workers over there for a 'long stand.' The new worker follows the instructions and goes over to the other side of the construction site and asks, 'Can I have a long stand?' to one of the men. The man says, 'Yes, just wait there a moment.' The new worker waits and waits. He doesn't know what to do. He waits for 30 minutes. The man does not return with

a 'long stand.' He waits for an hour. He waits for two hours. Finally, the man returns, smiles, and says, 'Did you enjoy your long stand?'
2. Ask students:

- 'What does the new worker think 'a long stand' means? '

Elicit from students – 'a tool to support something.' Ask students:

- 'What did 'a long stand' really mean?'

Elicit from students – 'standing in one position for a long time.' Ask students:

[Option] Explain that this is a typical practical joke played on new workers in some countries. Ask students if there are similar practical jokes played on people in their country.
3. Explain to students that the 'long stand' joke works via equivocation in which a key word is used in more than one way in an argument (usually) to confuse or mislead the listener.
4. Put students into pairs. Give each student a copy of the worksheet. Have them work through the task together.
5. Put pairs together to form small groups. Have them check their answers to the task on the worksheet together.
6. Elicit answers from each group. Answers are:

1	Faith – belief in God vs. faith – trust in someone to do something. By changing the meaning of 'faith,' the conclusion is misleading. The priest will not be happy as he wanted the person to be more religious.
2	Argue – evidence to support an idea vs. argue – verbal fight or strong exchange of opinions. By changing the meaning of 'argue' in the argument, the conclusion is misleading. The first meaning of argue is used in the first premise but the speaker concludes with the second and different meaning of argue.
3	Energy – heat vs. energy – the strength to do something. By changing the meaning of 'energy,' the conclusion is faulty as drinking the soda may not have the desired effect on giving the speaker the energy to do something.
4	Responsible – for one's behavior in general vs. responsible – for one single action. By changing the meaning of 'responsible,' the conclusion is misleading. The child is not being more responsible.
5	No – meaning no other vs. no – meaning none. By changing the meaning of 'no' in the second premise, the person can cleverly argue that their watch is better than a Rolex. However, this is fallacious.

7. [Option 1] Have groups search online for further examples of equivocation. Have them write them down and share their examples with the class.
8. [Option 2] Have groups make a list of homonyms – words that have the same spelling or pronunciation but have different meanings (e.g., right – not left/right – not wrong). Using the five examples on the worksheet as a guide, have students come up with their own example of an equivocation using one of the homonyms. Have each group write down their examples on a piece of paper. Have groups pass their examples to other groups to read, analyze, and work out how the different usage of the words changes the argument. For example:
'We should take the road on the right because it is right!'
9. Have students reflect on the activity and discuss what they have learned about equivocation and how it can be used to mislead or confuse the listener in an argument.

WORKSHEET

Task: Read the following examples of equivocation.

1) Circle the words being used in two different ways in the argument.
2) Discuss: a) the two different meanings of the word
                  b) how their usage changes the conclusion of the argument

Argument 1:

My priest told me that I should have more faith. I have a lot of faith that my baseball team will win tomorrow. Therefore, my priest will be really pleased with me.

Argument 2:

Some people think critical thinking will help you to argue better. However, there are too many people arguing all the time. I hate to see people fighting. Therefore, people should argue less.

Argument 3:

My teacher told me that calories are units of energy. There are lots of calories in this soda. I need lots of energy right now. Therefore, I'm going to drink two cans of it.

Argument 4:

My parents told me to be more responsible. The other day I was responsible for breaking the vase in the living room. Therefore, I'm already being more responsible.

Argument 5:

No watch is better than a Rolex. My watch is better than no watch. Therefore, my watch is better than a Rolex!

Activity 66: Equivocation in Politics
Introduction

In this final activity focusing on the equivocation fallacy, learners analyze examples from the world of politics to understand how equivocation can be used by politicians. Learners then research and discuss further examples of equivocation to be aware of and better understand it.

Aim	To understand the use of equivocation in politics, to analyze quotations for equivocation, to research for further examples of equivocation
Level	Intermediate to Advanced
Time	60–70 minutes
Materials	Image for Step 1
Preparation	[Option] Have some examples of equivocation in politics ready for Step 11

Fallacy: Equivocation	
Definition	Using a word in two different ways to make an argument more unclear or ambiguous.
Example	The sign said, 'fine if I return this book to the library late.' I am late to return the book, so it is fine, right?

Procedure

1. Show an image to students of an object in which there is a debate about its color (e.g., prepare an image of the pink and white sneakers vs. teal and gray sneakers photograph that went viral on the Internet). Elicit what color students believe the object to be.

2. On the board, write:

    A) The sneakers are pink and white, in my opinion.
    B) I think they very well could be pink and white.

    Ask students, 'What is the difference between A and B?' Elicit that a) is a person's belief whereas b) expresses a possibility.
3. On the board, write:

    A) Politicians do not speak the truth, in my opinion.
    B) I think politicians very well could lie.

    Ask students again, 'What is the difference between A and B?' Elicit the same answer as Step 2 – ask them if they agree or disagree with the statement.
4. Tell students, you are going to give them a real example from a politician to analyze. On the board, write:

    > 'There are millions of people who voted illegally in the election, <u>in my opinion</u>.'

    Explain this is a quotation by a politician. Ask students, 'What is the politician's argument?' Elicit that millions of people voted illegally in the election.

    Next, write:

    > 'I didn't say that <u>there are</u> millions. But I <u>think there could very well be</u> millions of people.'

    Explain that this is a quotation by the same politician in the same interview. Ask students, 'What is the politician's argument later in the interview? How has the argument changed?' Elicit that the new argument has shifted from a belief of the politician to a mere possibility.
5. Explain that this is an example of the fallacy of equivocation. Equivocation is ambiguous language or a kind of 'doublespeak' that can often be used by politicians to make their argument unclear, misleading, or confusing for the listener. It can be intentional or sometimes, it can be unintentional. [Option: Provide students some examples of equivocation from Activities 64 and 65 to facilitate further understanding]
6. Explain to students that they will now analyze a very famous quotation to check for equivocation. On the board, write, 'And so, my fellow Americans: Ask not what your country can do for you – ask what you can do for your country.' Ask students if they know who said this quotation, when it was spoken, and what it means. Elicit answers. Answers are:

    - John F. Kennedy
    - 1961 at his inauguration

- The quotation is a call for action for Americans to contribute to the public good – to help their communities and country.

7. Put students into pairs or small groups. Ask them – 'Why is this an example of equivocation?' Have them analyze the quote for changes or shifts in meaning.
8. Elicit ideas from pairs or small groups. Answers are:
   - There is a shift in the meaning of 'country.' In the first use of the word, 'country' refers to the government of the land. In the second use of the word, 'country' refers to an individual's nation or homeland.
9. Ask pairs or small groups to discuss how they feel this may change the meaning of what JFK said. Ask them if they feel this was intentional or unintentional.
10. Elicit answers from pairs or small groups. Answers will vary.
11. Have pairs or small groups research online to find further examples of equivocation in politics (there are many!). Have them write down and analyze their examples.
12. Put pairs or small groups together to form bigger groups. Have students share their examples with other groups. Have them explain what is fallacious about the quotations they found online.
13. [Option] Move each pair or small group again to form new groups and repeat Step 12.
14. [Option] Set a homework task for students to watch or read the political news over the coming week and look out for examples of equivocation. Have students write down their examples and share them in the following lesson.
15. Have students reflect on the activity and discuss what they have learned about the use of equivocation in politics.

Appeal to Emotion

Activity 67: How Does It Make You Feel?

Introduction

As a first step to understanding the appeal to emotion fallacy, learners are introduced to emotion words. Learners then discuss how different advertisements make them feel and may appeal to certain emotions. Learners discuss the use of appeal to emotion in advertising.	
Aim	To learn positive and negative emotion words, to understand how advertising may appeal to certain emotions
Level	Elementary to Pre-intermediate
Time	50–60 minutes

Materials	Worksheet, pictures of six advertisements
Preparation	Copies of the worksheet for each student; six advertisements for Step 6 – search on the Internet and find advertisements that appeal to the emotions of belonging, happiness, trust, sadness, anger, and fear. Use advertisements that you feel are appropriate for your students in terms of language and recognition

Fallacy: Appeal to Emotion	
Definition	Using emotionally charged words or explanations that appeal to emotions such as fear rather than facts.
Example	If we let foreigners into the country, they will take all our jobs.

Procedure

1. On the board, write:

   Elicit positive and negative emotions from students (e.g., love, hate)
2. Put students into pairs. Give each student a copy of the worksheet. Have students work through Task 1.
3. Elicit the answers from each pair. Answers are:

   1) belonging
   2) fear
   3) anger
   4) happiness
   5) trust
   6) sadness

4. Have pairs work through Task 2 of the worksheet. Have them complete the table and then ask the questions to one another.
5. Elicit some of the answers for the Task 2 questions (Worksheet) from each pair.
6. Put students into small groups. Pre-teach 'advertising' and 'advertisement.' Tell students you are going to show them (or give them copies of) six advertisements. Have students discuss together how the advertisement makes them feel and why. For example, Picture 1 may be an advertisement for clothes which shows a group of friends together wearing the same kind of clothing and all having fun. This gives people a feeling of belonging. Picture 2 may be a cigarette advertisement which shows a dead body with a toe tag that states, 'smoking kills.' This gives people a feeling of fear.
7. Elicit answers from groups. Answers may vary.

8. Go through each of the six advertisements again. Ask students why they think the advertisement wants us to feel each emotion (anger, fear, belonging, trust, sadness, happiness) when we see it.
9. [Option] Have students search the Internet for other examples of advertisements that appeal to anger, fear, belonging, trust, sadness, and happiness. Have them share their examples in their groups.
10. Have students reflect on the activity and discuss what they have learned about emotions and the appeal to emotions in advertising.

WORKSHEET

Task 1: Look at the words in the box. Are they positive or negative emotions? Draw a ☺ or ☹ next to each word:

| Anger | Happiness | Belonging | Sadness | Fear | Trust |

Now complete each sentence with one of the words:

1) I am a member of a dance team at school. Everyone is nice, and I feel like an important member of the team. It gives me a feeling of _____.
2) I don't like flying. It gives me a feeling of _____.
3) When my friend is one hour late to meet me, it gives me a feeling of _____.
4) A sunny day gives me a feeling of _____.
5) My friend never lies to me. It gives me a feeling of _____.
6) When people are not nice to me, it gives me a feeling of _____.

Task 2: Look at the questions below and complete the table:

Noun:	Anger	Adjective:	
Noun:	Happiness	Adjective:	
Noun:	Belonging	Verb:	
Noun:	Sadness	Adjective:	
Noun:	Fear	Verb:	
Noun:	Trust	Verb:	

Now, ask the following questions to your partner:

1) What is something that makes you angry?
2) What is something that makes you happy?
3) What is something that you belong to?
4) What is something that makes you sad?
5) What is something that you fear?
6) Who is someone that you trust?

Activity 68: Be Afraid, Be Very Afraid

Introduction

In this activity, learners are introduced to the appeal to emotion fallacy and how it works. Learners analyze six 'appeal to emotion' statements and discuss the evidence that would be needed to support each claim. Then, learners think of and share their own appeal to emotion statements and discuss how they may be used to get the listener to accept the conclusion without evidence.

Aim	To understand how the appeal to fear fallacy works, to support arguments with evidence, to come up with further examples of appeal to emotion arguments
Level	Intermediate to Advanced
Time	60–70 minutes
Materials	Worksheet
Preparation	Copies of the worksheet for each student

Fallacy: Appeal to Emotion	
Definition	Using emotionally charged words or explanations that appeal to emotions such as fear rather than facts.
Example	If we let foreigners into the country, they will take all our jobs.

Procedure

1. On the board, write:

   a) If you don't stop smoking, you'll die by the time you're 40.
   b) I think you should stop smoking. The World Health Organization states that smoking contributes to an early death. In fact, 8 million people die each year because of smoking.

2. Put students into pairs or small groups. Ask them to discuss the two claims on the board and the differences between them.

3. Elicit responses and explain that statement a) is an appeal to emotion fallacy, namely appeal to fear. The argument provides no evidence for the conclusion. In other words:

> If you don't do X, Y will happen.
> As Y is terrible, X must be true.

People may accept the conclusion without thinking because it creates the emotion of fear. Explain that statement b) provides evidence to support the argument of not smoking.
4. Give each student a copy of the worksheet and have students work through the task.
5. Go through each argument on the worksheet and elicit answers. Possible answers are:

1	Conclusion – taxes will go up Appeals to fear – threat of less disposable income for everyone Possible evidence – quotations from the politician or party manifesto to say taxes will be increased.
2	Conclusion – the planet will be destroyed Appeals to fear – humanity will cease to exist or need to relocate to another planet Possible evidence – environmental studies on the effects of fossil fuels on climate change
3	Conclusion – something bad will happen to you if you visit the country Appeals to fear – we desire personal safety when traveling Possible evidence – travel advisory warnings issued by one's government
4	Conclusion – there is a possibility of having an accident of death Appeals to fear – people do not want to have accidents or die Possible evidence – research into road safety, statistics
5	Conclusion – domestic industry will be threatened Appeals to fear – people wish their domestic industries to prosper not fail Possible evidence – economic articles, quotations by economists
6	Conclusion – people can be easily deceived without CT Appeals to fear – people do not want to be deceived Possible evidence – educational articles, quotations by experts

6. [Option] Have students go through the statements again and decide if they agree or disagree with them.
7. Have students work together in their pairs or groups to make three or four of their own appeal to fear arguments. For example: 'If you don't study hard in this class, the teacher will fail you.'
8. Put pairs or groups together to make larger groups. Have them share their appeal to fear arguments. Have them think of how each argument appeals to fear and ways they could support each appeal to fear argument with evidence. Have them discuss whether they agree or disagree with the statements.

9. [Option] Have students think of other emotions that can be appealed to when arguing to get the listener to accept the conclusion without evidence. Examples are enthusiasm, sympathy, compassion, ambition, belonging, indignation, anger. Have them research online for examples in which the arguer appeals to the emotion without presenting evidence to support the conclusion. Have them share their examples together.
10. [Option] Set a homework task for students to listen out for appeal to fear arguments in the news or in real life. Have them write down the examples they hear and share them in the following lesson.
11. Have students reflect on the activity and discuss what they have learned about the appeal to fear fallacy and how it can be used to get the listener to accept the conclusion without evidence.

WORKSHEET

Task: Read the following appeal to fear statements. For each statement:

1) Underline the conclusion
2) Discuss how the argument appeals to fear
3) Think of evidence that could be used to support each claim

Argument 1:

If [Name of politician] gets into power, our taxes will go up.

Argument 2:

If we do not switch to alternative forms of energy immediately, we will need to find another planet to live on in the future.

Argument 3:

I wouldn't visit [Name of country]. You'll be mugged, kidnapped, or murdered.

Argument 4:

If you don't wear a helmet while riding a bike, you'll have a serious injury or die.

Argument 5:

We shouldn't buy imported goods. Our domestic industry will collapse.

Argument 6:

If you don't study critical thinking, you'll get tricked all the time.

Activity 69: So Many Emotions

Introduction

In this final activity focusing on the appeal to emotion fallacy, learners are introduced to how it may be used to persuade or manipulate people into supporting the claims being made. Learners analyze six arguments to identify different appeals to emotion and discuss how they can respond to appeal to emotion arguments.	
Aim	To understand how the appeal to emotion fallacy may be used to persuade or manipulate, to identify different appeal to emotion arguments, to discuss how to respond to appeal to emotion arguments
Level	High-intermediate to Advanced
Time	60–70 minutes
Materials	Worksheet
Preparation	Copies of the worksheet for each student

Fallacy: Appeal to Emotion	
Definition	Using emotionally charged words or explanations that appeal to emotions such as fear rather than facts.
Example	If we let foreigners into the country, they will take all our jobs.

Procedure

1. Tell students a story. Tell them that you have a petition you would like them to sign. Tell them that the petition is for comfortable chairs in the classroom. Claim that all teachers need a comfortable chair when teaching. Tell them that you met a teacher yesterday who had taught in the classroom for 40 years. Every day, she sat in an uncomfortable chair during her classes. By the time she retired she had bad back problems due to sitting in the uncomfortable chair. Tell students that you saw her yesterday trying to walk to the grocery store. She had a walking stick and was walking very slowly. She looked like she was in a lot of pain. She saw you, looked into your eyes, and said, 'Whatever you do, you need to teach in a comfortable chair. You can't have other teachers go through what I am going through. You should start a petition. You can make the government listen. They will give money to schools to buy all teachers a comfy chair. Then, you will not end up like me. She said to me, 'Get your students to sign the petition. Get your school to buy you a comfortable chair before it's too late for you.'

   Ask students for a show of hands, 'Who will sign my petition?'

2. Now, ask students, 'What was my argument?' Elicit your argument – all teachers need a comfortable chair while teaching.

   Ask students, 'What was my evidence?' Elicit responses. Accept all answers.
3. On the board, write:

   'Appeal to emotion fallacy:

   Argument X is made.

   Instead of evidence, emotion is used to persuade the listener that the claim is true and should be supported.

   Ask students to name the emotions that you appealed to in your story so that the students would agree to sign the petition. Possible answers are: (Negative) guilt, pity, fear (For you the teacher) and (Positive) empathy, kindness.
4. Put students into pairs or small groups. Ask them to make a list of positive and negative emotions that people may appeal to in place of evidence when arguing. Examples are:

Positive:	Negative:
Love	Fear
Trust	Anger
Empathy	Envy
Respect	Disgust
Gratitude	Guilt
Compassion	Pity

5. Have pairs or small groups work together through the task on the worksheet (see worksheet).
6. Form larger groups by putting different pairs or small groups together. Have them share their answers to the task on the worksheet.
7. Elicit task answers from each group. Possible answers are:

1	Argument – If people vote for the politician, the politician will bring back the coal mining jobs to the area. Appeals to people's desire to work and put food on the table for their family. It also appeals to the audience's compassion – they may feel concern and pity for coal miners who have lost their jobs. Emotions – Compassion, Pity, Trust Evidence – The politician would need to provide a concrete plan of how he or she will invest in or rejuvenate the mining industry

2	Argument – If the country leaves the EU, there will be less or no migration. Appeals to people's fear and distrust that foreigners may take their jobs or add to the population of a country increasing the burden on the state to provide healthcare, education, housing and so on. Emotions – Fear, Distrust, Anger Evidence – The politician would need to give evidence of a) actual figures of mass migration, b) statistics to support the argument that the country is at a financial breaking point
3	Argument – You should give money to the charity Appeals to empathy, compassion, and a desire to help other's less fortunate than oneself. It also makes people feel guilty for what they have. Emotions – Guilt, Compassion, Empathy Evidence – For it not to be an appeal to emotion, the charity could provide evidence of the number of starving children in a country, how the donations will be used to help the children.
4	Argument – The fast-food chain is the best Appeals to people's trust in a person and respect for that person. It appeals to a sense of religious connection and trust that if this person is a devout Christian and charitable, the product must also be trustworthy. Emotions – Trust, Respect, Evidence – The friend would need to provide evidence to support the claim such as the rankings of the fast-food chain, statistics on customer satisfaction, and so on.
5	Argument – The military needs to be abolished. Appeals to empathy and compassion of the listener and an understanding of her terrible situation. Emotions – Empathy, Compassion, Pity, Anger Evidence – The friend would need to provide evidence of the benefits of abolishing the military as well as a plan of how to defend the country without one.
6	Argument – We need to go on strike Appeals to anger about the new policy and the feeling of being exploited by a company Emotions – Anger, Disgust Evidence – Before agreeing with the colleague, one needs to know what the policy is, why it is unfair, why it was implemented, and what the possible advantages and disadvantages will be for the company and its employees

8. Have students return to their original pairs or small groups. Have them refer to the list of emotions they made in Step 4. Have them make their own appeal to emotion argument related to the emotions they have listed. For example: 'Empathy – We need to stop domestic violence happening. Children who witness domestic violence are scarred for life.'

9. Put pairs or groups together to make larger groups again. Have them share their appeal to emotion arguments together. Have listeners identify the emotion that is being appealed to in each argument.
10. Have groups discuss how they could respond to an appeal to emotion argument.
11. Elicit ideas from each group. Possible answers are:
    - Politely point out the lack of evidence in the other person's argument.
    - Politely explain how the other person's argument may be trying to manipulate someone's emotions.
    - Ask for more facts to support the argument/give facts to counter the argument.
    - Respond with a counter appeal to emotion argument to show how it is easy to manipulate people's emotions.
12. [Option] Set a homework task for students to listen out for appeal to emotion arguments in the news or in real life. Have them write down the examples they hear and share them in the following lesson.
13. Have students reflect on the activity and discuss what they have learned about the appeal to emotion fallacy and how it can be used to try to manipulate the emotions of the listener so that the listener accepts the conclusion without the need for evidence.

WORKSHEET

Task: Read the following appeal to emotion arguments. For each argument:

1) Discuss what the argument is
2) Discuss how it may appeal to emotion rather than provides evidence
3) Identify the emotion it appeals to
4) Discuss the evidence that could be provided to support the argument

Argument 1:

During a political rally, a politician wearing a hard hat used in coal mining states, 'We're going to put our great coal miners back to work in this city.'

Argument 2:

A politician unveils a poster for his latest political campaign. The poster shows a queue of migrants and refugees with the slogan 'Breaking point: the EU has failed us all.'

Argument 3:

An advertisement for a charity shows a young starving child looking deeply into the camera. The slogan states, 'He's starving. We're not.'

Argument 4:

Your friend states, 'This fast-food chain is the best as the CEO is a devout Christian and has started many charities.'

Argument 5:

Your friend states, 'The military needs to be abolished. The other day my friend lost her husband while he was on active duty overseas. It is an absolute tragedy. She now has to bring up three children on her own.'

Argument 6:

Your colleague states, 'I can't believe the new policy the company has introduced. It is totally unfair. They are trying to take advantage of us. We have to go on strike.'

D. Logical Fallacies: Mistaken Assumptions

The final 24 activities introduce students to eight logical fallacies related to mistaken assumptions (see Table 1.1 in Part I). For each logical fallacy, there are three activities that cater for different learner proficiency levels:

Level 1	Elementary to pre-elementary (A2–B1)
Level 2	Intermediate to advanced (B1–B2)
Level 3	High-intermediate to advanced (C1–C2)

The level of each activity can be found easily in Table 2.8 by referring to the shading of each column (Level 1, Level 2, Level 3). Please note that levels are only an estimated guide. It may be possible to adapt a level 3 activity for lower-level students. Similarly, there may be something of value for advanced students within a level 1 activity. Remember, you do not need to do every activity with your students. Please feel free to pick and choose from the 24 activities and adapt them where necessary to your individual teaching context and learners.

TABLE 2.8 Logical Fallacies: Mistaken Assumptions: Activity Titles and Aims

Activity/Fallacy:	Title:	Aim:
Activity 70 Gambler's 1	Heads or tails?	To understand the gambler's fallacy. To identify how false assumptions can be made based on the frequency of past events.
Activity 71 Gambler's 2	Monte Carlo	To understand the gambler's fallacy, to learn about the origin of the fallacy. To share examples of committing the fallacy. To consider ways to guard against the fallacy.
Activity 72 Gambler's 3	What would you do (Part 2)?	To understand the gambler's fallacy. To identify if students would commit the fallacy or not in example situations. To research or think of further example situations. To consider ways to guard against the fallacy.
Activity 73 Logical paradox 1	Is it a contradiction?	To understand and identify contradictory statements. To understand that some contradictory statements can be valid. To make short dialogs to show how a contradictory statement can be valid.
Activity 74 Logical paradox 2	The Abilene Paradox	To understand and identify contradictory statements. To experience, learn about, and discuss the Abilene Paradox. To share experiences of making collection decisions that are counter to the real wishes of the group.
Activity 75 Logical paradox 3	What's the paradox?	To understand a number of logical paradoxes. To discuss what the paradoxes are and to research for further examples of logical paradoxes. To consider why logical paradoxes are important.
Activity 76 Unwarranted assumptions 1	Is it warranted?	To understand the assumptions we make every day. To distinguish between warranted and unwarranted assumptions. To share examples of unwarranted assumptions.
Activity 77 Unwarranted assumptions 2	This morning's assumptions	To understand assumptions that we make every day. To distinguish between warranted and unwarranted assumptions. To share examples of unwarranted assumptions in the news or everyday life.

(Continued)

TABLE 2.8 Continued

Activity/Fallacy:	Title:	Aim:
Activity 78 Unwarranted assumptions 3	What have the Romans ever done for us?	To understand the assumptions we make every day; to distinguish between warranted and unwarranted assumptions. To share examples of believing something without evidence. To discuss ways to prevent unwarranted assumptions.
Activity 79 Genetic 1	Which is the better reason (Part 2)?	To consider whether reasons are good and bad for accepting or rejecting statements as true or false. To understand the genetic fallacy indirectly.
Activity 80 Genetic 2	Who said it?	To determine whether statements are true or false; to understand the genetic fallacy. To consider how we may accept statements to be true based on their origins rather than the arguments themselves.
Activity 81 Genetic 3	Origins	To understand the genetic fallacy. To consider how we may judge claims based on their origins rather than the arguments themselves. To research and share further examples of the genetic fallacy.
Activity 82 Common belief 1	True or false	To simulate the common belief fallacy in the classroom. To understand the common belief fallacy by experiencing it.
Activity 83 Common belief 2	Accept or reject	To simulate the common belief fallacy. To understand the common belief fallacy. To discuss whether to accept or reject people's claims based on a common belief that it is true.
Activity 84 Common belief 3	The things we believed	To understand the common belief fallacy. To discuss false beliefs that people had in the past. To think of examples of false beliefs that people may have today. To discuss ways to avoid committing the fallacy.
Activity 85 Slippery slope 1	Negative chains	To understand cause and effect. To understand, analyze, and make slippery slope arguments to demonstrate their fallacious nature (the unlikeliness of the first action leading to the final extreme action).

(Continued)

TABLE 2.8 Continued

Activity/Fallacy:	Title:	Aim:
Activity 86 Slippery slope 2	Can I have a chocolate?	To understand the structure of slippery slope arguments. To make, share, and discuss slippery slope arguments. To research online for further examples of the fallacy.
Activity 87 Slippery slope 3	Countering slippery slope arguments	To understand the structure of slippery slope arguments. To make, share, and discuss slippery slope arguments. To think of ways to counter slippery slope arguments.
Activity 88 Ignorance 1	Evidence or no evidence?	To understand the need for evidence to support conclusions. To understand the ignorance fallacy.
Activity 89 Ignorance 2	No evidence is no evidence!	To understand the need for evidence to support facts or conclusions. To understand the ignorance fallacy. To determine that as no evidence supports both sides of an argument it is invalid.
Activity 90 Ignorance 3	No evidence is evidence!	To establish the evidence to support one's argument; to understand the ignorance fallacy. To research and share examples of evidence to support one's arguments of no evidence.
Activity 91 Naturalistic 1	Is it good for us?	To discuss the assumption that it is natural therefore it is good. To categorize items as natural or not natural, good for us or bad for us. To understand the naturalistic fallacy indirectly.
Activity 92 Naturalistic 2	What is to what ought to be!	To understand value statements versus facts. To identify sound and unsound arguments. To determine what the naturalistic fallacy is from examples.
Activity 93 Naturalistic 3	That's just the way it is!	To analyze, identify, and understand different aspects of the naturalistic fallacy and the closely related appeal to tradition fallacy. To think of examples of the fallacy. To think of ways to counter the fallacy.

Gambler's Fallacy

Activity 70: Heads or Tails?

Introduction

In this activity, learners are introduced to a coin toss experiment to illustrate the gambler's fallacy to them. Learners then share examples in which false assumptions can be made based on the frequency of past events.	
Aim	To understand the gambler's fallacy, to identify how false assumptions can be made based on the frequency of past events
Level	Elementary to Pre-intermediate
Time	50–60 minutes
Materials	1 coin
Preparation	[Option] Examples for Step 8

Fallacy: Gambler's	
Definition	Assuming that something is likely or less likely to happen based on the frequency of past events.
Example	It has been really sunny for the last eight days. It's bound to rain tomorrow.

Procedure

1. Pre-teach the term, 'Coin toss.' Explain that a coin has two sides. In some countries, there is a head of a president or king or queen on one side. This side is called 'Heads.' Explain that the other side is called 'Tails.' We toss the coin to decide between two choices. For example, at the start of an American football game, there may be a coin toss to decide which gets first use of the ball.
2. Use a coin from your pocket and demonstrate coin tossing. Toss the coin a few times and each time say, 'Heads.' Toss the coin again and say, 'Wow, heads again!' Repeat about 10 times and say 'Heads' for each coin toss.
3. Tell students you will toss the coin one more time. Ask them if they think it will be heads or tails. Write down the number of students who say 'Heads' or 'Tails' on the board. It is expected a lot of students will say 'Tails.'
4. Toss the coin. If it lands on 'Heads,' announce the result and repeat Step 3 until it lands on 'Tails.' If it lands on 'Tails' announce the result and point to the number of students who thought that it would land on 'Tails.' Ask

students, 'Why did you think it would land on tails?' Expected answers are 'because it landed on heads ten times before.'
5. On the board, write, 'Because the coin has landed on heads ten times before, it will land on tails the next time.'

   Elicit the conclusion – 'It will land on tails the next time.'
   Elicit the reason – 'Because the coin has landed on heads ten times before.'
6. Put students into pairs or small groups. Have them discuss what is wrong with the argument. Elicit responses from each pair or small group. Explain that the argument is wrong because a coin toss has two possible outcomes – heads or tails. Every time someone tosses a coin, it can either be 'heads' or 'tails.' The current coin toss has no connection to past coin tosses. However, people can believe or assume that something will or will not happen because of what has happened before. Therefore, the argument 'The coin will land on tails because it has landed on heads ten times before' is wrong.

   [Option] You may wish to explain to students that this is called the Gambler's fallacy.
7. Have students test this argument out. Have one student take a coin from their pocket. Have them designate a side of the coin as 'Heads' and the other side as 'Tails.' Have students take turns to toss the coin 11 times and make a record of how many times it landed on 'heads' or 'tails.' Go around each pair or group and elicit the results of the experiment.
8. Have students think of other examples in which people may believe something will or will not happen because of how many times it has occurred in the past. Examples are:

    > 'They have three daughters so the next baby will be a girl.'
    > 'My team has won ten games in a row. They will win tomorrow.'
    > 'Every time I do my washing on a Saturday, it rains. I will do my washing on a Tuesday instead.'
    > 'Every time I take my lucky pencil with me to a test, I pass. I have my lucky pencil, so I will pass the test.'
    > 'I have failed my driving test five times in a row. I'll never pass.'

   [Option] You may wish to prepare a list of four or five examples for students. Then, they can discuss why each argument is faulty reasoning.
9. Have students share their examples with the class.
10. Have students reflect on the activity and discuss what they have learned about the gambler's fallacy and assuming something will or will not happen because of how many times it has happened before.

Activity 71: Monte Carlo

Introduction

In this activity, learners are introduced to the gambler's fallacy and the story of the Monte Carlo fallacy. Learners then share examples of committing the gambler's fallacy in their lives and discuss ways they can guard against committing the fallacy in the future. Important – if gambling is not a suitable topic for your learners, please feel free to use the coin toss example from Activity 70 at the start of the game. You may also wish to skip the story of the Monte Carlo fallacy and provide your own real-life examples of times that you have committed the gambler's fallacy to illustrate the point.

Aim	To understand the gambler's fallacy, to learn about the origin of the fallacy, to share examples of committing the fallacy, to consider ways to guard against the fallacy
Level	Intermediate to Advanced
Time	60–70 minutes
Materials	None
Preparation	Examples of the gambler's fallacy for Step 8

Fallacy: Gambler's	
Definition	Assuming that something is likely or less likely to happen based on the frequency of past events.
Example	It has been really sunny for the last eight days. It's bound to rain tomorrow.

Procedure

1. On the board, write 'gambling' and elicit examples of gambling. Examples may be horse racing, casinos, blackjack, poker, mah-jongg, the lottery, and scratch cards. Have students discuss their experience of gambling (or what they have seen about gambling in movies or on television).
2. Find a suitable online roulette wheel simulator to show your students (for example:
    https://www.online-stopwatch.com/chance-games/roulette-wheel/).
   Ask students if they think the ball will land on red or black. Spin the wheel. Ask students again and repeat a few more times. [Option 1] Share the link and have students play in small groups. [Option 2] Instead of a roulette wheel, use the coin toss example from Activity 70 and then proceed to Step 4.
3. Ask students if the ball landed on black five or six times in a row, what color would they choose for the next spin of the wheel and why.

From Implications to Application 253

4. Show Monte Carlo on a map. Explain to students that you are going to tell them the story of the Monte Carlo fallacy; an event that occurred on August 18, 1913. Have them take notes. Explain that on August 18, 1913, after noticing that the ball had landed on black five or six times in a row, gamblers noticed the pattern. They believed that this streak would end soon. Therefore, they started to bet on red. Ask students, 'What do you think happened next?' Elicit some answers. Then, explain that they spun the wheel and it landed on black again. Ask, 'What do you think the gamblers did?' Elicit some answers. Then, explain that they bet on red again. Ask students, 'What do you think happened next?' Elicit some answers. Then, explain that it landed on black again. Ask students, 'How many times do you think it landed on black?' Have them guess. Then, explain it happened 26 times in a row. The ball landed on red on the 27th spin of the wheel. Statistically speaking this is a 1 in 66.6 million occurrence. Many gamblers lost millions that night believing that the ball had to land on red sooner or later. The gambler's fallacy gets its name from this event.
5. Put students into pairs of small groups. Have them retell the story from their notes. Have them work together to write a definition of the gambler's fallacy.
6. Elicit definitions from some of the pairs or small groups. An example definition is: The gambler's fallacy is the mistaken assumption that something is more or less likely to happen based on a series of previous events. However, these events are independent to and have no causal relation to the present event.
7. Share some examples with your students of times in your life you have committed the gambler's fallacy.
8. Have students think of times in their lives that they or someone they know have committed the gambler's fallacy. For example:

> 'I bought a scratch card in a store and won some money. The next day, I won again. I thought I was on a lucky streak, but I didn't win on the third scratch card.'

> 'The team I support lost five games in a row. I believed their bad streak would end, so I kept paying to go to the games. They lost another three games in a row.'

> 'It hadn't rained for five days in the summer, and my father believed it would rain on the sixth day. It didn't, so he had to water the grass in the front garden.'

9. Have students share their examples in their groups.
10. [Option] Put students into new groups and repeat Step 10.

11. Have students discuss what they can do to guard against the committing the gambler's fallacy in the future. Answers will vary.
12. Have students reflect on the activity and discuss what they have learned about the gambler's fallacy and what they may do to guard against making mistaken assumptions about what may or may not happen in the future.

Activity 72: What Would You Do (Part 2)?

Introduction

In this final activity focusing on the gambler's fallacy, learners examine five situations to help them understand the gambler's fallacy. Learners then research or think of further example situations to share with their classmates. Finally, learners discuss ways to guard against committing this fallacy (Note: The activity is similar to and shares the same name with Activity 45 which focuses on the sunk cost fallacy. Therefore, this activity has been named 'Part 2.')	
Aim	To understand the gambler's fallacy, to identify if students would commit the fallacy or not in example situations, to research or think of further example situations, to consider ways to guard against the fallacy
Level	High-intermediate to Advanced
Time	70–80 minutes
Materials	Worksheet
Preparation	Copies of the worksheet for each student

Fallacy: Gambler's	
Definition	Assuming that something is likely or less likely to happen based on the frequency of past events.
Example	It has been really sunny for the last eight days. It's bound to rain tomorrow.

Procedure

1. Give students a copy of the worksheet. Put them into pairs or small groups and have them work through Task 1.
2. Put pairs or small groups together to form larger groups. Have them share their answers to Task 1.
3. Elicit answers from each group. Answers will vary.
4. Go through each of the five situations and explain the gambler's fallacy to students:

1	An investor may feel that as the stock price continues to rise, there will be a sudden crash and the price will go spiraling down. However, this 'gut feeling' or assumption is fallacious unless supported with evidence. The past action of the stock price increasing has no influence or connection by itself to the occurrence of a sudden drop in price.
2	Although we have flown many times before, we may feel that we are riding our luck and that we will one day be involved in a plane crash. This is fallacious as the statistics of being in a plane crash are 1 in 11 million. The past outcome of a recent plane crash is almost always independent to all over flights that take off and land successfully. However, there may be cases where a fault occurs with a specific type of plane resulting in it being grounded pending further investigation.
3	Research has shown that loan officers may reject a loan application because they have accepted several applications in a row and 'feel' it is time to reject one. Similarly, in this example, a teacher may feel that it is time to give an essay a B just because they have given 6 As in a row. This is fallacious. As with loan applications, each essay should be judged independently and according to a set of criteria. The essay has no relationship with essays that have already been graded.
4	We may have an irrational belief that can jinx our team; that if we go to watch our team live or on television, they will lose. In reality, each game is an independent event. The team has the chance to win or lose (or draw) the particular game. A team may currently be in form, however, the influence of an individual spectator to affect the outcome of a game is fallacious.
5	Once again, we may have an irrational belief that we are on a lucky streak and that we should not ride this luck too long. We may feel that if we stay open for 30 more minutes, a customer may appear who does not purchase a car and therefore ruins our lucky streak. However, this is fallacious. In reality, every visit by a customer provides the salesperson with the opportunity to make or sale or not. There is no connection with the 12th customer to the prior 11 successful sales. Each is an individual event with the possibility of success or failure.

[Option 1] Use the examples of the coin toss from Activity 70 and the roulette wheel from Activity 71 to explain further about the gambler's fallacy.
[Option 2] Have students come up with a definition for the gambler's fallacy based on Task 1

5. Have students work individually to research online or come up with other examples of the gambler's fallacy. Using Task 1 (worksheet) as a guide, have them complete Task 2 on the worksheet.
6. Have students work in their groups to read out their situations and ask students, 'Would you X or Y?' (As students now know about the gambler's fallacy, remind them to be truthful with their responses!)

7. [Option] Have students think of times in their lives that they or someone they know have committed the gambler's fallacy.
8. Have students discuss what they can do to guard against the committing the gambler's fallacy in the future. Answers will vary.
9. Have students reflect on the activity and discuss what they have learned about the gambler's fallacy, how they may commit the fallacy in everyday life, and what they may do to guard against making mistaken assumptions about what may or may not happen in the future.
10. Set students a homework task to listen for examples of the gambler's fallacy in their everyday conversations and/or on the television over the following week and to make a note of any they hear. Students can then report their findings in the next lesson.

WORKSHEET

Task 1: Look at the following situations and discuss with your group what you would do and why?

Situation 1:

You are an investor. You have invested in some stock. Over the week, the stock has made a series of huge gains on the stock market. You fear the stock price will crash soon. Would you hang on to the stock or would you sell?

Situation 2:

There is a terrible plane crash. Tragically, many people are killed. You are scheduled to fly out of the same airport tomorrow using the same airline. Would you still fly or cancel your flight?

Situation 3:

You are the teacher of this class. You are marking critical thinking essays. You have marked six great essays in a row so far. Each one has scored an 'A' grade. You are reading the seventh essay. It is also of a similar standard. Would you give it an A or a different score?

Situation 4:

Your favorite sports team is on a winning streak. They have won 12 games in a row. It is a record in the league. You hate to watch your team lose. Last time you went to the live game, they lost, and you swore that you'd never go again. In fact, you think you are a jinx on your team. Your friend has tickets to the 13th game and invites you to go with her. Would you accept or reject the invitation?

Situation 5:

You are a car salesperson. You are having a great day. You have made a sale with the last 11 customers who have visited your showroom. It's 5 p.m. You could finish for the day or stay open a little while longer in case more customers show up. However, you do not want to ruin the streak you are on. Would you close for the day, or would you stay open?

Task 2: Research or think of other examples in which people commit the gambler's fallacy. Write your examples below. Include a 'Would you X or Y?' question at the end of your example:

Situation 6:

Situation 7:

Situation 8:

Get ready to share your example situations with your classmates.

Logical Paradox

Activity 73: Is It a Contradiction?

Introduction

> As an introduction to logical paradoxes, this activity focuses on contradictory statements. Learners identify contradictions in statements and consider whether the statement can be valid in particular situations. Learners then make short dialogs to show how a contradictory statement may be valid.

From Implications to Application

Aim	To understand and identify contradictory statements; to understand that some contradictory statements can be valid; to make short dialogs to show how a contradictory statement can be valid
Level	Elementary to Pre-intermediate
Time	70–80 minutes
Materials	Worksheet
Preparation	Copies of the worksheet for each student

Fallacy: Logical Paradox	
Definition	Assuming an idea is valid when it is contradictory.
Example	Sorry, I don't speak any English.

Procedure

1. Pre-teach the term, 'contradiction.' Give some examples of contradictory statements. For example:

   'I don't like fish, but I like tuna.'
   'My sister doesn't like me because I am an only child.'

2. Explain that these statements cannot be true. For example, you either like tuna and you like 'some' fish, or you don't like tuna and you don't like fish.
3. On the board, write, 'You can save money by spending it.' Ask students, 'What is the contradiction?' Explain that if you are spending money, you are not saving it.
4. Tell students that this statement is a contradiction. However, it can be true in some situations. Ask them if they can think of a situation in which the statement might be true. Elicit some responses.
5. Give some example situations in which the statement can be true. For example: 'You are in the supermarket buying soda. You can buy two cans of soda for $0.75 each. Each can of soda contains 500ml. A second choice is you can buy a 2-liter bottle of soda for $2. You have to spend $0.50 more than buying the cans but you get double the soda! This saves you buying soda the next day – you save money by spending it.'
6. Put students into pairs or small groups. Give each student a copy of the worksheet. Have them work through Task 1 together.
7. Put students together to make larger groups. Have them share their answers for Task 1.

8. Go through the answers together. Possible answers are:

1	a) Tennis is a sport, so the person must play sports. b) This statement cannot be true.
2	a) The person just spoke English, so contradicts themselves! b) This statement can be true.
3	a) Pink is #1 but blue is #1! b) This statement cannot be true.
4	a) The person just repeated themselves. b) The statement can be true.
5	a) The person cannot call if they do not get the message. b) The statement cannot be true.
6	a) If the restaurant is busy, people go there. b) The statement can be true.
7	a) How can you raise your hand if you are not there? b) The statement cannot be true.
8	a) But he is somebody by the very nature of existing. b) The statement can be true.

9. Have larger groups work through Task 2 together.
10. Elicit answers from each group. Possible answers are:

2	The person means that they only know how to say, 'I'm sorry but I don't speak English' and has no more language ability.
4	The person means that they never repeat themselves in a specific situation. The situation might be as a manager giving instructions to a subordinate and used as a warning to listen carefully to the manager.
6	'Nobody' is not used to mean no person whatsoever but to mean the speaker and possibly the speaker's friends too. In other words, the speaker doesn't want to go there because they don't like crowded places.
8	Of course, the person in question is 'somebody.' The speaker uses 'nobody' to mean the person in question is not important.

11. Put students back into pairs. Have pairs look again at Statements 2, 4, 6, or 8 from the worksheet. Have them work together to turn the statements into short skits to perform in front of the class. For example:

   A: Who's the guy over there?
   B: The guy in red?
   A: Yes.
   B: Oh, don't worry about him. He's nobody.
   A: Nobody?
   B: Yeah, he's not part of the project group.
   A: Oh, okay then.

Give students some time to make their skits and then call on pairs to perform their skits. Have the group listen for the contradiction and how it can be used in everyday conversation.

12. Have students reflect on the activity and discuss what they have learned about statements that can appear to be contradictory at first but can be valid.

WORKSHEET

Task 1: Look at the following statements and the answer the following two questions:

a) What is the contradiction?
b) Can the statement be true?

1. 'I don't play any sports, but I love to play tennis.'
2. 'I'm sorry but I don't speak English.'
3. 'My favorite color is pink, but I like blue the best.'
4. 'Let me say this again: I never repeat myself.'
5. 'If you don't get this message, call me.'
6. 'That restaurant is always busy. Nobody goes there.'
7. 'If you are not here, raise your hand.'
8. 'Don't worry about him. He's nobody.'

Share your answers with your group.

Task 2: Check your answers to Task 1 with your teacher.

Write down the number of the four statements that can be true below. For each statement, think of a situation in which it can be used:

Number:	Situation:

Get ready to share your answers!

Activity 74: The Abilene Paradox

Introduction

	In this activity, the Abilene Paradox is simulated with the learners. Through the experience, they learn about the paradox and share experiences of making collective decisions that many be counter to the real wishes of the group. Learners discuss experiences of the Abilene Paradox and ways to avoid committing it.
Aim	To understand and identify contradictory statements; to experience, learn about, and discuss the Abilene Paradox, to share experiences of making collection decisions that are counter to the real wishes of the group
Level	Intermediate to Advanced
Time	70–80 minutes
Materials	Worksheet
Preparation	Copies of the worksheet for each student

Fallacy: Logical Paradox	
Definition	Assuming an idea is valid when it is contradictory.
Example	Sorry, I don't speak any English.

Procedure

1. Pre-teach the word 'contradiction' to the class.
2. Put students into groups of four or five. Tell students that today you will do an experiment. Write on the board, '1. I'll be back in a second.' Have students choose one student from each group to stand up and leave the classroom for a few minutes.
3. Have the chosen student say to their group, 'I'll be back in a second.' Instruct each chosen student to wait outside of the classroom.
4. When the chosen students from each group have left the classroom, tell the students still in the classroom that you will write some sentences on the board. Tell them that each sentence will be a contradiction. You will ask the question, 'Is this a contradiction?' Tell them to answer 'Yes,' to the first example (I'll be back in a second) and 'No,' to Examples 2 to 5. Explain that the real experiment is to see if their classmate who is waiting outside will agree with the group or not.
5. Bring the students waiting outside back into the classroom and have them rejoin their groups.
6. Ask 'How long were you waiting outside?' and elicit responses from the chosen students. Say, 'But you said – 'I'll be back in a second' – Is this a contradiction?' Have groups discuss and elicit responses. If everything goes to plan and Step 4 has been successful, students will all answer 'Yes.'

7. Write on the board, '2. I don't play any sports, but I love to play tennis.' Ask students, 'Is this a contradiction?' Have groups discuss and elicit responses. If everything goes to plan and Step 4 has been successful, students will say 'No.' When you elicit responses, call on the students who were outside to answer to give the group answer.
8. Repeat Step 7 with the following statements:

   3. My favorite food is pizza, but I like curry the best.
   4. Honestly speaking, I'm a liar.
   5. I'm going to be more positive, but I know it won't work.

9. Reveal to the class that all five statements were in fact contradictions. Explain the real experiment was to see if the chosen group members who waited outside would go along with the incorrect answers of their group members and agree with them. Comment on the results of the experiment. If students did in fact go along with their classmates and give the wrong answers, have them discuss why in their groups. If they decided to disagree with their classmates, have them discuss why they chose to disagree in their groups.
10. Elicit some responses from each chosen student.
11. Explain the Abilene Paradox to the class and have them take notes on the explanation:

    > 'One day, a husband and wife are visiting the parents of the wife. It is a very hot day. After a short time of being there, the father-in-law suggests that they drive 50 miles to a town called Abilene for lunch at a restaurant. The wife says, 'Sounds like a good idea.' She really doesn't want to go but thinks that nobody will agree with her. The son-in-law is tired. The car has no air-conditioning. The drive will be awful. However, he does not want to appear rude. He says okay. Everyone assumes that the mother-in-law wants to go, too. They drive to the restaurant. It is long. The car is hot. To make matters worse, the food in the restaurant is awful. On the way back home, the husband says, 'This wasn't a great idea, was it?' His wife replies, 'I thought my mother really wanted to go.' The mother-in-law says that she was happy staying at home. Then, the father-in-law says that he only suggested the trip because everyone looked bored. Everyone was confused to why they had driven to Abilene in the first place.'

    Have students discuss the story and why they think the situation happened.
12. Elicit ideas from each group.
13. Explain that the Abilene Paradox is an experience that happened to a professor called Jerry Harvey and he wrote about it in his 1974 article. The paradox is that people in a group may sometimes make a decision that is counter to the group because they assume it is the real wish of the group.

They do not want to go against the will of the group but choose to go along with what has been decided even if it is incorrect or undesirable.
14. Have students think of time in their lives they have gone along with a group decision even if they thought it was the wrong thing to do.
15. Have students reflect on the activity and discuss what they have learned about contradictions and the Abilene Paradox. Have them think of ways they can avoid the paradox (e.g., not making assumptions, asking each member for an honest opinion, listening to one another, expecting disagreement).

Activity 75: What's the Paradox?

Introduction

In this final activity focusing on logical paradoxes, learners examine seven logical paradoxes and discuss what the paradoxes are. Learners research for further examples of logical paradoxes and consider why logical paradoxes are important to study.	
Aim	To understand a number of logical paradoxes, to discuss what the paradoxes are, to research for further examples of logical paradoxes, to consider why logical paradoxes are important
Level	High-intermediate to Advanced
Time	60–70 minutes
Materials	Worksheet
Preparation	Copies of the worksheet for each student

Fallacy: Logical Paradox	
Definition	Assuming an idea is valid when it is contradictory.
Example	Sorry, I don't speak any English.

Procedure

1. On the board, write:

    'This statement is written in English.'

    Ask students if the sentence is true. Elicit responses. The answer is it is true.

    Next, write:

    'This statement is grammatically correct.'

    Ask students if the sentence is true. Elicit responses. The answer is it is true.

    Next, write:

    'This statement is false.'

Ask students if the sentence is true. Elicit responses. Explain you will give the answer in the next task.
2. Introduce students to the term, 'logical paradox.' Put students into pairs or small groups. Have them work together to explain what the paradox of 'This statement is false' is. Elicit responses. The answer is:

> 'The statement is false.' If the statement is true, then by the very meaning it is trying to convey, the statement is false. However, if the statement is false, then we have a paradox. If 'The statement is false' is false, then the statement is actually true.

3. Give a copy of the worksheet to each student. Have them work through the task together.
4. Put pairs or small groups together to form larger groups. Have students share their answers to the task in their groups.
5. Elicit answers from each group. Possible answers are:

1	The paradox is that if we know nothing, then we must know something – that we know nothing. This is a famous quotation by the philosopher, Socrates. However, this may be interpreted as meaning that we should question everything as we cannot be certain about what we know.
2	This phrase is from Shakespeare's *Hamlet*. Although it may be paradoxical in the sense of being cruel is not kind, it is often used to mean that I may have to something which is painful to benefit someone in the long run.
3	If you accept the mission, you have failed the mission. If you don't accept the mission, you have failed the mission – an interesting paradox with no easy solution.
4	The moment you try and locate the movement of an arrow in flight, it is no longer moving. At every moment of its flight, it exists in an exact location. Therefore, it cannot move at any given moment of it being located.
5	If a being is omnipotent, it can create anything. Therefore, the being can create a stone that it cannot lift. However, if the being creates a stone that it cannot lift, then the being is not omnipotent. Therefore, the being is not omnipotent.
6	The mother says, 'You will not return the child.' Therefore, if the crocodile keeps the child, the crocodile breaks the promise, so must return the child. However, if the crocodile gives back the child, the guess by the parent has been falsified, and so the crocodile must keep the child. There is no easy solution to this paradox.

6. Have students research online to find more examples of logical paradoxes. Have them write down their examples and share them in their groups.
7. Call on groups to share the logical paradoxes they found and to explain the paradox.
8. Have students reflect on the activity and discuss what they have learned about logical paradoxes. Have them think about why learning about logical paradoxes is important.

WORKSHEET

Task: Look at the following logical paradoxes.
　　　For each one, explain what the paradox is.

Paradox 1:

'All I know is that I know nothing.'

Paradox 2:

'I must be cruel to be kind.'

Paradox 3:

'Your mission is to not accept the mission.'

Paradox 4:

If you fire an arrow at a target, how do you know it is moving?

Paradox 5:

Can an omnipotent being create a stone that they cannot lift?

Paradox 6:

Imagine that a crocodile snatches a young child from its mother. The crocodile promises to return the child if the mother can correctly guess what the crocodile will do with the child. The mother says, 'You will not give the child back.'

Unwarranted Assumptions

Activity 76: Is It Warranted?

Introduction

In this activity, learners discuss the assumptions we make every day and determine whether they are warranted or unwarranted assumptions. Learners examine ten assumptions and decide if they are warranted or unwarranted assumptions. Then, they share examples of unwarranted assumptions from their own lives.	
Aim	To understand the assumptions we make every day; to distinguish between warranted and unwarranted assumptions; to share examples of unwarranted assumptions
Level	Elementary to Pre-intermediate
Time	60–70 minutes

Materials	Worksheet
Preparation	Copies of the worksheet for each student

Fallacy: Unwarranted Assumptions	
Definition	A truth or condition is believed to exist when in fact it does not.
Example	I pressed the power button, but my phone won't turn on. It must be broken.

Procedure

1. Pre-teach the term, 'assumption' – an assumption is something we expect or believe to be true or will be true without the need for evidence.
2. Put students into pairs or small groups. Have them make a list of five assumptions that they have about today's class. For example:
   - The class will finish at the regular time.
   - The class will be in the same room as always.
   - The same students as last week will be in the group.
   - The teacher will be the same as last lesson.
   - The teacher will have a lesson plan.
   - We will be studying critical thinking.
   - There will be homework at the end of the lesson.
3. Put pairs or small groups together to form larger groups. Have them share their assumptions together.
4. Call on groups to share some of their assumptions about the class.
5. Pre-teach the terms 'warranted' and 'unwarranted' – a warranted assumption is having a good reason to believe something without the need for evidence based on custom; an unwarranted assumption is not having a good reason to believe it.
6. Put students into new pairs or small groups. Give each student a copy of the worksheet. Have them work through the task together.
7. Put pairs or small groups together to form larger groups. Have them share their answers together.
8. Go through the answers together. Possible answers are:

1	**Warranted** – We can assume from the custom of inviting people for dinner that the guest will not need to pay for the food.
2	**Unwarranted** – We can assume that we have to pay for the service unless we have a voucher for free food or are good friends with the owner.
3	**Unwarranted** – Our usual expectation is that milk will turn sour if opened and left for a long time.

4	**Warranted** – We expect that when we buy food or drink from the supermarket that the items will be fresh. If not, we can return to the supermarket and complain.
5	**Unwarranted** – Although we can assume that some businesses will be open on national holidays, it is safe to assume the post office will be closed.
6	**Warranted** – We can assume that the post office will be open during regular working hours.
7	**Unwarranted** – If the coffee maker is new, from all the reasons why it may not be working at that moment this would be the most extreme assumption.
8	**Warranted** – If the coffee maker is new, it is reasonable to assume the simplest reason for the machine not working.
9	**Warranted** – We can assume that teachers can be delayed from time to time due to traffic, problems with the train, students asking questions in the corridor on the way to class and so on.
10	**Unwarranted** – Like the coffee maker example, this would be an extreme assumption to jump to.

9. [Option] Have students think of their own examples of warranted or unwarranted assumptions and share them with their classmates.
10. [Option] Have students think of time in their lives they have made unwarranted assumptions. Have them share their experiences together.
11. Have students reflect on the activity and discuss what they have learned about warranted and unwarranted assumptions.

WORKSHEET

Task:	Read the following assumptions.
	Which do you think is warranted and which is unwarranted?
	Check the correct box ✓

	Assumption	Warranted	Unwarranted
1	You are invited to your friend's house for dinner. You assume you will not have to pay for the meal.		
2	You go to a restaurant with your friend. You assume you will not have to pay for the meal.		

3	You buy some milk from the supermarket. You open it and leave it in your refrigerator for three weeks. You assume it will be okay to drink.		
4	You buy some milk from the supermarket. You open it when you get home. You assume it will be okay to drink.		
5	You go to the post office to post a letter on a national holiday. You assume the post office will be open.		
6	You go to the post office to post a letter on a regular weekday. You assume the post office will be open.		
7	You press the power button on your new coffee maker. It does not turn on. You assume the coffee maker is broken.		
8	You press the power button on your new coffee maker. It does not turn on. You assume the coffee maker is not plugged in.		
9	The teacher is late for class. You assume the teacher has been delayed and will arrive soon.		
10	The teacher is late for class. You assume the teacher has quit the school and there will be no lesson today.		

Activity 77: This Morning's Assumptions

Introduction

In this activity, learners consider the assumptions we make every day and distinguish between warranted and unwarranted assumptions. Learners share examples of unwarranted assumptions in the news or from everyday life to understand more about the fallacy. Finally, learners discuss how to avoid making unwarranted assumptions.

Aim	To understand the assumptions we make every day; to distinguish between warranted and unwarranted assumptions; to share examples of unwarranted assumptions in the news or everyday life
Level	Intermediate to Advanced
Time	60–70 minutes
Materials	None
Preparation	[Option] Examples of unwarranted assumptions in the news for Step 8

Fallacy: Unwarranted Assumptions	
Definition	A truth or condition is believed to exist when in fact it does not.
Example	I pressed the power button, but my phone won't turn on. It must be broken.

Procedure

1. Pre-teach the word 'assumption' to the class.
2. Have students think about their morning. Ask them to write a list of five or six assumptions they have made so far today. For example:

   'The water will be running when I turn the tap on.'
   'My smartphone will work when I turn it on.'
   'The train or bus I take to school will be running.'
   'The money I left in the bank will be there when I use the ATM.'
   'Today's lesson will be on.'

3. Put students into groups of three or four to share their assumptions.
4. Pre-teach the terms 'warranted' and 'unwarranted' – a warranted assumption is having a good reason to believe something without the need for evidence based on custom; an unwarranted assumption is not having a good reason to believe it. Give students some examples of warranted assumptions and unwarranted assumptions from Activity 76.
5. Have students look back at the list they made in Step 2. Have them consider whether the assumptions they have made this morning were warranted and why. For example:

   'The water will be running when I turn the tap on – this is warranted because I have paid my water bill. I have not received notification from the water company that they will switch the water off for maintenance. I can expect the water to be running from my previous experiences of turning the tap on each morning. It is a custom, so I expect the same thing to happen.'

Give students time to think about their assumptions and have them share their answers with their group members.

6. Have students look again at the list they made in Step 2. Have them use their imagination to change their warranted assumptions to unwarranted assumptions. Have them make a list of unwarranted assumptions. For example:

'The water won't be running when I turn the tap on. My pipes will have a leak or a blockage.'

'My smartphone won't turn. It is broken.'

'The train or bus won't be running. There is a strike.'

'The money I left in the bank is gone. Somebody has hacked my account.'

'Today's lesson won't be on. The teacher has quit and moved to Bali.'

7. Have them share their unwarranted assumptions with their group members. Have them discuss why they are unwarranted assumptions. For example:

'Everything was working fine when I brushed my teeth last night so it would be unwarranted to assume that the water would not be running in the morning.'

8. [Option] Have groups work together to think about and discuss the current news in the world. What are some unwarranted assumptions that are being made? For example:

'A politician gives advice about how best to treat COVID-19 with an existing drug that treats a different disease. An unwarranted assumption may be that the politician has consulted health experts and scientists before making the claim.'

9. [Option] Have students think of time in their lives they have made unwarranted assumptions. Have them share their experiences together.
10. Have students reflect on the activity and discuss what they have learned about warranted and unwarranted assumptions. Have them think of how they can avoid making unwarranted assumptions in their arguments (e.g., checking for evidence, not to take things for granted without good reason to do so, to question our assumptions).

Activity 78: What Have the Romans Ever Done for Us?
Introduction

	In this final activity focusing on unwarranted assumptions, learners discuss the assumptions they make every day and determine if they are warranted or unwarranted. Learners analyze an excerpt from a famous British comedy to determine the unwarranted assumptions being made. Learners share examples of times they have believed something without evidence and then discuss ways to avoid making unwarranted assumptions.
Aim	To understand the assumptions we make every day; to distinguish between warranted and unwarranted assumptions; to share examples of believing something without evidence; to discuss ways to prevent unwarranted assumptions
Level	High-intermediate to Advanced
Time	60–70 minutes
Materials	Worksheet, Video clip of Monty Python's 'What Have the Romans Done for Us' (Jones et al., 1979). Available online at the YouTube Monty Python Channel
Preparation	Copies of the worksheet for each student

Fallacy: Unwarranted Assumptions	
Definition	A truth or condition is believed to exist when in fact it does not.
Example	I pressed the power button, but my phone won't turn on. It must be broken.

Procedure

1. On the board, write:

    'Assumptions.'

    Elicit the meaning of the terms, 'assume' and 'assumptions' from students.
2. Tell students an assumption that you have already made today. For example, 'I assume everyone has done their homework.' Have students share with the class one assumption they have already made today.
3. Put students into groups of four. Have them discuss if making assumptions is good or bad. Elicit responses. Answers will vary.
4. On the board write: 'Warranted' and 'Unwarranted.' Explain that a warranted assumption is an assumption in which we have a good reason to believe something without the need for actual evidence. This is often based on custom, expectation, prior experience. These assumptions help us to function in daily life (e.g., When we get out of the bed, the floor will be

there; When we set of for school, we assume the train is running). An unwarranted assumption is an assumption that we do not have a good reason to believe. It can be a false assumption that we have acquired without thinking more deeply about it. [Option] Give some examples of unwarranted assumptions from Activity 76.
5. Tell students that you are going to make an assumption about them. Based on what you know about your students, you can say one of the following statements:

> 'I assume you have heard of Monty Python.'
> 'I assume you haven't heard of Monty Python.'

If students have heard of Monty Python, elicit what they know. If they haven't heard of Monty Python, explain they were a famous British comedy group from the 1970s. They made several movies including the controversial *Life of Brian* in 1979. Explain that today, we will perform a famous scene from that movie.
6. Beforehand, using your preferred internet search engine, enter 'Monty Python Life of Brian Script'. Choosing from the various websites containing the script, search down to the section where Reg (The Leader) asks the question, 'And what have they given us in return?' Select the text down to the point where Reg says scornfully, 'yes … now shut up!'
7. Paste or write this section of the script into a word processing program. Change the question of 'And what have they given us in return?' to 'What have the Romans ever done for us?'
8. Leave Reg's name and dialog intact. Change the names of other characters (Xerxes, Stan, Francis, Mattias, General, and other voices) to PFJ1, PFJ2, and PFJ3. You will need to incorporate some of the dialog of these characters into one or the other of the three new character headings.
9. Go to the official Monty Python YouTube channel, and search for the video clip entitled 'What have the Romans done for us?'
10. Give a copy of the worksheet to each student. Have them read through Task 1 and check understanding.
11. Direct the students to do Task 2. Using the resources provided by your school that will enable you to show the YouTube video to the class, watch the scene (approximately 90 seconds in length). Ask the students to find the places where their script is different from what the characters say in the video.
12. Have the students work through Task 3 (Worksheet). Note: If one group has three students, only have one student take on the role of PFJ1 and PFJ3.
13. Instruct the students to work through Task 4 (Worksheet). Elicit answers from each group. Possible answers are:

1	The unwarranted assumption is that the Romans have not done anything for the people of the region.
2	They have made improvements to sanitation, medicine, education, public order, irrigation, roads, health, and introduced wine and a freshwater system.
3	The comedy comes from Reg's continued insistence that the Romans have done nothing for the people (his unwarranted assumption) even when the evidence provided by the other members of the rebel group says otherwise.

14. Have students consider the unwarranted assumption within the question of 'What have the Romans ever done for us?' Have them think of situations in which they or people they know have made similar assumptions; they believe someone or an organization has done nothing for the people when in reality improvements have been made. Have them share their experiences in their group.
15. Have students discuss the possible dangers of unwarranted assumptions and how people can prevent making them. For example:

    'One possible danger is people assuming something to be true without any evidence and then sharing this false assumption via social media where it can spread and be believed by others. One possible way to prevent unwarranted assumptions is to seek evidence that supports it.'

16. Elicit responses. Answers will vary.
17. Have students reflect on the activity and discuss what they have learned about unwarranted assumptions and how to prevent them.

WORKSHEET

Task 1: Read the following information:

Life of Brian is a 1979 movie by the comedy group Monty Python. It is set in the time of the Roman occupation of Judea (around 28–32 CE). The scene is a meeting between a rebel group, 'People's Front of Judea (PFJ)' who wish to end the Roman occupation of their region.

Task 2: Give each student the script excerpt. Play the video clip as the students watch and read along. Ask the students to find the places in their script that is different from the video dialog. After playing the video clip, allow students to form groups to compare what they found to be different. It may be necessary to play the video a couple of times for all of the students to better understand. Then, ask the students to read through the script individually and look up any unknown words.

Task 3: Put the students into groups of four. Decide who will be Reg (The Leader), PFJ1, PFJ2, and PFJ3. If one group has three students, one of the students will read PFJ1 and PFJ3. Allow the students to read out the scene. If more practice seems necessary, ask the students to switch roles and read again.

Task 4: Think about the scene. Discuss the following questions:

1. What is the unwarranted assumption being made?
2. Why is it unwarranted?
3. What makes this scene funny?

Genetic Fallacy

Activity 79: Which Is the Better Reason? (Part 2)

Introduction:

In this activity, learners evaluate the reasons given for accepting or rejecting statements as true or false. Learners discuss a series of statements and decide which is the better reason and why. The activity introduces learners indirectly to the genetic fallacy. (Note: The activity is similar to and shares the same name with Activity 28 which focuses on the 'begging the question' fallacy. Therefore, this activity has been named 'Part 2'.)	
Aim	To consider whether reasons are good and bad for accepting or rejecting statements as true or false; to understand the genetic fallacy indirectly
Level	Elementary to Pre-intermediate
Time	50–60 minutes
Materials	Worksheet
Preparation	Copies of the worksheet for each student

Fallacy: Genetic	
Definition	Assuming something is true (or false) because of its origin or source.
Example	My teacher told me that you cannot end sentences with prepositions, so it must be true.

Procedure

1. On the board, write:

    '**Argument 1** – My friend says that riding a bicycle to work is very safe these days. He drives a car to work. So, I don't believe him.'

2. Put students into pairs and have them discuss whether they think this is a good or bad reason to not believe the friend. Elicit responses.
3. On the board, write:

   '**Argument 2** – My friend says that riding a bicycle to work is very safe these days. However, I read a study by the University of Glasgow that said there is a higher chance of having an accident than driving. So, I don't believe my friend.'

4. Have pairs discuss whether they think this is a good or bad reason not to believe the friend. Elicit responses.
5. Explain that Argument 1 focuses on attacking the friend and not on the friend's argument. For example:

   Friend says X.
   Friend does not use X and is therefore a bad source.
   Therefore, X is false.

   Explain that Argument 2 focuses on the friend's argument to attack it.

   Friend says X.
   University of Glasgow study says Y
   Therefore, X is false.

6. Give each student a copy of the worksheet. Have pairs look at the ten statements on the worksheet and underline any words that they do not know. Have them check their meanings together, in a dictionary, or by asking the teacher.
7. Have pairs work through the task together.
8. Put pairs together to form small groups. Have them check their answers together.
9. Elicit answers from each group and go through the task with the whole class. Possible answers are:

1–2	Reason 2 is the better reason. Reason 1 focuses on rejecting Jimmy's claim because of something bad he did in the past. This is unrelated to the argument of the dog eating the homework and commits the genetic fallacy. Reason 2 focuses on the fact that Jimmy has no pets so must be telling a lie.
3–4	Reason 4 is the better reason. In Reason 3, we accept the claim as being true because of the source; the famous movie star. However, we commit the genetic fallacy as it is unrelated to whether the coffee maker is good or not. In Reason 4, we check the evidence for ourselves by reading many reviews.
5–6	Reason 6 is the better reason. In Reason 5, we accept the claim as being true just because our teacher told us. This again is the genetic fallacy. It does not address the argument itself. In Reason 6, we have statistical evidence to support the claim.

7–8	Reason 8 is the better reason. In Reason 7, we accept the claim as being true just because the politician told us. This again is the genetic fallacy. In Reason 8, we check the claim for ourselves and support it with evidence.
9–10	Reason 9 is the better reason. In Reason 10, we reject the doctor because he or she smokes. This commits the genetic fallacy as it is unrelated to whether they can treat the sickness or not. In Reason 9, we have a valid reason for wanting a different doctor.

10. [Option] Have students think of a time in their lives they have assumed something to be true or false based on who said it rather than thinking about the argument itself. Have them share their stories together.
11. Have students reflect on the activity and discuss what they have learned about not accepting statements to be true or false solely based on who has said them.

WORKSHEET

Task:	1. Read the ten statements below and underline any words that you do not know. 2. Check the meaning of these words. 3. For statements 1–2, 3–4, 5–6, 7–8, 9–10, decide which is the better reason and why.

1	Jimmy said his dog ate his homework. But, he cheated on his math test. So, I don't believe him.
2	Jimmy said his dog ate his homework. But, he has no pets. So, I don't believe him.
Which is the better reason, 1 or 2 and why?	
3	I bought this coffee maker because a famous movie star said it was excellent.
4	I bought this coffee maker because I read many good reviews about it online.
Which is the better reason, 3 or 4 and why?	
5	My teacher told me that young people are very bad drivers. They drive too fast. It must be true.
6	Many young people drive too fast. According to the police, 30% of car accidents last year were caused by teenagers driving too fast.
Which is the better reason, 5 or 6 and why?	

7	I believe that newspaper has many fake stories. [Name of politician] said so on television, so it must be true.
8	I believe that newspaper has many fake stories. I ran them through a fact-checking site and 80% of the stories were false.
	Which is the better reason, 7 or 8 and why?
9	My doctor does not know much about my sickness. I want to see a different doctor.
10	My doctor smokes 40 cigarettes a day. I want to see a different doctor.
	Which is the better reason, 9 or 10 and why?

Activity 80: Who Said It?

Introduction

In this activity, learners rank statements for believability based on who has said them. Learners are made aware that the statements are all false and can understand the genetic fallacy and how it works. Learners consider how we may accept statements to be true based on their origins rather than the arguments themselves.

Aim	To determine whether statements are true or false; to understand the genetic fallacy; to consider how we may accept statements to be true based on their origins rather than the arguments themselves
Level	Intermediate to Advanced
Time	40–50 minutes
Materials	Worksheet
Preparation	Copies of the worksheet for each student

Fallacy: Genetic	
Definition	Assuming something is true (or false) because of its origin or source.
Example	My teacher told me that you cannot end sentences with prepositions, so it must be true.

Procedure

1. Give each student a copy of the worksheet. Put students into groups of four. Have students work through Task 1. Have them look at the five statements on the worksheet and underline any words that they do not know.

Have them check their meanings together, in a dictionary, or by asking the teacher.
2. [Option] Have students look again through the five statements and discuss if they think each statement is true or false.
3. Pre-teach the term, 'rank.'
4. Have students work through Task 2 on the worksheet together.
5. Put two members from each group together with two members from a different group to form new groups. Have them share their answers and reasons together.
6. Elicit answers from each group. Answers will vary.
7. Ask students to discuss which statements they believe are true. Elicit some answers and then tell students that all five statements are false.
8. Ask students to think about why they believed some statements to be true. Elicit some answers. For example:

    'I thought Statement 1 was true, especially if a doctor said it.'

9. Explain that we may sometimes accept or assume that a statement is true (or false) because of who said it rather than thinking about the argument itself. Explain that this is called the 'genetic' fallacy.
10. [Option] Ask students whether they believed some statements to be true because the teacher asked them to do the worksheet tasks. This then would be an example of the genetic fallacy as students assumed some statements would be true due to the origin of the instructions.
11. [Option] Have students look again at the five false statements and think about the evidence that would be needed to make them true. For example: 1) medical research, 2) statistics, 3) scientific research, 4) proof from astronauts who have been to space, 5) a grammar rule that most people agree with.
12. Have students reflect on the activity and discuss what they have learned about the genetic fallacy and not accepting statements to be true or false solely based on who has said them.

WORKSHEET

Task 1: Read the five statements below and underline any words that you do not know. Check the meaning of the words you do not know:

1. Eating sugar causes cancer.
2. Older drivers have more car accidents than younger drivers.
3. The Sun is orange.
4. You can see The Great Wall of China from space.
5. You cannot start a sentence with 'and.'

Task 2: Look again at the five statements. Decide who you would believe the most if they said this statement.

Rank the people from 4 (most believable) to 1 (least believable).

Think about reasons for your answers:

1. Eating sugar causes cancer.			
A politician says it.		A doctor says it	
An athlete says it.		A neighbor says it.	

2. Older drivers have more car accidents than younger drivers.			
A retired taxi driver says it.		A car salesperson says it.	
A student says it.		A police officer says it.	

3. The Sun is orange.			
A teacher says it.		A friend says it.	
A parent says it.		A scientist says it.	

4. You can see The Great Wall of China from space.			
A politician says it.		A teacher says it.	
An astronaut says it.		A neighbor says it.	

5. You cannot start a sentence with 'and.'			
A teacher says it.		A writer says it.	
A doctor says it.		A parent says it.	

Activity 81: Origins

Introduction

In this final activity focusing on the genetic fallacy, learners examine eight arguments to determine what is wrong with each one. Through this, learners are made aware of the genetic fallacy and consider how we may judge claims based on their origins rather than the arguments themselves.

Aim	To understand the genetic fallacy; to consider how we may judge claims based on their origins rather than the arguments themselves; to research and share further examples of the genetic fallacy
Level	High-intermediate to Advanced
Time	50–60 minutes
Materials	Worksheet
Preparation	Copies of the worksheet for each student

Fallacy: Genetic	
Definition	Assuming something is true (or false) because of its origin or source.
Example	My teacher told me that you cannot end sentences with prepositions, so it must be true.

Procedure

1. Ask students what makes a good argument. Elicit some responses.
2. Put students into small groups of three or four. Give each student a copy of the worksheet. Have students go through the task on the worksheet.
3. Assign each student in the group a number and form new groups with number 1s, number 2s, number 3s, and number 4s. Have new groups share their answers to the task on the worksheet.
4. Elicit responses from each group. Possible answers are:

1	The person who makes the argument judges the product solely on its origin. Although we may assume Japanese televisions are high-quality products, we need more evidence to make the claim that the television is great.
2	The person argues that the claim of seeing in the dark is valid solely on its origin. The assumption is that the teachers were a reliable and trusted source, therefore the claim they made must have been true. It does not support the argument itself. [Background information] The story about carrots may have originated from a British government propaganda campaign in World War II to try and fool the Germans into thinking that carrots were helping the RAF to shoot down enemy planes at night and keep the new radar technology they had developed a secret.
3	The person argues that the claim of plucking gray hairs is valid solely on its origin. The assumption being made is that the grandmother is a reliable and trusted source, therefore the claim must be true. In fact, it is a myth.

4	The person argues that the claim of knowing what is best for the economy is valid solely on the politician being a self-made billionaire. It may be true that a self-made billionaire is an expert on economic strategies. However, it may also be false. More evidence is required to support the claim being made.
5	The person argues that the theory of evolution is NOT valid solely on its origin. The argument being made is that as Darwin does not believe in the existence of God, that his theory is also invalid. However, this is fallacious – one must argue against the theory itself rather the person who put forward the theory.
6	The person argues that the claim of terrible cars is valid solely on its origin. The argument being made is that as the company was founded by the Nazis, the cars are not good quality products. However, the history of the company bears no relation to the company today nor to supporting the argument that their cars are indeed terrible. The argument is fallacious. Related evidence would need to be put forward to support the claim.
7	The person argues that the claim of opposing tax cuts is valid solely on the origin of its support; that is, extremely wealthy people. However, no evidence is provided to support why the tax cuts should be opposed or whether they would benefit or be detrimental to the country in question.
8	The person (a past president of the US!) claims that being treated unfairly in court is due to the heritage of the judge and the person's current policies of building (or strengthening) the border wall between Mexico and the US. This is fallacious as it suggests the judge was biased but provides no actual evidence to support the claim itself.

5. Explain that the eight arguments from the worksheet task are all examples of the genetic fallacy. Explain that we may sometimes accept or reject a claim or assume that something is true or false because of who said it rather than addressing the argument itself.
6. [Option] Have students research online for more examples of the genetic fallacy. Have them share their examples together.
7. [Option] Have students think of times in their lives that they have committed the fallacy by assuming something to be true or false based on who said it rather than thinking about the argument itself. Have them share their stories together.
8. Have students reflect on the activity and discuss what they have learned about the genetic fallacy.
9. Set students a homework task to listen out for the genetic fallacy in everyday life, news, advertising, and television. Have them write down the example and share it in the following class.

WORKSHEET

Task: Read the following arguments and discuss what is wrong with each one:

Argument 1:

This television must be great as it is made in Japan.

Argument 2:

My teachers at elementary school told me that if I eat a lot of carrots, I will be able to see in the dark. That is why I eat so many carrots.

Argument 3:

I never pluck my gray hairs. My grandmother told me not to pluck my gray hairs; otherwise, more will grow in their place.

Argument 4:

Since he is a self-made billionaire, he must know what is best for the country's economy.

Argument 5:

We cannot really believe the theory of evolution as Charles Darwin was an atheist.

Argument 6:

You know Volkswagen cars were founded by the Nazi party. They are terrible cars.

Argument 7:

Most support for tax cuts come from those who are extremely wealthy, so it is obvious that we oppose these cuts.

Argument 8:

I think the judge has treated me very unfairly in the lawsuit. He's of Mexican heritage and I am building a wall between Mexico and the United States.

Common Belief Fallacy

Activity 82: True or False

Introduction

In this activity, the common belief fallacy is simulated in the classroom. Through the simulation, learners are made aware of the fallacy and reflect on how people may believe something is true because many other people believe it to be so.	
Aim	To simulate the common belief fallacy in the classroom; to understand the common belief fallacy by experiencing it
Level	Elementary to Pre-intermediate
Time	40–50 minutes
Materials	None
Preparation	Statements about the class members for Step 1; statements about the teacher for Steps #5 to 8

Fallacy: Common Belief	
Definition	Because everyone believes something to be true, it must be true.
Example	Most of my classmates think the exam is on Tuesday, so it must be on Tuesday.

Procedure

1. Tell students you are going to play a game and see how much the students know about each other. Make some statements about students in the class. Some that are true and some that are false. For example:

    'Olivia has three younger sisters.'
    'Juan plays the saxophone.'
    'Lena used to live in New York.'

    After each statement, have students decide if the statement is true or false. NB: Make sure the student featured in the statement does not give the answer away.

2. Tell students that in the next game, you are going to see how much the students know about the teacher. Explain that before you play the game, you are going to choose three or four students in the class. Choose three or four students in the class and ask them to leave the classroom for a few minutes. At this stage, don't explain why they need to leave the classroom, let their imaginations run wild!

3. When the chosen students from each group have left the classroom, tell the students that are still in the classroom that you are going to make some

statements about yourself. Explain that every student should choose 'True' for every statement even if they know the answer is 'False.'
4. Bring the students waiting outside back into the classroom and have them return to their seats.
5. Ask students to stand up. Explain that you are going to start the game and if students think the statement about the teacher is 'True' to move to the front of the classroom. Explain that if they think the statement is 'False' to move to the back of the classroom. Give the first statement and have students move. NB: Make the first statement true and very easy for students to know the answer. For example, 'I am [Nationality].'
6. After giving the first statement, have students return to the middle of the room and give the second statement. NB: Again, make the second statement true and very easy for students to know the answer. For example, 'I have a pet [cat].'
7. After the second statement, have students return to the middle of the room and give the next statement. NB: For the remaining statements, make them all false. However, make sure they are statements that the students may possibly know about you. Example statements could be about children, hobbies, abilities, favorites, travel experience, work experience and so on. For example, 'I can speak four languages: English, Spanish, Chinese, and Russian.' The key here is that the students you gave instructions to in Step 3 will choose 'True' no matter what! In this step, it is important to pay attention to the choices of the students who you instructed to leave the classroom in Step 2. Keep a note of whether they follow the other students and choose, 'True,' or they go against the majority and choose, 'False.'
8. Repeat Step 7 using three to five more false statements about you.
9. Have students return to their seats. Go through the answers to the game (the first two statements are true, but the remaining students are false). Reveal the real reason for the game. Explain that the students who stayed in the classroom in Step 3 were instructed to choose 'True' to each answer.
10. Focus on the students who were chosen to leave the classroom in Step 2. Did they follow the other students and choose, 'True,' or did they go against the majority and choose, 'False'? If they chose, 'True' for the false statements ask them why. Ask them was it because they didn't know whether the statement was true or false or was it because they believed the majority to be the correct answer.
11. Explain about the 'common belief' fallacy to students. Explain that sometimes we may believe something to be true because many other people believe it to be true. However, that can be a dangerous way to judge the information we receive every day.
12. Have students reflect on the activity and discuss what they have learned about the common belief fallacy.

Activity 83: Accept or Reject

Introduction

In this activity, the common belief fallacy is simulated in the classroom. Through this, learners can understand how the fallacy works. Learners then read six arguments and discuss whether they should accept or reject each claim and give reasons to support their answers. Learners then reflect on the activity and the need to seek further evidence before accepting claims that many people believe to be true.	
Aim	To simulate the common belief fallacy; to understand the common belief fallacy, to discuss whether to accept or reject people's claims based on a common belief
Level	Intermediate to Advanced
Time	60–70 minutes
Materials	Worksheet
Preparation	Copies of the worksheet for each student

Fallacy: Common Belief	
Definition	Because everyone believes something to be true, it must be true.
Example	Most of my classmates think the exam is on Tuesday, so it must be on Tuesday.

Procedure

1. Tell students that you are thinking of getting a new smartphone but cannot decide between android or iOS. Tell students you want them to help you decide.
2. Put students into groups of four or five. Have students discuss which is best, android or iOS. As you are listening to the group discussions, slip a secret note to most of the groups (e.g., if you have ten groups, slip the secret note to eight groups). The secret note may read:

    'SECRET – When I ask your group, say you think android is the best.'

3. Go around the groups and elicit their answers. However, make sure to elicit responses from all the groups you slipped a secret note to BEFORE you elicit responses from the remaining groups. Of course, the groups you slipped a secret note to will choose android. What is important here is the choice of the remaining groups. Make a note of whether they follow suit and choose android or whether they go against the crowd and choose iOS.

4. Ask the groups that you did not slip the secret note to – 'Did you choose android because it really is best, or did you choose android because the other students chose it first?' [Note:] Adapt Steps 1 to 4 according to your context and students. For example, you could ask about cats vs. dogs for a pet, whether or not to have a test in class today, the best store to buy clothes in town, and so on.
5. On the board, write, 'Common belief fallacy' and explain that sometimes we may accept that something is true because most other people believe it to be true. Sometimes, this can be fallacious. On the board, write:

    'Many people believe/think X,
    Therefore, X must be true.'

    Explain that sometimes there may be good evidence to believe it. However, sometimes there isn't. We must think carefully before accepting claims to be true without any evidence to support it.
6. Give a copy of the worksheet to each student. Have groups work through the worksheet task together.
7. Assign each student in the group a number and form new groups with number 1s, number 2s, number 3s, and number 4s. Have new groups share their answers to the task on the worksheet.
8. Elicit responses from each group. Possible answers are:

1	Reject. Just because many people are going to get the new smartphone, there is no evidence to support the claim that it will be better than the speaker's current phone.
2	Reject. Just because the movie is successful and many people have paid to see it, it doesn't make it a good movie. In my experience, many box office movies are terrible.
3	Reject. Just because many people are saying this online, it doesn't make it true. The speaker would need to give clear evidence to support the argument that the election had been rigged or stolen by the winning party.
4	Accept. Although I would research this more to get evidence to support the claim before agreeing to the vaccination, I would expect clinical trials to have taken place by medical experts to evaluate the safety of the vaccine.
5	Reject. Just because 54% of people believe it, it doesn't make it true. Evidence is needed to support the claim of the existence of demons.
6	Accept. Although I would need to research this more to confirm the claim, climate scientists are experts in their field. Thus, if 97% have reached consensus on this matter, it would be wise to believe them.

9. [Option] Have students think of times in their lives they have committed the common belief fallacy. Have them share their examples in their groups.
10. Have students reflect on the activity and what they have learned about the common belief fallacy and accepting or rejecting people's claims based on a common belief that something is true.
11. Set students a homework task to listen out for the common belief fallacy in everyday life, news, advertising, and television. Have them write down the example and share it in the following class.

WORKSHEET

Task: Look at the following six arguments. Do you accept or reject the speaker's claims? Why?

Argument 1:

'Everyone is going to get the new smartphone when it is released. It must be better than my current one. I think I will get one, too.'

Argument 2:

'This movie is a box office hit, so it must be good.'

Argument 3:

'I think the election was stolen. Many people are saying this online.'

Argument 4:

'Nearly all doctors say the new vaccinations are safe, so I'm going to take one. How about you?'

Argument 5:

'I read about this survey done with republicans and democrats in the US – 54% of republicans asked said that they believe in demons. I see a lot of evil in the world, so there must be something to this, right?'

Argument 6:

'Around 97% of climate scientists agree that humans are the cause of global warming. I agree with them.'

Activity 84: The Things We Believed

Introduction

In this final activity focusing on the common belief fallacy, learners discuss beliefs that people had in the past. Learners think of the connection between the eight beliefs and are introduced to the common belief fallacy. Learners then think of current false beliefs that people have and discuss ways to avoid committing this fallacy.

Aim	To understand the common belief fallacy; to discuss false beliefs that people had in the past; to think of examples of false beliefs that people may have today; to discuss ways to avoid committing the fallacy
Level	High-intermediate to Advanced
Time	50–60 minutes
Materials	Worksheet
Preparation	Copies of the worksheet for each student. [Option] Prepare some current examples for Step 9

Fallacy: Common Belief	
Definition	Because everyone believes something to be true, it must be true.
Example	Most of my classmates think the exam is on Tuesday, so it must be on Tuesday.

Procedure

1. Ask students to name something that they believe and why they believe it. For example:

    'I believe today is Tuesday because I checked my calendar when I woke up, and we have critical thinking class today.'

2. Put students into pairs or small groups. Give each student a copy of the worksheet. Have them work through Task 1.
3. Do not elicit answers for Task 1 but explain to students that the answers to 1 to 8 are false. Have students think about the connection between the 8 statements. Ask students: 'What do they all have in common?' Have them discuss in their pairs or small groups.
4. Elicit answers from pairs or groups. Explain that the connection is that the statements were all sadly considered to be true by people at one time in history.
5. Have students discuss why they think people believed them to be true.
6. Elicit answers from pairs or groups. Answers will vary.

7. Explain the common belief fallacy to students. Sometimes we may accept that something is true because many other people believe it to be true. As can be seen by the eight statements on the worksheet, this can be fallacious. On the board, write:

   'Many people believe/think X,
   Therefore, X must be true.'

8. [Option] Have students research online more things that people believed in the past. Put students into new groups to share what they find.
9. Have students think of current examples of things that people accept to be true because many other people believe them to be true. For example – the 2020 Big Lie about the US election, Flat Earth, anti-vaxxers, Facebook owns the photographs that people upload.
10. Have students share their examples with the class.
11. Have students think of ways to avoid the common belief fallacy. For example – examining the arguments more closely and looking for evidence to support or dispute the claims being made.
12. Have students reflect on the activity and what they have learned about the common belief fallacy and how people may falsely believe something because many other people believe it, too.
13. Set students a homework task to listen out for the common belief fallacy in everyday life, news, advertising, and television. Have them write down the example and share it in the following class.

WORKSHEET

Task: Look at the following statements. Do you think they are true or false?

1. The Earth is flat.	T or F
2. The Earth is the center of the universe.	T or F
3. Women are too emotional to vote.	T or F
4. African Americans have no rights and can be bought and sold.	T or F
5. People with mental illnesses are possessed with demons.	T or F
6. Smoking is good for your health.	T or F
7. Doctors do not need to wash their hands before surgeries.	T or F
8. Taking a train can cause people to go insane.	T or F

Slippery Slope Fallacy

Activity 85: Negative Chains

Introduction:

As a first step to understanding the slippery slope fallacy, learners are introduced to cause and effect to create negative chains of events. Leaners make and analyze arguments to understand their fallacious nature.	
Aim	To understand cause and effect; to understand slippery slope arguments; to make and analyze slippery slope arguments to demonstrate their fallacious nature (the unlikeliness of the first action leading to the final extreme action)
Level	Elementary to Pre-intermediate
Time	50–60 minutes
Materials	None
Preparation	A list of causes for Step 9

Fallacy: Slippery Slope	
Definition	The assumption that a small action will lead to bigger negative actions.
Example	If you have one cookie now, you will want five cookies tomorrow, and ten cookies the next day. Before you know it, you will have gained weight.

Procedure

1. Pre-teach 'cause' and 'effect.'
2. On the board, write:

    'Cause: You skipped class.'

3. Elicit the effect from students. For example: You skipped class, so you missed some important information.
4. Write the effect on the board as the next cause to create a chain of increasingly negative events. For example:

    'Cause: You missed some important information.'

5. Elicit the next effect from students. For example: You missed some important information, so you couldn't do the assignment.
6. Repeat Steps 4 and 5 several more times. For example:

    Cause: You skipped class
    Effect: So, you missed some important information.
    Cause: You missed some important information.

Effect: So, you couldn't do the assignment.
Cause: You couldn't do the assignment.
Effect: So, you failed the class.
Cause: You failed the class.
Effect: So, you couldn't graduate.
Cause: You couldn't graduate.
Effect: You couldn't get a job.
Cause: You couldn't get a job.
Effect: You had no money.
Cause: You had no money.
Effect: You were hungry and homeless.

7. Explain to the students the argument in this cause-and-effect chain results in – 'If you skip class, you may be homeless.' Ask students how likely the final action is. Ask if this is a good argument or not.
8. Explain that a 'slippery slope' argument is fallacious. It includes a chain of actions that get worse and worse. The final action 'being homeless' is used to argue that the first action, 'skipping class,' is bad.
9. On the board, write a list of causes appropriate to the level of your students. For example:

    Cause: You buy one donut from the store.
    Cause: You miss your train.
    Cause: You use your smartphone while walking.
    Cause: You buy a lottery ticket.
    Cause: You drink coffee to stay awake while studying.

10. Put students into groups of four. Have each group choose one cause from the board. Have them work together to make a cause-and-effect chain in which each action gets worse (as with the example in Step 6 of this activity). Students should start with the cause they have chosen (Cause 1) and think of an effect (Effect 1). Then, they write this effect (Effect 1) as the next cause in the chain (Cause 2) and think of the next effect (Effect 2) and so on.
11. Once they have completed a chain of seven or eight cause-and-effects, they should write an argument at the end of the chain – If (Cause 1), you will (Effect 8). For example:

    If you buy one donut from the store, the next thing you know you will be in hospital.

12. Assign each student in the group a number and form new groups with number 1s, number 2s, number 3s, and number 4s. Have each student explain their cause-and-effect chain and their slippery slope arguments to each other.

13. Have students discuss how likely each final action in the chain is and why each slippery slope argument is probably a bad argument.
14. Have students reflect on the activity and discuss what they have learned about the slippery slope fallacy and how people may use it to make bad arguments.

Activity 86: Can I Have a Chocolate?

Introduction

In this activity, learners are introduced to a slippery slope argument and then analyze and understand how slippery slope arguments work. Learners make and share their own slippery slope arguments. Finally, learners discuss the fallacious nature of each argument.

Aim	To understand the structure of slippery slope arguments; to make, share, and discuss slippery slope arguments; to research online for further examples of the fallacy
Level	Intermediate to Advanced
Time	60–70 minutes
Materials	None
Preparation	None

Fallacy: Slippery Slope	
Definition	The assumption that a small action will lead to bigger negative actions.
Example	If you have one cookie now, you will want five cookies tomorrow, and ten cookies the next day. Before you know it, you will have gained weight.

Procedure

1. Ask students to imagine that they bring some chocolates to class (you could use an example of a branded chocolate that students may know). Ask students how many chocolates are usually in one bag, tube, or pack. For example, the British chocolate 'Rolo' has about seven chocolates in one tube (please do a Google search for 'Rolo').
2. Put students into pairs. Have students imagine they open their chocolate just before the start of class. The person sitting next to them asks for a chocolate. Have students discuss the question, 'Would you give the person sitting next to you a chocolate?'
3. Elicit responses from pairs. Answers will vary.
4. Draw a quick map of the classroom on the board. Point to one of the tables and two circles to represent two people sitting at the table. Explain that

one person has some chocolates, and the other person asks for one chocolate. Write:

> 'If I give the person sitting next to me a chocolate …'

Elicit possible consequences or effects from students. Then, draw two circles on the table located behind the two people sitting and elicit:

> 'If I give the person sitting next to me a chocolate, I'll have to give the people sitting behind me one chocolate each, too.'

Next, draw two circles at the table positioned to the right of the first table. Elicit from students what the next possible consequence will be:

> 'If I give the person sitting next to me a chocolate, I'll have to give the people sitting behind me one chocolate each, too. If that happens, I'll have to give the people sitting to the right of me one chocolate each, too.'

Next, draw two circles at the table positioned to the left of the first table and elicit from students what the next possible consequence will be:

> 'If I give the person sitting next to me a chocolate, I'll have to give the people sitting behind me one chocolate each, too. If that happens, I'll have to give the people sitting to the right of me one chocolate each, too. Then, I'll have to give the people sitting to the left of me one chocolate each, too.'

Elicit from students what the final negative outcome is – 'You have no chocolates for yourself.'

Finally, elicit from students what the conclusion of the argument will be – 'So, I'm not going to give a chocolate to the person sitting next to me!'

5. On the board, write:

> 'If A, then B'

Elicit from students that in the example from Step 4, A stands for giving a chocolate to the person next to you and B stands for the people sitting on the table behind seeing the action of giving a chocolate and you feeling compelled to give them both a chocolate. Write:

> 'If B, then C'

Elicit that B stands for giving chocolates to the students sitting behind and C stands for the people sitting on the right seeing the action of giving chocolates, so you feel compelled to give them both a chocolate. Write:

> 'If C, then D'

Elicit that C stands for giving chocolates to the students sitting on the right and D stands for the people sitting on the light seeing the action of giving chocolates, so you feel compelled to give them both a chocolate. Write:

'If D, then E'

Elicit that D stands for giving chocolates to the students sitting on the light and E stands for having no chocolates left for yourself.

6. On the board, write, 'Slippery slope fallacy' and ask each pair to work out from the example in Step 4 and explanation in Step 5 what the fallacy is. Elicit that the slippery slope fallacy means assuming that a small action will lead to bigger negative actions or outcomes.
7. Have pairs discuss why they think such an assumption is fallacious. Elicit answers from pairs or groups. Explain that such an argument assumes that each chain of event will indeed happen; that A will lead to B and B will lead to C and so on. Explain that it also assumes that the outcome is indeed negative – I mean sharing chocolates with your classmates is a good thing, isn't it?
8. Have pairs think of their own slippery slope chains using the example in Step 4 and the structure in Step 5 as a model.
9. Put one student from each pair together to form groups of three or four. Have each student share their examples in their group. Have students listen to each example and decide if they feel the argument is fallacious or a likely possibility given the chain of events.
10. [Option] Have students search online for more examples of slippery slope arguments. Have them share their examples in their groups.
11. Have students reflect on the activity and what they have learned about the slippery slope fallacy and how people may use it to make fallacious arguments.
12. Set students a homework task to listen out for the slippery slope fallacy in everyday life, news, advertising, and television. Have them write down the example and share it in the following class.

Activity 87: Countering Slippery Slope Arguments

Introduction

In this final activity focusing on the slippery slope fallacy, learners analyze how slippery slope arguments work. Learners then discuss ways to counter various slippery slope arguments.	
Aim	To understand the structure of slippery slope arguments; to make, share, and discuss slippery slope arguments; to think of ways to counter slippery slope arguments

Level	High-intermediate to Advanced
Time	50–60 minutes
Materials	Worksheet
Preparation	Copies of the worksheet for each student

Fallacy: Slippery Slope	
Definition	The assumption that a small action will lead to bigger negative actions.
Example	If you have one cookie now, you will want five cookies tomorrow, and ten cookies the next day. Before you know it, you will have gained weight.

Procedure

1. On the board, write:

    If A, then B,
    If B, then C,
    If C, then D,
    If D, then Z

2. Ask students to imagine that there is a jar of cookies on the table, but you are on a diet. Next to 'If A, then B' on the board, write:

    'If I have on cookie now, I'll want another one later today.'

    Elicit from students the B–C chain. Encourage them to think of a progressively worse outcome for each chain. For example:

    'If I eat another cookie later today, I'll want three cookies tomorrow.'

    Elicit from students the C–D chain. For example:

    'If I eat three cookies tomorrow, I'll want five cookies the next day.'

    Elicit from students what the most negative outcome could be of eating so many cookies. For example:

    'If I eat so many cookies, I'll put on weight, get sick, and end up in a hospital bed.'

3. On the board, write, 'Slippery slope fallacy' and have students work out what the fallacy is from the example in Step 2. Elicit from students that the slippery slope fallacy means assuming that a small action will lead to bigger negative actions or outcomes.

4. Put students into pairs or small groups. Have them imagine their friend argues, 'If I eat one cookie today, I'll go out of control, eat many cookies, put on weight, and end up in hospital.' Have them discuss how they would counter this slippery slope argument – How would you respond to your friend?
5. Elicit answers from pairs or small groups. Answers will vary. One possible answer is to point out that eating one cookie does not necessarily lead to eating another cookie later. One could eat a cookie and have a friend take away the cookie jar. Another argument would be eating a jar of cookies would not put you in hospital unless the action was repeated daily over a period of time.
6. Give a copy of the worksheet to each student. Have students read through the five arguments and check any unknown words or phrases in a dictionary, by asking their partner or group members, or by checking with the teacher.
7. Have pairs or small groups work through the worksheet task together.
8. Put students into new pairs of groups to share their answers to the worksheet task.
9. Go through the answers together. Possible answers are:

1	The argument is fallacious as it assumes that everyone must be granted the same exception to the deadline regardless of circumstance. To counter the argument, it is possible to point out that accepting the essay after the deadline will not set a dangerous precedent and usurp the deadline rule for future assignments.
2	The argument is fallacious as no evidence is provided to support the claims and past immigration has not resulted in such a negative outcome. To counter the argument, it is possible to ask the person for evidence or to point out that immigration usually has benefits for a country and stating what those benefits are.
3	This argument is fallacious as it assumes that the removal of controversial statues will lead to the censorship of truth. To counter the argument, it is possible to point out that the history of the controversial figure will still be available in books and on the Internet for people to study if they so wish. A statue may be considered a celebration of the person's life and achievements, so in some cases it may be appropriate to remove statues as we learn more about the controversial actions of certain historical figures.
4	This argument is fallacious as there is no evidence that providing free healthcare encourages people to want other things for free, thus resulting in the economic collapse of a country. To counter this argument, it is possible to ask for evidence to support the claim or provide evidence of countries that successfully provide healthcare to its citizens and their healthy economies.

| 5 | This argument is fallacious as it tries to change the definition of a union between two humans to include animals and inanimate objects. To counter this argument, it is possible to restate the dictionary definition of 'marriage' and show how it does not include animals and objects and to point to countries in which gay marriage has been legalized and show there has been no legal marriages to animals or objects in these countries. Also, to counter this argument, one can point to Japan in which same-sex marriage is not yet legal, yet a man was able to marry a hologram! |

10. [Option 1] Have students come up with their own slippery slope arguments. Have them share their examples with their partner or group and think of ways to counter the arguments.
11. [Option 2] Have students search online for more examples of slippery slope arguments. Have them share their examples in their groups and think of ways to counter the arguments.
12. [Option 3] Have pairs make a short dialog in which Speaker A makes a slippery slope argument and Speaker B gives a counterargument. Have them perform their dialog in front of the class. Have group members listen and evaluate how effective the counterargument is.
13. Have students reflect on the activity and what they have learned about the slippery slope fallacy, how people may use it to make fallacious arguments, and how we may counter such arguments.
14. Set students a homework task to listen out for the slippery slope fallacy in everyday life, news, advertising, and television. Have them write down the example and share it in the following class.

WORKSHEET

Task: Look at the five slippery slope arguments. How would you counter them?

Argument 1:

I know you were only five minutes late turning your essay in and you had some computer problems, but I am going to have to fail you on it. I cannot make an exception for five minutes. Then, I would have to give an exception for somebody turning it in an hour late and then two hours late and then a day late and so on. Then there would be no point having a deadline. I may as well just say to everyone turn in your work whenever you feel like it. I'm sorry the deadline is the deadline.

Argument 2:

We shouldn't let any more foreigners into our country. If we keep letting them in, there won't be any room for us. More immigrants will be a burden on the health system. We already have overcrowding in schools. Also, they'll take our jobs. Give it a few years and we'll all be out of work and living on the streets.

Argument 3:

We've got to stop people removing statues from public places because they are controversial. We should keep them to remind people of the past. I mean one minute they're taking down the statues and the next minute they'll be rewriting the history books and censoring the truth.

Argument 4:

People need to pay for healthcare. If we give it to them for free, what else will they want? Next thing, they'll want free housing, free utilities, free food, and a free television. There will be no reason for anyone to work and the country will be in economic ruin.

Argument 5:

If we allow gay marriages, where does it stop? Next thing you know people will want to marry their pet cats or they will want to marry their kitchen table. Quite simply, marriage is the union between a man and a woman.

Ignorance Fallacy

Activity 88: Evidence of No Evidence?

Introduction

In this activity, learners discuss the need for evidence to support conclusions. Learners are then introduced to the ignorance fallacy and identify which statements commit this fallacy.

Aim	To understand the need for evidence to support conclusions; to understand the ignorance fallacy
Level	Elementary to Pre-intermediate
Time	70–80 minutes
Materials	Worksheet
Preparation	Copies of worksheet for each student [NB: Copy the worksheet so that Task 1 is on the front and Task 2 is on the back of the sheet]

Fallacy: Ignorance	
Definition	Assuming something is true as no one has proved it to be false.
Example	Nobody has proved ghosts do not exist, so it makes sense to believe in them, right?

Procedure

1. On the board, draw a picture of a big bottle with lots of small balls inside of it. [Option] If you can bring a bottle into class with lots of small balls inside of it. Write:

    'There are 438 balls in the bottle.'

2. Ask students if they think the statement is true or false and why.
3. Pre-teach 'evidence.'
4. Ask students what evidence could be used to support the statement. Elicit some ideas.
5. On the board, write:

    '1. I counted them by hand and there are 438 balls in the bottle.'
    '2. Nobody has counted them but there are 438 balls in the bottle.'

    Ask students which statement has evidence and which statement has no evidence. Elicit the answer that Statement 1 has evidence as you have counted them to check.

6. Put students into small groups of three or four. Give a copy of the worksheet to each student. Have students work together to complete Task 1 on the worksheet.
7. Elicit ideas from each group.
8. Have students turn the worksheet over and work together to complete Task 2 on the worksheet.
9. Put groups together to share their answers to Task 2 (Worksheet).
10. Go through each statement with the whole class and elicit answers. Possible answers are:

1	No evidence – you don't know if you got the job or not at this stage.
2	Possible evidence – it is possible that the position has been filled.
3	Evidence – you asked and got permission.
4	No evidence – you do not know if it is okay or not.
5	Possible evidence – as John has seen the action of the person taking the money it is likely true (unless the person has a reasonable explanation).
6	No evidence – not being able to prove you didn't do the action is not evidence that you did.

300 From Implications to Application

7	No evidence – you don't know if the person is interested in you or not.
8	Possible evidence – long periods of eye contact is a sign that someone may be interested in you
9	Possible evidence – scientists finding water on Mars indicates a possibility that there was life on Mars.
10	No evidence – not being able to prove there wasn't life on Mars is no evidence that there was life on Mars.

11. Explain the ignorance fallacy to students. On the board, write:

    'X is true because there is no evidence that it is false.'

    Have students look again at Task 2 and identify which statements commit the ignorance fallacy. Answers are:

1	I didn't get the job because there is no evidence that I got the job.
4	I'm using the computer because there is no evidence that I can't.
6	You stole the money because there is no evidence that you didn't steal it.
7	The person is interested in me because there is no evidence they are not.
10	There was life on Mars because there is no evidence there wasn't.

12. Have students reflect on the activity and discuss what they have learned about the ignorance fallacy and the need for evidence to support one's conclusions.

WORKSHEET

Task 1: What evidence can you give to support each conclusion?

1	, so I guess I didn't get the job.
2	, so I'm using my sister's computer.
3	, so I guess you stole the money.
4	, so I'm going to ask him/her on a date.
5	, so I believe there was life on Mars.

Task 2: Read the ten statements and decide if they have evidence to support their conclusion or have no evidence.

1	I didn't get a phone call from the coffee shop, so I guess I didn't get the job. Evidence or no evidence?
2	I saw somebody new working at the coffee shop, so I guess I didn't get the job. Evidence or no evidence?
3	I asked her and she said it was okay, so I'm using my sister's computer. Evidence or no evidence?
4	She didn't say I couldn't use it, so I'm using my sister's computer. Evidence or no evidence?
5	John saw you put the money in your pocket, so I guess you stole the money. Evidence or no evidence?
6	You cannot prove that you didn't steal the money, so I guess you stole the money. Evidence or no evidence?
7	The person has never said they don't like me, so I'm going to ask him/her on a date. Evidence or no evidence?
8	The person always looks and smiles at me, so I'm going to ask him/her on a date. Evidence or no evidence?
9	They found water on the planet, so I believe there was life on Mars. Evidence or no evidence?
10	Nobody can prove that there wasn't life on Mars, so I believe there was life on Mars. Evidence or no evidence?

Activity 89: No Evidence Is No Evidence!

Introduction

In this activity, learners discuss the need for evidence to support facts or conclusions. Learners work in groups to read and discuss five arguments and come together to share their answers. Through the activity, learners understand about the ignorance fallacy and determine that as no evidence supports both sides of an argument it renders it invalid.

Aim	To understand the need for evidence to support facts or conclusions; to understand the ignorance fallacy; to determine that as no evidence supports both sides of an argument it is invalid
Level	Intermediate to Advanced
Time	50–60 minutes
Materials	Worksheet A and B
Preparation	Copies of worksheet A for half of the class; copies of worksheet B for half of the class

Fallacy: Ignorance	
Definition	Assuming something is true as no one has proved it to be false.
Example	Nobody has proved ghosts do not exist, so it makes sense to believe in them, right?

Procedure

1. Pre-teach 'proof' and 'prove.'
2. Give an example to students of something you can prove and how you can prove it. For example, 'I work at this school' and show your identification card. Ask students, 'What is something you can prove?' Elicit some answers and evidence.
3. Refer students back to Activity 1 'Prove it' – [Option] Repeat Steps 5 and 6 of Activity 1.
4. Put students into groups of four. (If you have odd numbers in the class, make one group of three or five members.) Give each group a number. Give a copy of Worksheet A to each student in groups 1, 3, 5, 7, 9 and so on. Give a copy of Worksheet B to each student in group 2, 4, 6, 8 and so on.
5. Have students read through the five arguments and check any unknown words or phrases in a dictionary, by asking their partner or group members, or by checking with the teacher.
6. Have students work through the task on the worksheet together and answer the five questions. Students should take notes of their answers.
7. Assign a number to students in the Worksheet A groups (e.g., 1, 2, 3, 4, 5, 6 and so on). Assign a number to students in the worksheet B groups (e.g., I, 2, 3, 4, 5, 6 and so on). Put students into pairs by putting 1s together, 2s together, 3s together and so on. Make sure each pair has a student who worked on Worksheet A and a student who worked on Worksheet B. (If you have odd numbers in the class, make one group of three.)

8. Have pairs share their answers together to Step 6.
9. Go through the worksheet task with the whole class and elicit answers from each pair. Point out to students that each argument is fallacious or is an example of poor reasoning as there is no evidence for each conclusion. Therefore, we do not have enough information to agree or disagree with the argument. The only evidence provided to support each conclusion is that there IS no evidence. Therefore, if the argument is valid, it can support both sides of the argument. For example:

Argument 1: There is no evidence that ghosts exist or not. Therefore, they may exist, or they may not exist.

Argument 2: There is no evidence that aliens exist or not. Therefore, they may exist, or they may not exist.

Argument 3: There is no evidence that black cats are lucky or unlucky. Therefore, they may be lucky or unlucky.

Argument 4: There is no evidence about how teachers feel about my work at school. Therefore, I may be doing well, or I may not be doing well.

Argument 5: There is no evidence that the mountain is safe or dangerous to climb. Therefore, it may be safe or dangerous to climb.

10. Explain to students that the fallacy is called the 'ignorance' or 'appeal to ignorance' fallacy.
11. [Option] Using the worksheet examples as a model, have students think of other examples of the ignorance fallacy. For example:

'Nobody can prove that Santa Claus does not exist. Therefore, Santa Claus exists.'

12. Have students reflect on the activity and discuss what they have learned about the ignorance fallacy and how having NO evidence does not provide support for one's conclusions in an argument.

WORKSHEET A

Task: Look at the five arguments and answer the five questions.

Argument 1:

Nobody can prove ghosts do not exist. Therefore, it makes sense to believe in them.
 Do you agree or disagree?

Argument 2:

Nobody can prove aliens exist. Therefore, I think they don't exist.
   Do you agree or disagree?

Argument 3:

Nobody can prove that black cats are lucky. Therefore, I believe it.
   Do you agree or disagree?

Argument 4:

Nobody has praised my work. I must not be doing well at school.
   Do you agree or disagree?

Argument 5:

Nobody has told me it is dangerous. Therefore, it is safe to climb the mountain.
   Do you agree or disagree?

WORKSHEET B

Task: Look at the five arguments and answer the five questions.

Argument 1:

Nobody can prove ghosts exist. Therefore, it makes sense to not believe in them.
   Do you agree or disagree?

Argument 2:

Nobody can prove aliens do not exist. Therefore, I think they do exist.
   Do you agree or disagree?

Argument 3:

Nobody can prove that black cats are unlucky. Therefore, I believe it.
   Do you agree or disagree?

Argument 4:

Nobody has complained about my work. I must be doing well at school.
   Do you agree or disagree?

Argument 5:

Nobody has told me it is safe. Therefore, it is dangerous to climb the mountain.
　　Do you agree or disagree?

Activity 90: No Evidence Is Evidence!

Introduction

In this final activity focusing on the ignorance fallacy, learners determine the evidence needed to support an argument. Learners are made aware of the ignorance fallacy and analyze an example from the news. Learners then come up with their own fallacious examples to illustrate the ignorance fallacy. Finally, learners research and share further examples in which there is evidence to support an argument of no evidence.

Aim	To establish the evidence to support one's argument; to understand the ignorance fallacy; to research and share examples of evidence to support one's arguments of no evidence
Level	High-intermediate to Advanced
Time	60–70 minutes
Materials	None
Preparation	Prepare some example topics for Step 11

Fallacy: Ignorance	
Definition	Assuming something is true as no one has proved it to be false.
Example	Nobody has proved ghosts do not exist, so it makes sense to believe in them, right?

Procedure

1. Ask students, 'What do you know about elections and voter fraud?' Elicit some responses.
2. Put students into pairs or small groups and have them make a list of what evidence they would look for to establish voter fraud had or had not occurred in an election. Possible answers are:

Voter fraud occurred:	Voter fraud did not occur:
People impersonated registered voters.	Voters had to show photo ID and signatures on mail-in ballots were double-checked.

People who had passed away were able to vote.	Ballots were checked against public records. Very few mistakes were found. Sometimes, people had the same name as somebody who had passed away.
Computer software was hacked.	Computer software was checked by experts and no evidence of hacking was found.
Ballots were tampered with.	Ballots were checked many times and there is no evidence of ballots being tampered with.
Votes were miscounted.	In a close vote, there is always a recount to recheck the tally.
A state has more ballots than registered voters.	After investigation, it was found that the information about number of registered voters is outdated.

3. On the board, write:

   Reporter: 'But there's no evidence of widespread voter fraud in the election.'
   Politician: 'There's no evidence that there's not either.'

4. Have pairs or small groups discuss the two arguments put forward by the reporter and politician. Explain that one argument is fallacious. Have students work together to discuss which argument they feel is fallacious and why.
5. Elicit responses from each pair or small group.
6. Explain that the politician's argument is fallacious. Explain that it is an example of the ignorance fallacy. The fallacy occurs when an argument is put forward as being true because there is no evidence against it not being true. In other words:

   X is true because you cannot prove that it is false.
   X is false because you cannot prove that it is true.

   The politician is arguing that voter fraud is true because there is no evidence that it is false. Explain that following this logic, one can argue that monsters dance in the park near my apartment every night because I have no evidence that they do not. Therefore, we can say that having no evidence is NOT evidence to support the conclusion of one's argument.
7. Have students come up with some of their own fallacious examples using the logical forms in Step 6. (e.g., monsters dancing in the park!). Have them share their examples with the class.
8. Ask students to look again at the reporter's statement in Step 3 and ask them that if no evidence is NOT evidence to support the conclusion of one's argument, the reporter also argues there is no evidence of widespread voter fraud, so is this also fallacious? Have students discuss in pairs and small groups.
9. Elicit responses from each pair or small group.

10. Explain that the statement is not fallacious because having evidence of there being no evidence is evidence to support the conclusion of one's argument. Refer students back to the list they made in Step 2 and explain that supporting the statement with evidence such as ID checks, signature checks, computer software checks, recounts, and so support the claim that there is no evidence of voter fraud. In other words:

    X is false because we can prove that it is false.

11. Have pairs or small groups think of and research other examples where no evidence is evidence (X is false because we can prove that it is false) (e.g., the efficacy of homeopathic remedies, vaccinations cause autism, sugar is addictive, the Pizzagate conspiracy theory).
12. Put pairs or small groups together to form larger groups. Have them share their examples from Step 11.
13. [Option] Have students research online for other examples of the ignorance fallacy. Have them share these examples with the class.
14. Have students reflect on the activity and what they have learned about the ignorance fallacy and how having no evidence is NOT evidence to support a conclusion but having evidence of no evidence is.

Naturalistic Fallacy

Activity 91: Is It Good For Us?

Introduction

In this activity, learners discuss the assumption that as something is natural it must be good for us. Learners categorize items as natural or not natural, good for us, or bad for us and give reasons for their choices. Through the activity, learners are introduced indirectly to the naturalistic fallacy.	
Aim	To discuss the assumption that it is natural therefore it is good; to categorize items as natural or not natural, good for us or bad for us; to understand the naturalistic fallacy indirectly
Level	Elementary to Pre-intermediate
Time	50–60 minutes
Materials	Worksheet
Preparation	Copies of worksheet for each student. [Option] Prepare some examples of the naturalistic fallacy for Step 13

Fallacy: Naturalistic	
Definition	Assuming that if something is natural it must be good or cannot be wrong.
Example	It's natural for humans to eat meat, so you should do it.

Procedure

1. Pre-teach 'nature' and 'natural'
2. On the top of the board, write:

    'It is natural therefore it is good.'

    [Note] You will return to this statement in Step 10.
3. Ask students whether they agree or disagree with the statement and why. Elicit some responses.
4. Put students into pairs or small groups. Give each students a copy of the worksheet. Have students read through the 15 words in Task 1 on the worksheet and check any unknown words in a dictionary, by asking their partner or group members, or by checking with the teacher.
5. Have pairs or small groups work through Task 1 on the worksheet.
6. Elicit Task 1 answers from pairs or small groups. Answers are:

    1. Natural
    2. Not natural
    3. Natural
    4. Natural
    5. Not natural
    6. Natural
    7. Not natural
    8. Natural
    9. Natural
    10. Natural
    11. Not natural
    12. Natural
    13. Not natural
    14. Natural
    15. Natural

7. Have pairs or small groups work through Task 2 on the worksheet. Answers may vary.
8. Put students into new pairs or groups to share their answers to Task 2 and discuss why they chose each category. For example: 'I chose 'good for us' for water as we need water to live.'
9. Have pairs or small groups work through Task 3 on the worksheet.
10. On the board draw six boxes – Good for us (Natural), Good for us (Not natural), Bad for us (Natural), Bad for us (Not natural), Both good and bad

for us (Natural), Both good and bad for us (Not natural). Elicit answers for Task 2 and 3 (worksheet) from pairs or small groups and write the answers on the board in the correct boxes. For example:

Good for us (Natural)	Good for us (Not natural)
Bad for us (Natural)	Bad for us (Not natural)
Both good /bad for us (Natural)	Both good/bad for us (Not natural)

11. Return to the statement you wrote on the board in Step 2. Ask students if they still agree with the statement and why. Elicit some responses.
12. Explain that people often argue that if something is natural, it must be good. Point to the 'Good for us (Not natural)' and Bad for us (Natural) boxes. Point to the 'Both good and bad for us' boxes. Explain that this is not always true.
13. [Option] Have students work together in their pairs or small groups to add words to each of the boxes in Task 2 on the worksheet.
14. [Option] Introduce examples of the naturalistic fallacy for students to discuss. For example:

> 'Lions eat meat, so we ought to eat meat. Do you agree?'
> 'Sicknesses are a natural part of life, so we shouldn't use medicine. Do you agree?'

15. Have students reflect on the activity and discuss what they have learned about the assumption, 'It is natural, so it is good,' and the naturalistic fallacy.

WORKSHEET

Task 1: Decide if the following are natural or not natural (man-made):

1. Water	Natural/Not natural
2. Glasses	Natural/Not natural
3. Earthquakes	Natural/Not natural
4. Coal	Natural/Not natural
5. Medicine	Natural/Not natural
6. Trees	Natural/Not natural
7. Bottles	Natural/Not natural
8. Tobacco	Natural/Not natural
9. Hurricanes	Natural/Not natural
10. Salt	Natural/Not natural
11. Clothes	Natural/Not natural
12. Lions	Natural/Not natural
13. Books	Natural/Not natural
14. Vegetables	Natural/Not natural
15. Mushrooms	Natural/Not natural

Task 2: Match the words into the following categories:

Good for us	Bad for us	Both good and bad for us

Get ready to give reasons for your answers.

Task 3: Use two different color pens. Look again at the three categories in Task 2. Circle the 'natural' things using one color. Circle the 'not natural' things with a second color.

Activity 92: What Is to What Ought to Be!
Introduction

In this activity, learners understand the difference between value statements and facts. They analyze eight arguments to identify if they are sound or unsound and then determine what the naturalistic fallacy is. Through the activity, learners can understand how people can move fallaciously from an argument of what is (a fact) to what ought to be (a moral imperative).

Aim	To understand value statements versus facts; to identify sound and unsound arguments; to determine what the naturalistic fallacy is from examples
Level	Intermediate to Advanced
Time	70–80 minutes
Materials	Worksheet
Preparation	Copies of worksheet for each student

Fallacy: Naturalistic	
Definition	Assuming that if something is natural it must be good or cannot be wrong.
Example	It's natural for humans to eat meat, so you should do it.

Procedure

1. Pre-teach the concept of 'moral rightness.'
2. Elicit examples from students of something that is morally right or morally wrong. For example:

    'It's morally right for crime to be punished.'
    'It's morally wrong to steal.'

    Write examples on the board.
3. Put students into pairs or small groups. Have them discuss whether they consider the statements to be facts or opinions. Elicit responses from pairs or small groups.
4. Explain that the examples are value statements. They are beliefs or opinions that we have developed in our lives about standards of behavior and what we consider to be right or wrong.
5. Give students a copy of the worksheet. Have them work through the task on the worksheet.
6. Put pairs or small groups together to form larger groups and have them share their answers to the task on the worksheet.
7. Elicit some responses from each group.

8. Share the answers to the task to students. Answers are:

   Argument 1 – is fallacious

   Argument 2 – is fallacious

   Argument 3 – is a sound argument. Based on empirical evidence the speaker believes it is in the best interest for the person to stop smoking.

   Argument 4 – is fallacious

   Argument 5 – is fallacious

   Argument 6 – is a sound argument. The statement is an opinion and the subsequent use of 'ought to' is an extension of the opinion. The speaker feels because the headphones have good sound quality the listener should also get a pair.

   Argument 7 – is fallacious.

   Argument 8 – is a sound argument. The statement is an opinion, a prediction of the weather and the subsequent use of 'ought to' show that it would be a good idea to take an umbrella.

9. Now students have the answers, have them focus on Arguments 1, 2, 4, 5, and 7. Ask them to discuss why they are fallacious.
10. Elicit some responses from each group.
11. Go through the answers with the students. Answers are:

Argument 1	The argument moves from what is (a fact that some animals eat meat) to a moral imperative of what ought to be (humans ought to eat meat) without providing a reason why that ought to be. It also assumes that as eating meat is natural it is morally right.
Argument 2	The argument moves from what is (a fact that breastfeeding is natural) to a moral imperative of what ought to be (mothers ought to breastfeed) without providing a reason why that ought to be. It also assumes that as baby formula is not natural it is bad.
Argument 4	The argument moves from what is (a fact that some animals are promiscuous) to a moral imperative of what ought to be (humans ought to be promiscuous) without providing a reason why that ought to be. It also assumes that what happens in nature is morally right.
Argument 5	The argument moves from what is (a fact that vaccinations are man-made) to a moral imperative of what ought to be (humans ought NOT to get vaccinated) without providing a reason why that ought to be. It also assumes that because vaccinations are man-made, they are bad.

Argument 7	The argument moves from what is (a fact that wars have always occurred throughout history) to a moral imperative of what ought to be (humans ought to accept wars as inevitable) without providing a reason why that ought to be. It also assumes that as wars are 'natural,' they are morally acceptable.

12. Explain to students that the fallacy is called the 'naturalistic fallacy,' and takes the form:

    X is.
    Therefore, X ought to be morally right.

    X is not.
    Therefore, X ought not to be morally right.

13. [Option] Have groups think of their own examples of the naturalistic fallacy and share their examples with the whole class.
14. Have students reflect on the activity and discuss what they have learned about the naturalistic fallacy and how people may move to what is to what ought to be in an argument without providing an adequate reason.

WORKSHEET

Task: Look at the following arguments. For each one, decide if it is a good argument or not.

Argument 1:

Vegetarians have got it so wrong! Animals eat meat. Therefore, we ought to eat meat.
    Is this a good argument? Why or why not?

Argument 2:

Baby formula is not natural. Breastfeeding is. Therefore, mothers ought to breastfeed their babies.
    Is this a good argument? Why or why not?

Argument 3:

You've been coughing a lot recently and not looking well. You really ought to quit smoking.
    Is this a good argument? Why or why not?

Argument 4:

Did you know that many animals in the animal kingdom are promiscuous? Therefore, it ought to be okay for people to have as many partners as they want.
    Is this a good argument? Why or why not?

Argument 5:

You know that vaccinations aren't natural, right? Therefore, we ought not to get vaccinated. It could be harmful for our body.
    Is this a good argument? Why or why not?

Argument 6:

I love my new headphones. I think the sound quality is great. You ought to get some.
    Is this a good argument? Why or why not?

Argument 7:

There have always been wars throughout history. They are inevitable. We ought to just accept that they will always happen.
    Is this a good argument? Why or why not?

Argument 8:

I think it's going to rain today. You ought to take an umbrella with you.
    Is this a good argument? Why or why not?

Activity 93: That's Just the Way It Is!

Introduction

In this final activity focusing on the naturalistic fallacy, learners analyze, identify, and understand different aspects of the naturalistic fallacy and the closely related appeal to tradition fallacy. Learners think of their own examples to illustrate the naturalistic fallacy, Finally, learners consider ways to counter the fallacy.	
Aim	To analyze, identify, and understand different aspects of the naturalistic fallacy and the closely related appeal to tradition fallacy; to think of examples of the fallacy; to think of ways to counter the fallacy
Level	High-intermediate to Advanced

From Implications to Application 315

Time	70–80 minutes
Materials	None
Preparation	[Option] Find the song 'The Way It Is' by Bruce Hornsby; print out the lyrics and make a gap-fill activity

Fallacy: Naturalistic	
Definition	Assuming that if something is natural it must be good or cannot be wrong.
Example	It's natural for humans to eat meat, so you should do it.

Procedure

1. Explain to students that today we will look at the 'naturalistic' fallacy and focus on a fallacy that is closely related – an appeal to tradition.
2. On the board, write:

   'It says 100% natural on the packaging, so this food must be good for us.'
   'Diseases are a natural part of life, so we shouldn't use medicine.'

3. Put students into pairs or small groups. Have them discuss the arguments on the board. Ask students to work out what the assumptions are in each argument and why they are fallacious. Elicit some responses.
4. Explain that one aspect of the naturalistic fallacy is an appeal to nature. Here, the arguer assumes that anything natural is good and anything artificial is secondary, wrong, or bad. Have students think of their own 'appeal to nature' examples and share with the class. [Note] Activity 91 focuses on appeal to nature, so you may wish to incorporate some of the steps from Activity 91 in this lesson.
5. On the board, write:

   'It says 100% natural on the packaging, so we ought to eat this.'
   'Diseases are a natural part of life, so we ought not to treat people with medicine.'

6. Have pairs or small groups discuss the arguments. Ask students to work out what the assumptions are in each argument and why they are fallacious. Elicit some responses.
7. Explain that another aspect of the naturalistic fallacy is a move from a fact – 'It says 100% natural on the packaging' to a moral imperative – 'people ought to eat this.' Here, the arguer does not provide a reason or explanation but jumps to an assumption of what we ought to do or ought not to do based only on a fact from nature. Have students think of their own

'what is ought to be' examples and share with the class [Note] Activity 92 focuses on the move from what is to what ought to be, so you may wish to incorporate some of the steps from Activity 92 in this lesson.

8. On the board, write:

> 'The poor will always be poor. That's just the way it is.'
> 'This medicine has been used for years to treat this disease, so it must be effective.'

9. Have pairs or small groups discuss the arguments. Ask students to work out what the assumptions are in each argument and why they are fallacious. Elicit some responses.
10. Explain that a closely related fallacy to the naturalistic fallacy is the appeal to tradition. Like an appeal to nature, the arguer will appeal to a belief, tradition, state or how things have always been done to argue that we can assume it is good, acceptable, or not possible to change.
11. Have students think of their own 'appeal to tradition' examples and share with the class.
12. [Option 1] Find the song 'The Way It Is' by Bruce Hornsby (1986) on Spotify or YouTube and play it to students. Have them listen to the lyrics and discuss them. Ask how Bruce Hornsby suggests we should counter the appeal to tradition fallacy (Answer – 'Don't you believe them!'). [Option 1.1] You may also wish to print out the lyrics and do a gap-fill activity with students.
13. [Option 2] Have students research further examples of the naturalistic fallacy (appeal to nature, is/ought to, appeal to tradition fallacies) and share further examples with the class.
14. [Option 3] Have students share their own experiences with group members in which someone has argued to them, 'That's the way it is.' For example:

> 'In a meeting, I suggested we use a different book distributor for English textbooks at the school as they offered students a 15% discount. After some discussion, my suggestion was rejected, and I was told that we would use the usual book distributor. When I asked why, I was greeted with the response, 'That's just the way it is!'

15. Have students reflect on the activity and what they have learned about different aspects of the naturalistic fallacy. Have students think of ways they could counter the fallacy when they experience it. Answers will vary.

PART III
From Application to Implementation

Introduction

In Part II, we explained 93 activities that can be used to help learners develop a disposition toward critical thinking, consider more carefully the information they receive from others, be aware of a variety of logical fallacies, and begin to discern possible weaknesses within the arguments presented to them. In Part III, we focus on ways that educators may implement the activities into their language classrooms. Section A looks at how you may use the CT activities to build your own unique CT course that addresses the needs of your learners or to get your learners involved in negotiating the course content (Boon, 2011). Section B offers ideas about how you may use the CT activities to supplement an existing course. Section C reminds readers of the objectives of the activities in Part II and discusses how you may approach using them in your classes or choose to modify the content to suit your teaching context. It also suggests encouraging your learners to keep a CT learning diary. You may wish to use the CT activities as a springboard to develop your own ideas. Section D suggests ways you may further research CT, introduce students to some of the logical fallacies not covered in Part II, and possibly how to create your own CT material.

A. Creating a Critical Thinking Course

One way to implement the activities in Part II into the language classroom is to design a critical thinking course for your learners. Taking into consideration the needs, wants, and interests of your learners and the time available to achieve the CT learning outcomes you have identified, you can begin to map out the course by picking and choosing from the activities from Part II that you feel would be most relevant and beneficial to include in your CT course.

DOI: 10.4324/9780429059865-3

A.1 Making Your Own CT course

For example, if you were to design a CT course for B1 learners that were to meet for 90 minutes each week over a 15-week period (15 lessons), you may wish to include the following elements as shown in Table 3.1:

TABLE 3.1 Example CT Syllabus

Lesson	Activities	Title	Aim
The CT Cycle: Developing Dispositions			
1	1 & 2	Prove it The 'why' game	To help students begin to develop CT dispositions. To raise learner awareness about the need to check facts and reliability. To raise learner awareness about the need to support one's opinion. To break the ice in the first class.
The CT Cycle: Receiving			
2	7 & 9	Show me you're listening Picture what I'm saying	To raise learner awareness about positive body language when listening. To help learners focus on the message being communicated to them by another speaker.
The CT Cycle: Reasoning			
3	12 & 14	Rank it! Spot the problem!	To identify premises and conclusions to other people's arguments. To listen for and evaluate the strength of other people's arguments. To raise learner awareness of misleading or unproven claims.
The CT Cycle: Responding			
4	16 & 19	Reflecting Correct me!	To listen carefully to and restate a speaker's argument to show understanding. To be able to correct mistakes and point out weak arguments made by others politely.
Logical Fallacies: Faulty Conclusions: Non Sequitur			
5	22	Does it follow?	To review the CT cycle. To identify whether statements logically follow one another or not.
Logical Fallacies: Faulty Conclusions: Begging the Question			
6	28	Which is the better reason?	To review the CT cycle and previous fallacy. To learn about and be able to identify statements that beg the question.
Logical Fallacies: Faulty Conclusions: Hasty Generalization			
7	34	All students in this class…	To review the CT cycle and previous fallacies. To use quantifiers to make statements about classmates. To be aware of and correct generalizations.

(Continued)

TABLE 3.1 Continued

Lesson	Activities	Title	Aim
Mid-semester Review/Test			
8	–	–	To evaluate what students have learned in Lessons 1 to 7.
Logical Fallacies: Questionable Reasons: Ad Hominem			
9	46	Don't attack me!	To review the CT cycle and previous fallacies. To be aware of the strategies used in an argument to attack a person. To learn about disagreeing by addressing the argument and providing a reason.
Logical Fallacies: Questionable Reasons: Red Herring			
10	49	Avoiding the question	To review the CT cycle and previous fallacies. To identify when someone is answering or avoiding a question. To learn about the red herring fallacy.
Logical Fallacies: Questionable Reasons: Either/Or			
11	58	The third option	To review the CT cycle and previous fallacies. To understand the either/or fallacy. To challenge questions in which only two options are presented and offer alternative options.
Logical Fallacies: Mistaken Assumptions: Common Belief			
12	82	True or False	To review the CT cycle and previous fallacies. To simulate the common belief fallacy in the classroom. To discuss whether to accept or reject people's claims based on a common belief that it is true.
Logical Fallacies: Mistaken Assumptions: Slippery Slope			
13	85	Negative chains	To review the CT cycle and previous fallacies. To understand cause and effect. To understand, analyze, and make slippery-slope arguments to demonstrate their fallacious nature.
Logical Fallacies: Mistaken Assumptions: Naturalistic			
14	91	Is it good for us?	To review the CT cycle and previous fallacies. To discuss the assumption that it is natural therefore it is good for us. To categorize and analyze items.
End-of-Semester Review/Test			
15	–	–	To evaluate what students have learned in Lessons 9 to 14.

The example syllabus in Table 3.1 introduces learners to the CT cycle, helping them to question the reliability of the facts that they hear or read, support their opinions with evidence, listen to and evaluate what others say to them, and respond politely to point out potential weaknesses in other people's arguments. It then focuses on nine different logical fallacies (three from each of the three areas identified in the Common Logical Fallacies Table 1.1), so that learners can increase their awareness of the potential fallacious argumentation that they may be exposed to during the reading or listening process.

The syllabus also gives room for teachers to review previous lessons, adapt other activities from Part II, and/or develop their own activities to supplement individual lessons in situations where their learners get through the material more quickly than anticipated or it is possible to cover more material within the allotted time. The syllabus in Table 3.1 should serve as a guide only. It can be extended as necessary and alternative activities from Part II can be selected by educators as they build a CT course that best suits their learners.

A.2 Negotiating a CT Course

Another way you may choose to design a CT course is by negotiating the content with your learners. After introducing your students to some of the activities in Part II, Section 1, relating to the CT cycle, you may wish to work through Activity 21: Introduction to Logical Fallacies with them. This activity introduces students to Tu quoque and the 24 common logical fallacies outlined earlier in Table 1.1. Go through the steps outlined in Activity 21 and determine which fallacies your learners would like to learn more about in the remainder of the CT course. Then, design the latter part of your course based on the learners' requests. Your negotiated CT course may include the following three stages:

- **Stage 1:** Introductory lessons related to the CT cycle.
- **Stage 2:** A lesson to introduce learners to common logical fallacies and negotiate which of them to focus on in the course.
- **Stage 3:** Lessons related to the chosen logical fallacies.

Alternatively, you may wish to divide Activity 21 into three discrete lessons. Then, your CT course may include the following seven stages:

- **Stage 1:** Introductory lessons related to the CT cycle.
- **Stage 2:** A lesson to introduce students to Tu quoque and eight common logical fallacies related to faulty conclusions. Negotiate which logical fallacies to focus on in the next few lessons of the course.
- **Stage 3:** Lessons related to the chosen logical fallacies for faulty conclusions.
- **Stage 4:** A lesson to introduce students to eight common logical fallacies related to questionable reasons. Negotiate which logical fallacies to focus on in the next few lessons of the course.

- **Stage 5:** Lessons related to the chosen logical fallacies for questionable reasons.
- **Stage 6:** A lesson to introduce students to eight common logical fallacies related to mistaken assumptions. Negotiate which logical fallacies to focus on in the remaining few lessons of the course.
- **Stage 7:** Lessons related to the chosen logical fallacies for mistaken assumptions.

B. Using the Activities to Supplement a Course

Your intention may not be to create a CT course. You may just wish to read through the activities in Part II to add to your knowledge and your pedagogical 'bag of tricks.' As you read through the CT activities, it may spark ideas within you. You may begin to make connections to lessons that you already teach. You may start to see how you could use or adapt the activities to incorporate critical thinking skills into an existing course, to supplement a coursebook that you have adopted for your classes, or to use the activities within an upcoming course. For example:

- You may be teaching a lesson about giving opinions or using follow-up questions to get extra information and decide to use or adapt Activity 2 for your class.
- You may be teaching a lesson on basic research skills that requires your learners to categorize and organize their data or a lesson on writing a classification essay and decide to use or adapt Activity 11 for your class.
- You may be teaching a lesson on quantifiers and decide to use or adapt Activity 34 for your class.
- You may be teaching a lesson on cause and effect and decide to use or adapt Activity 85 for your class.
- You may decide to dedicate a period of class time away from your syllabus each week to work through some of the activities in Part II.

Remember, it may not always be possible to supplement your existing course(s) fully with CT activities. However, what we offer in Part II are some possibilities to do so.

C. Implementing Critical Thinking Activities into Your Classroom

We believe that the CT cycle (see Figure 1.5) can provide a systematic approach to helping learners become better critical thinkers.

C.1 Using the CT Cycle Activities as an Introduction

A useful starting point to CT learning is to introduce your learners to some or all of the activities from 1 to 20 in Part II. Activities 1 to 5 can be used to help learners begin to develop a CT disposition, to understand the need to check the many facts that are presented to them, to become more aware of their own beliefs, assumptions, and biases, and to support their own claims with evidence. Activities 6 to 10 can help learners to really listen carefully and respectfully to other people as they receive incoming information from them. Activities 11 to 15 can assist learners in thinking more deeply about the information they receive, critically analyzing the information, and determining the strengths and weaknesses of other people's arguments. Finally, activities 16 to 20 can equip learners with skills to reflect back the incoming information to show they have truly understood it, to politely and diplomatically respond and point out any possible weaknesses within the information, to engage in discourse that leads to better understanding and deeper thinking for both parties, and to reflect on the CT cycle as a whole as they work toward further developing their CT dispositions.

C.2 Using Activity 21 as a Needs Analysis

As mentioned earlier in Part III, Activity 21 can be used as a tool for negotiating a CT syllabus with your learners with regard to them selecting the logical fallacies they would like to learn about during the course. However, it can also be used as a tool for determining the current CT level of your learners and their particular CT learning needs. If students are able to identify successfully the problems or errors in reasoning in each of the eight arguments in Tasks 1 to 3 of the worksheet for Activity 21, and/or are familiar with the particular logical fallacy, then you may wish to focus valuable class time on the logical fallacies that are not known by your learners.

We should also reiterate the point that Activity 21 can be divided into three discrete needs analysis lessons. It is possible to do a needs analysis regarding the logical fallacies related to faulty conclusions, and then choose several activities from 22 to 45 to use with your learners. After, you may return to Activity 21 for a second needs analysis session regarding the logical fallacies related to questionable assumptions, and then choose a number of activities from 46 to 69. Finally, you may return to Activity 21 for a third needs analysis session regarding the logical fallacies related to mistaken assumptions, and then choose a number of activities from 70 to 93.

C.3 Using the Logical Fallacy Activities

In Part II, Activities 22 to 93 focus on raising learner awareness of 24 common logical fallacies (see Table 1.1) that can be used to misrepresent, twist, or change the conclusions, reasons, and assumptions within an argument. We feature logical fallacies that:

- Further faulty conclusions,
- Engage in questionable reasoning, and
- Rely on mistaken assumptions (see Part I).

For each of the three areas, there are eight fallacies featured. For each fallacy, there are three activities that are aimed at different levels of learner proficiency. When deciding on an activity to use with your learners, read carefully through the introduction, procedure, and worksheet (if provided) and consider your particular teaching context. Imagine how the activity may work in your class with your particular learners. Remember, it may be possible to adapt a Level 1 activity to use with higher-level students. Likewise, it may be possible to use parts of a Level 2 or 3 activity with lower-level students.

Think about any preparation or research you will need to do prior to teaching the lesson. For example, you may need to read up on each logical fallacy that you introduce to your learners. Think about the examples provided in this book – are they suitable for your learners or do they need adapting to your context? For example, you may teach in a country in which gambling is prohibited. In that case, you may need to modify Activities 70 to 72 (Gambler's Fallacy), omit the Monte Carlo gambling story, and focus on the probability aspect of the fallacy.

You may also wish to use alternative examples to the ones featured in the book to illustrate a particular logical fallacy. These examples may come from your own experiences, from more current news or media stories, or by searching for supplementary examples on the Internet. The activities in Part II also encourage learners to make connections between the fallacies and their own lived experiences. We truly hope that you and your learners have fun working through these activities and they inspire your learners to think more critically about the information they read or hear.

C.4 Returning to the CT Cycle

Although we have recommended using the CT cycle Activities 1 to 20 as an introduction, we believe that the four stages associated with the CT cycle permeate all aspects of the CT learning process. As your learners work through Activities 21 to 93 of the book, they should remember to remain open to developing a CT disposition; to be more cautious of what they believe and why they believe it. They should remember to listen carefully and respectfully to others whilst receiving information. They should remember to use reasoning to evaluate the strength of the arguments they read or hear.

Finally, they should remember to show understanding, respect, and diplomacy when responding directly to any inconsistencies in another person's argument. In the example CT syllabus (see Table 3.1), we have suggested a regular review of the activities related to the CT cycle so that learners can reorient themselves to the skills that we believe will benefit their critical thinking and their engagement with others.

C.5 Reflecting on Learning

Encouraging self-reflection at the end of lessons can be an important tool for helping learners to think critically about their learning, to consider the individual effort they have put into lessons (Boon, 2012), and to make connections between the lesson content, their experiences, and the world outside of the classroom. With this in mind, each activity in Part II (except for Activity 21) ends with a self-reflection task. This gives learners the opportunity to think more deeply about what they have learned in relation to critical thinking via the process of undertaking the particular activity.

C.6 Keeping a CT Diary

Encouraging your learners to keep a critical thinking diary can be a further way for students to reflect on their learning experiences in your classes, to keep notes of their classroom learning, to consider their progress, to ask themselves questions, and to record examples of logical fallacies they experience in their daily lives.

In fact, many of the logical fallacy activities in Part II suggest optional homework tasks for your learners in which they listen out for and identify examples of logical fallacies they come across in everyday conversations, readings, or news stories outside of the classroom. They may also begin to recognize some of the logical fallacies they may use themselves in their daily lives. A CT diary offers learners a space to record and write about such examples as they occur and to build their confidence in identifying fallacious arguments. Having students keep a CT diary during the length of the course and submit it to you on a regular basis can be a means for you to check that CT learning is taking place and of providing an opportunity for you to offer some words of encouragement to each learner.

D. Going Beyond the Activities in the Book

Although by the time you get to this sentence in the book you will have read a lot of information about critical thinking, as you can guess, there is always more to learn.

D.1 Researching CT

Following up on some of the references in the list at the back of the book can help you develop a greater understanding of the critical thinking field. Part IV also includes suggestions for methods and procedures you may wish to employ to undertake and publish your own research studies of CT pedagogy. However, at this stage, you may just wish to do more research on the logical fallacies that we have featured in Part II to gain a deeper understanding of them. With a simple search on the Internet, you will be able to find many useful websites with descriptions and examples of each fallacy that may help you and your learners. Alternatively, you may wish to check video-sharing platforms, such as YouTube, which have some great video explanations of the logical fallacies featured in Part II.

D.2 Finding More Fallacies

As we mentioned in Part I, there are literally hundreds of logical fallacies. In Activities 22 to 93, we have chosen to focus on 24 common logical fallacies only. The aim is to provide a solid foundation for you to work with in order to help improve the critical thinking skills of your learners. However, you may wish to introduce your learners to alternative logical fallacies not featured in this book. Again, a simple Internet search with the keywords 'logical fallacies' will yield numerous pages for you to check and discover the names, definitions, and examples of other logical fallacies. There are many great websites out there. And yet, I provide no evidence to support this claim. I leave the burden of proof with you (which is itself a logical fallacy that we did not feature in this book!).

D.3 Creating Your Own CT Activities

We believe that the activities in Part II offer you some great ideas for introducing critical thinking to your students. However, why stop there? After reading this book, you may wish to research different logical fallacies and go on to create your own CT activities for your learners. You may wish to create your own examples of each different fallacy for your learners to analyze and determine what the problems or errors in reasoning are. You may wish for your learners to think of the times they have come across the fallacy in their lives or to consider ways that they can avoid committing the fallacy within their own arguments. You may also wish to refer your learners back to the CT cycle to discuss how best to respond to another person who commits the fallacy.

E. A Final Note

In Part I, we stated that while we are not experts in CT, we are avid students. In this respect, we believe that CT is an ongoing skill for both teachers and learners that evolves with awareness, commitment, and practice. As you embark on this CT journey, you may begin to notice logical fallacies everywhere you turn. Don't worry. This is a good thing. Question everything – even this!

PART IV
From Implementation to Research

Introduction

Doing research on critical thinking takes more work than making a questionnaire at the end of the course and asking your students whether they feel that their CT skills have improved. Critical thinking is a mental construct, like motivation or student anxiety, and we cannot see or measure these directly. To get findings that are convincing and credible, your investigation needs to be focused, well-planned, and methodologically sound. Without a clear and specific idea of what it is you want to explore in a construct as multifaceted as CT, you will end up chasing shadows. Answers to your questions will always be just beyond your reach.

In this final part of the book, we will suggest procedures for avoiding this situation. You will learn ways of investigating your language learners' CT skills and research strategies for checking on their improvement. We do this through an integrated action research approach using a mixed methods research design. After unpacking these terms, we will go into greater detail on research procedures that, when used in a critical and consistent manner, have potential for helping you to find focus and clarity as you seek to improve the quality of CT instruction in your second-language classes. We will then finish with a discussion of the important final stage – that of sharing your findings with others who also want to encourage their learners to become better critical thinkers.

A. Integrating Methodologies

We will briefly explain the background and rationale of action research and mixed methods research. Then we will show how synthesizing these two

DOI: 10.4324/9780429059865-4

approaches to research can give you a means of focusing your thoughts, actions, and interpretations.

A.1 Action Research

The term action research (AR) was popularized by the social psychologist Kurt Lewin (1946), who proposed an interaction of 'action, research and training as a triangle' (p. 42) for finding solutions between groups whose goals, racial perspectives, and beliefs were at odds with each other. Starting in the early 1990s, the pragmatic nature of AR began to appeal to second-language teachers and continues to be a popular research methodology in ELT today.

Burns (2010, p. 2) describes AR as a 'self-reflective, critical, and systematic approach to exploring your own teaching contexts … in AR, a teacher becomes an 'investigator' or 'explorer' of his or her own personal teaching context, while at the same being one of the participants in it.' The teacher-investigator finds issues in their classes and tries to either improve or understand them: '[T]he goals of AR,' she explains, 'are to work towards educational improvement and more effective outcomes for our students by reflecting on and observing current classroom practices' (Burns, 2010, p. 33).

Numerous graphic representations have been created for visualizing the AR process. In our opinion, most have been inspired by Kemmis and McTaggart's (1988) dynamic flowchart, which presents recurring patterns of planning, acting, observing, reflecting, and then the creation of a revised plan if the outcomes of the first attempt are found to be unsatisfactory. Action research begins at that moment when you as a teacher notice something taking place with your learners that seems to be either a barrier to learning or something that sparks within you a sense of curiosity. You go back and maybe you read some books or research articles about the problem or curious behavior, and then you develop a plan for addressing the issue among your learners. You put your plan into action, and observe your learners' response. You find out more by using certain tests or interview protocols. Based upon what you learn from your students, you then consider whether or not your intervention has worked. If not, then you build upon what you have learned to make a better strategy for addressing what you see as affecting the quality of learning among your students. This process is repeated, each time bringing you closer to a satisfactory outcome.

However, AR is not simply a systematic means of problem-solving. Edge (2001), Burns (2019), and Hadley (2003) state that AR also aids in 'the reflective language teacher's organized and ongoing search for classroom solutions and professional insight' (Hadley, 2003, pp. ii–iii). AR helps teachers to become wiser as they learn to reflect upon their current teaching practices and to deepen their understanding of the lived experiences of their learners.

Kemmis and McTaggart's (1988) visual representation of AR posits the search for understanding in a top-down manner. For us, symbolically at least,

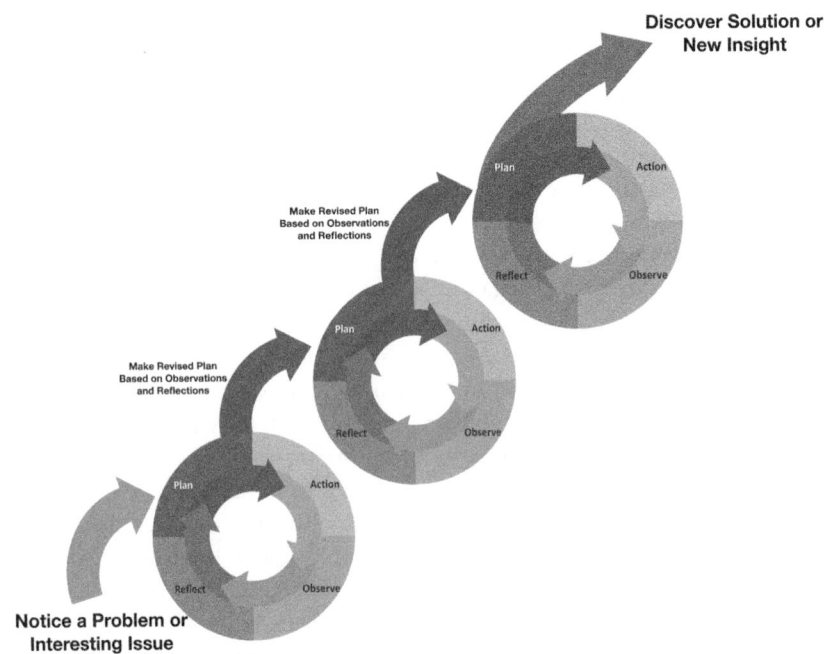

FIGURE 4.1 Action Research Process

this seems to point in the wrong direction. Our depiction of AR, which incorporates ideas from Edge (2001) and Burns (2019), positions the process as a progressive climb toward your goal (Figure 4.1). Our model shows three cycles, because most action researchers engage in multiple iterations of planning, acting, observing, and reflecting. This is a symbolic representation, however, because you may have to do more cycles, or fewer. But nevertheless, while the process is iterative, it won't be endless. You will eventually progress to a point where you have gained new solutions or know-how that will improve the quality of your students' educational experiences.

One particular feature that we like about AR is its flexibility, in that it can accommodate quantitative, qualitative, or a combination of methods. Some research tools and procedures may be more appropriate than others, depending upon the situation, so your methodological decisions still need to be well-informed. Otherwise, getting answers to your questions might end up becoming a difficult uphill struggle.

A.2 Mixed Methods Research

To investigate the CT issues in your classes, you need procedures that are more nuanced than a simple qualitative or quantitative approach. Research methodologists (Creswell, 2015; Creswell & Plano Clark, 2018; Rose et al., 2019) explain that when you want to study complex concepts, it is better to use a combination of data collection methods. This is why we also want to introduce the use of mixed methods research (MMR) to help you investigate CT in your classes.

Tashakkori and Creswell (2007, p. 4) define MMR as an approach 'in which the investigator collects and analyses data, integrates the findings, and draws inferences using both qualitative and quantitative approaches or methods in a single study or a program of inquiry.' Many models for MMR abound, but Creswell and Plano Clark's (2018) three organizational models for carrying out an MMR project are clear, elegant, and accessible:

- Convergent design: Quantitative and qualitative data are collected and analyzed at the same time, then merged for a fuller comparative interpretation of the issue under study.
- Exploratory sequential design: This begins with qualitative research. The findings are used to develop a quantitative tool or some system of measurement. This quantitative research is then administered to informants in the field, and the findings are used to better understand the qualitative findings.
- Explanatory sequential design: Quantitative research is followed by qualitative research. The findings and new questions created by the quantitative research guide the qualitative investigation. The findings of both sequences are integrated at the end of the study.

We believe that Creswell and Plano Clark's (2018) exploratory and explanatory designs are most helpful for our purposes and interpret their overarching concerns as focusing on exploration, verification, and integration. Let us see how this works with AR in the next section.

A.3 Putting It Together

Combining the processes of exploration, verification, and integration with AR gives us an action framework for exploring issues, solving problems, and gaining insights. Figure 4.2 presents this framework to show how the conceptual undercurrents of MMR and AR enhance each other as they help classroom researchers focus their thoughts, make informed decisions, and engage in prudent actions.

We can see that at the beginning of the process, exploration consists of planning followed by action. While this seems obvious, it is common for teachers to jump into some research project or do something without really thinking things through. Research that produces good outcomes requires careful, thoughtful planning. This leads to actions that are both purposeful and meaningful.

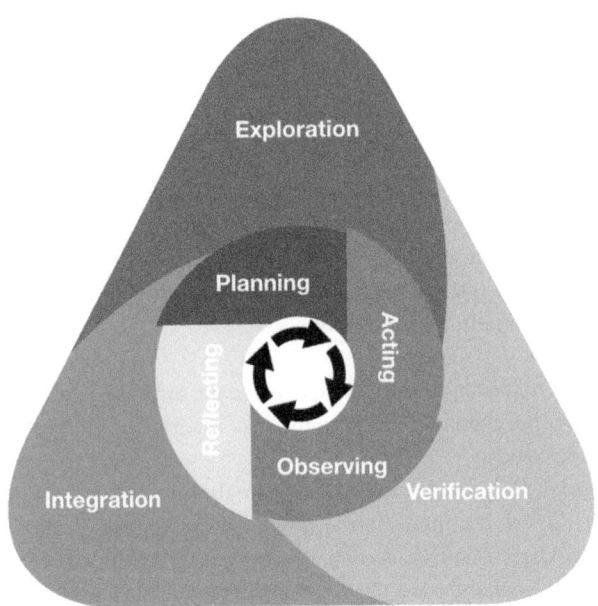

FIGURE 4.2 Synthesizing the Rationale of Mixed Methods with Action Research

Action eventually transitions toward the task of verification. It is not simply a case of doing what you have planned to do. You must monitor how your learners are responding to the action plan. Observing doesn't mean only watching, however. It also includes any other data collection methods you use for finding out either what is going on or what has taken place as a result of your CT lessons.

Observant verification then crosses over into integration, which is carried out in a reflective manner. Reflective integration of the data means first looking at the qualitative and quantitative data together in order to find out how they give you a fuller, richer story about what is happening with your learners. Creswell (2020) describes data integration using the metaphor of baking bread. Different ingredients go into the loaf, but the bread is much more than yeast, water, and flour. It has become something much more than the sum of its parts. Similarly, with integration it is not a case of just having qualitative and quantitative data sitting side-by-side. It is what you learn when you put them together. Look for how the qualitative data helps to explain the quantitative findings, and vice versa. Be open to any surprises or new questions that emerge.

The reflective part of integration requires you to take a hard look at how you interpret your findings. This begins with asking yourself some hard questions, such as, 'Is my interpretation of the integrated datasets a reflection of what is really happening in the data (as communicated by the students), or am I projecting my own issues on the data?' Standing behind questions like this is the concern of confirmation bias. Confirmation bias is in play when you decide beforehand that a certain issue exists among your learners and, regardless of what your data says, you interpret it as proving what you thought was the problem in the first place. Most of the time this is more nuanced. We can be influenced by earlier words, actions, or events that took place in class that, for one reason or another, we either didn't like or felt at the time as somehow problematic. These events then slip out of our conscious memory but lurk in the background of our minds, where they can shape the questions we ask and color our interpretations of the data. All we are suggesting is that you should not 'force' your data into something you want it to be. Let the data speak to you. Let it enhance, adjust, or transform any perspectives that you had at the beginning of the project.

Reflective integration of the data is not an entirely inward journey, though. Outwardly, it asks you to remember that even if you find an issue that is affecting your students' CT skills, the learners will likely not have seen this as problematic. Transitioning from reflection back to a new action plan means developing strategies for convincing your learners that a problem does in fact exist. It is only after enough of your learners become convinced of the problem that you can work together with a class to find better ways of learning. This results in an integration of your combined efforts as you all gain greater experience and deeper insight.

B. The 'PEAR' Approach

The MMR designs as described by Creswell and Plano Clark (2018) are consistent, well-thought-out, and easy to follow. The only problem we see is that the linear nature of these models does not easily complement the iterative processes of AR. What we have done, then, has been to modify the architecture of Creswell and Plano Clark's (2018) models in order to create what we playfully describe as the PEAR approach to classroom research. The PEAR approach consists of two designs: progressive exploratory action research and progressive explanatory action research. Let's study these in more detail.

B.1 Progressive Exploratory Action Research

We have seen that before you can do anything in AR, you must notice something of interest or concern taking place within your class. When it comes to CT, however, it can be difficult to notice such issues right away. Often you are faced with a sense that something is going on, but it is difficult to put your finger on what that 'something' is. In this situation, we suggest that you start out by using the progressive exploratory action research design (Figure 4.3).

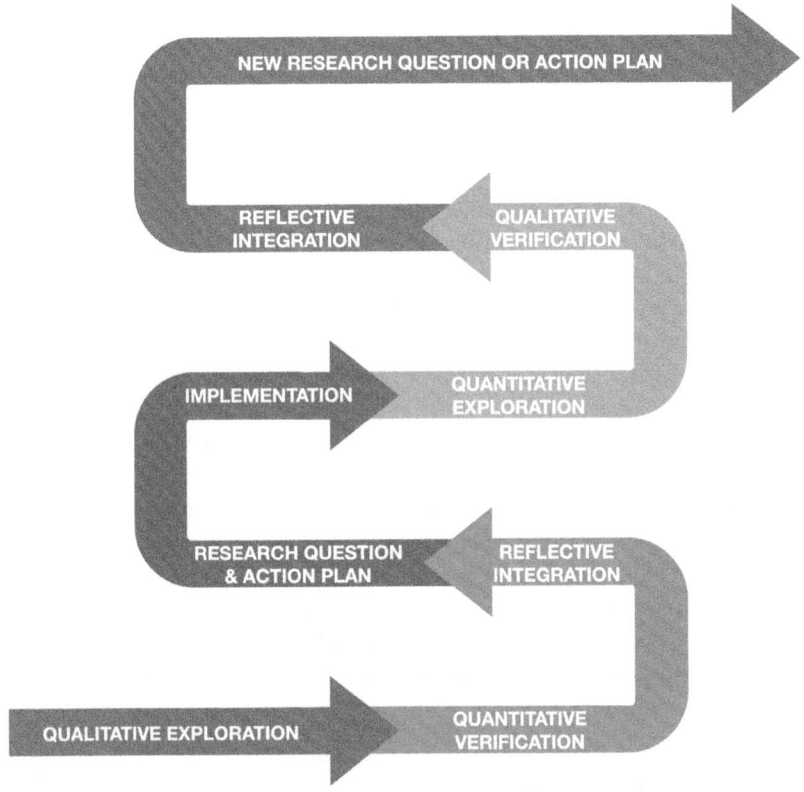

FIGURE 4.3 Progressive Exploratory Action Research Process

Progressive exploratory action research starts out in an open-ended qualitative manner. The goal is to keep your eyes open and ask yourself questions such as, 'What seems to be happening here?' Begin by keeping a regular journal for a few weeks about what you observe in class and what you find in any written assignments from your students. Or you could make audio recordings of your lessons and make notes about what you learn from listening to what took place in class. One helpful means for explanation that we like is called a diary study, because it often helps to focus your attention on avenues for research that you may not have noticed earlier.

There are many books and articles in ELT that explain how to conduct a diary study and most books on qualitative research methods have chapters that give more details on how to keep journals or diaries. A couple of good recent books on this subject are Rose et al. (2019) and Hyers (2018). But doing a diary study is straightforward, and you can certainly get started as you do some necessary background reading.

Bring a notebook with you to class while you assess student writing assignments. As you teach, pay attention to what is happening, for example, in the students' reactions or in your own teaching practices. In CT activities, what are you or they doing and saying? In student essays or other written work, do you see any issues related to critical thinking?

Your account of student words and actions at this stage should be as descriptive as possible. Avoid writing judgment statements. For example, if you observe a student who is listening while crossing his arms while another student is explaining their reasons for their argument, it would be inappropriate to write that the student was being closed-minded or uncritical. Rather, you would simply note what you saw. You should also have a section below every diary entry where you can write questions and express your interpretations and other ideas for future investigation. But keep these separate from the section that has your observations of what your students are doing, saying, and writing. After writing each entry, you should also take time to code this data. Charmaz (1983) describes coding as 'simply the process of *categorizing* and *sorting* data' in order to 'summarize, synthesize, and sort many observations made out of the data' (pp. 111–112). There is no one 'right way' to code qualitative data, and Saldaña (2016) has an excellent book that will show you many of the different ways of breaking your data into manageable bits. Probably the simplest way that we would suggest is for you to read what you or your students have written, and to underline what seem to be important observations or statements about CT. You would then give these underlined sections of data a name or label, and then write these labels in a right-hand margin column of your journal. An example of this from a hypothetical study can be found in Figure 4.4.

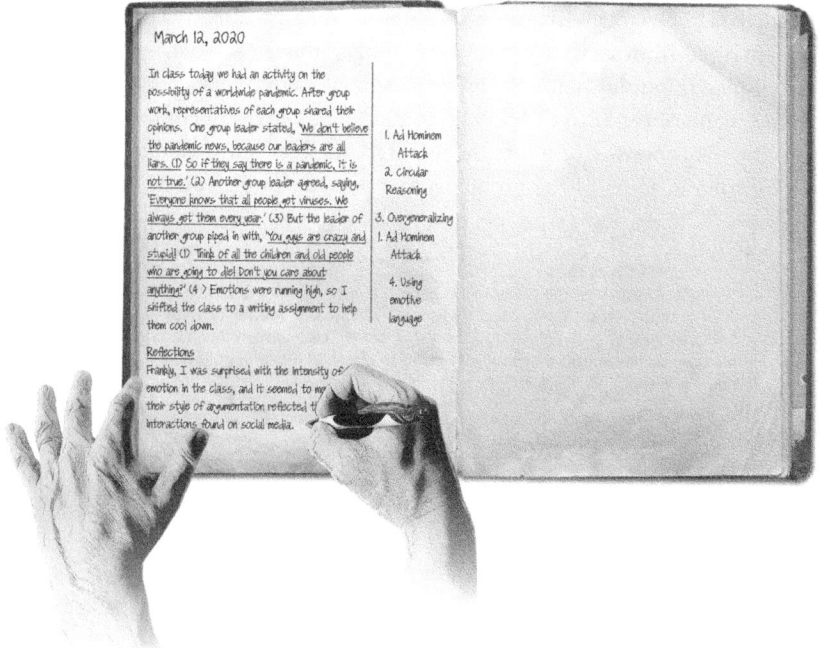

FIGURE 4.4 Example of a Coded Diary Study Entry

After a short period of writing and coding journal entries, you will notice patterns and problems starting to occur on a regular basis. At this point, you should stop collecting data, otherwise you might fall into the trap of constantly wanting to get more qualitative data. This will end badly, because you will risk either drowning in your own data or feeling overwhelmed. It is enough for the moment to have found some interesting patterns and themes. This is progress.

Study these and choose some that you think are most common or conceptually important. For example, in our imaginary study, a teacher decided that among their learners, overgeneralizing, using circular reasoning, engaging in ad hominem attacks, and using emotive language seemed to be common problems. With the discovery of some themes and factors, it is possible to shift toward quantitative verification. During this phase, turn the themes into an instrument that measures how many students in your class have these problems. You could create a short critical thinking test, one where the students would be presented with short paragraphs featuring examples of both fallacious and critically aware thinking. A five-point Likert scale would help you measure the degree to which your learners lean one way or the other on the problems you are investigating (Figure 4.5).

After collecting your quantitative data, you can then transition toward integration. Integration is where MMR really adds value to reflection, because it brings your research datasets together in a way that allows for the possibility of new insight emerging. Integrated data is presented as 'joint display' – that is, a table that juxtaposes the key themes with the findings of qualitative and quantitative data. The table will also contain a space for any reflective inferences that have emerged from studying your data comparatively. Table 4.1 shows what a joint display might look like from our imagined study.

Now you are ready to develop questions and an action plan to explore further. You may choose to explore the use of focused teaching methods and activities for solving some of the problems that you have uncovered. The question

> 4) "We should arrest all the people who enter our country without permission. A lot of these people are criminals who are hiding in our country anyway, and because they all entered our country illegally, they have broken the law, and they are now criminals. So that's why we need to arrest all those people who enter our country without permission."
>
> *In your opinion, how convincing is the statement above? (Circle One)*
>
> Very Unconvincing • Somewhat Unconvincing • Uncertain • Somewhat Convincing • Very Convincing
> 1 2 3 4 5

FIGURE 4.5 Sample Critical Thinking Test Question

TABLE 4.1 Example Joint Display after First Stage of Exploratory Cyclical AR Investigation

Themes and Issues	Qualitative Display	Quantitative Display	Reflective Inferences
Overgeneralizing	'We always get this sort of thing every year.'	12% Very Convincing 10% Slightly Convincing 5% Uncertain 51% Slightly Unconvincing 22% Very Unconvincing	Most students seem to be able to identify such generalizations, but enough learners are missing it to the point to justifying work on it in some activities.
Circular Reasoning	'Our leaders always lie to us, so what they are saying now is also a lie.'	39% Very Convincing 35% Slightly Convincing 10% Uncertain 21% Slightly Unconvincing 5% Very Unconvincing	Circular reasoning occurs in most often in written essays. This suggests that even with time to think about an argument, this fallacy is widespread in this class.
Emotive Language	'Think about all the children and old people that will die! Don't you care?'	12% Very Convincing 40% Slightly Convincing 24% Uncertain 16% Slightly Unconvincing 8% Very Unconvincing	Given the other issues, addressing emotive language warrants less attention for now. However, it seems that emotive language has a certain 'pull' among many of the learners.
Ad Hominem Attacks	'He is a liberal and socialist – so he is not only wrong but also an enemy of our country.'	41% Very Convincing 21% Slightly Convincing 12% Uncertain 18% Slightly Unconvincing 6% Very Unconvincing (87% of male students found Ad Hominem attacks as either slightly or very convincing.)	This needs to be addressed. Maybe male students view argumentation as a form of verbal battle, where some measure of 'trash talk' is acceptable?

for our sample study might be posed as: What teaching practices help to resolve the problem of circular reasoning and ad hominem attacks among my learners? Or, you may wish to gain deeper insight into the problem by asking: What factors (social, cultural, emotional, educational, religious, political, etc.) contribute to circular reasoning and ad hominem attacks among my learners?

If exploring the problem is the path you wish to take, from here your action plan would be to read books and research articles on the various cultural and other institutional factors that influence your learners. You would interview people who represent your students' cultures to get added insight and talk with some of your students or their peers to get a better understanding of their worldview and values. The factors that you uncover would then become the basis for another questionnaire to confirm the strength of student beliefs on these issues. The questionnaire would also need a space for students to qualitatively write their reasons for believing certain things or what they think about issues affecting their CT skills. The qualitative and quantitative data is integrated again into a joint display, and you would then develop a new action plan for how to teach in order to address the factors and concerns of students.

If, after this first cycle of exploration, verification, and integration, you wish to focus on addressing the problems, then your action plan would entail reading up on teaching techniques. For example, since, in our imaginary study, the students were engaging in circular reasoning most often during writing assignments, would a process writing approach help in encouraging students to challenge their assumptions and to see the illogicality of circular reasoning? What activities from this book could be used, modified, or expanded upon to solve the issue of ad hominem attacks? After some weeks of classes, you could then administer the same CT test that you created earlier, except now you would also provide a section for students to explain their reasons for why they found the different situations to be convincing or unconvincing (Figure 4.6).

4) "We should arrest all the people who enter our country without permission. A lot of these people are criminals who are hiding in our country anyway, and because they all entered our country illegally, they have broken the law, and they are now criminals. So that's why we need to arrest all those people who enter our country without permission."

In your opinion, how convincing is the statement above? (Circle One)

Very Unconvincing • Somewhat Unconvincing • Uncertain • Somewhat Convincing • Very Convincing
1　　　　　　　　2　　　　　　　3　　　　　　　4　　　　　　　5

In the space below, please explain why you were either convinced, unconvinced, or uncertain

FIGURE 4.6 Sample of Critical Thinking Test Question with Space for Qualitative Responses

The joint display would then set out the new data that has been collected. There is no predetermined format for joint displays, so this time in our simulated study, the teacher has placed the findings of the first quantitative study next to the second stage of findings in order to highlight any changes (see Table 4.2). Sample quotes from the second stage of qualitative data are included to further illustrate dynamics in the class. As before, a column for reflection and inferences about the data is included. In our imagined study, the teacher finds that the students have improved their CT skills in most of the factors addressed in class, but that the students still struggle emotionally, culturally, and sometimes religiously with the challenges posed from thinking critically. These discoveries will be of some encouragement to the teacher, in that the students did learn to recognize examples of fallacious thinking, but the teacher also wonders about the degree to which the students have really improved. Are they thinking more critically or are more of the students providing answers they have learned to be pleasing to the teacher? Pursuing this question and framing the procedures would put the teacher and learners into another cycle of AR, and closer to finding better ways of teaching CT to learners in this educational context.

B.2 Progressive Explanatory Action Research

In this approach, the process of the progressive exploratory AR design has been inverted. This design is useful for when you have a clearer idea about what aspect of CT you want to measure. For example, you may be interested in assessing whether your learners are able to identify the parts of an argument. Alternatively, you may want to explore their susceptibility to certain logical fallacies or identify the degree to which they exhibit CT dispositions, such as their level of awareness about their own biases and assumptions. Whatever you choose to investigate, you will want to know more about the reasons for the findings – especially for any that you find to be puzzling or particularly interesting.

As we can see in Figure 4.7, progressive exploratory action research starts quantitatively by assessing your students' proficiency in the preselected features of CT. This is followed by qualitative analysis, and then both datasets are integrated into a joint display. After reflecting on the findings and developing an action plan for addressing some of the problems you have uncovered, you conduct another qualitative study to explore whether your strategies have worked and verify your findings with quantitative assessment. With further integration and reflection, new surprises will serve as forward momentum for new ideas and teaching plans. After a few more iterations, we are confident that you will have gained deeper insight and experience about how to help your second-language learners become better critical thinkers.

Many of the procedures used in the progressive explanator AR design are like those we read about earlier for the exploratory version, so we will limit our

TABLE 4.2 Sample Joint Display from Second Cycle

Themes and Issues	Quantitative Display (First Cycle)	Quantitative Display (Second Cycle)	Qualitative Display (Second Cycle)	Reflective Inferences
Overgeneralizing	12% Very Convincing 10% Slightly Convincing 5% Uncertain 51% Slightly Unconvincing 22% Very Unconvincing	4% Very Convincing 5% Slightly Convincing 1% Uncertain 32% Slightly Unconvincing 59% Very Unconvincing	Convinced: 'There are general rules to life. Why can't we say them in class?' Unconvinced: 'When I think about a situation, I think there are many exceptions that are possible.'	It certainly seems that most students have moved even further along in seeing how an overgeneralized argument can be effectively inaccurate and faulty.
Circular Reasoning	39% Very Convincing 35% Slightly Convincing 10% Uncertain 21% Slightly Unconvincing 5% Very Unconvincing	7% Very Convincing 20% Slightly Convincing 7% Uncertain 31% Slightly Unconvincing 35% Very Unconvincing	Convinced: 'Sometimes a fact is true no matter how people say it.' Unconvinced: 'I learned we need to have reasons and evidence to help prove an argument.'	More of the students seem now to be able to recognize a circular argument when they see it, and they are using them less in writing, but I am wondering if some students are avoiding circular reasoning for me in this class? This is something that may warrant further investigation.

Themes and Issues	Quantitative Display (First Cycle)	Quantitative Display (Second Cycle)	Qualitative Display (Second Cycle)	Reflective Inferences
Emotive Language	12% Very Convincing 40% Slightly Convincing 24% Uncertain 16% Slightly Unconvincing 8% Very Unconvincing	8% Very Convincing 10% Slightly Convincing 34% Uncertain 39% Slightly Unconvincing 9% Very Unconvincing	Convinced: 'The way other people feel is important. I can't ignore it.' Unconvinced: 'The facts are more important, but I don't want to be cold to other people.'	Students have learned to focus more on facts that are presented in arguments, but both the qualitative and the quantitative data show that the pull of emotions is still causing them some feelings of dissonance.
Ad Hominem Attacks	41% Very Convincing 21% Slightly Convincing 12% Uncertain 18% Slightly Unconvincing 6% Very Unconvincing (87% of male students found ad hominem attacks as either slightly or very convincing.)	19% Very Convincing 31% Slightly Convincing 8% Uncertain 32% Slightly Unconvincing 10% Very Unconvincing (56% of male students found ad hominem attacks as either slightly or very convincing.)	Convinced: 'Bad people have bad ideas. I think it is good to be honest about their bad character.' Unconvinced: 'It feels strange to believe reasons and facts from people who are unbelievers. But the teacher said we must accept what is true, even from unpleasant people. I will try.'	Students have shown more tendency to notice and avoid ad hominem attacks, and it seems that the group activities in class have had a positive effect, but still over half of the learners find them to be moderately convincing, and several of those willing to reject such attacks are doing so with great struggle, with cultural and religious issues at play.

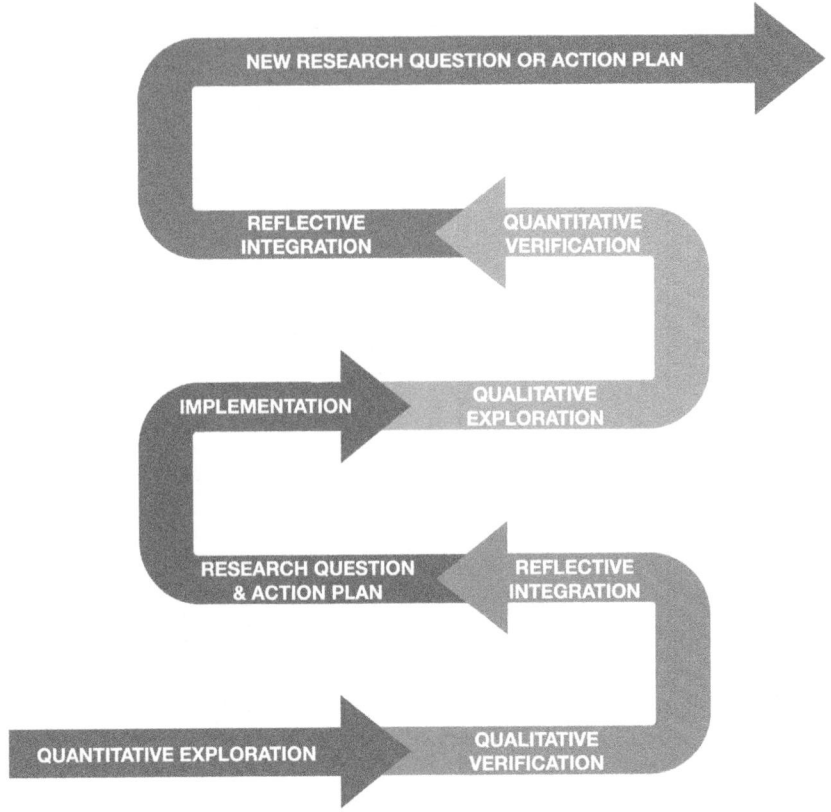

FIGURE 4.7 Progressive Explanatory Action Research Process

discussion to issues that pertain more specifically to this design. We will focus on quantitative and qualitative strategies we believe to be helpful in the quest for good data.

The first thing that you will need to decide before starting quantitative exploration is whether you will use a professionally designed CT assessment inventory, such as the Watson-Glaser Critical Thinking Appraisal (Watson & Glaser, 2002), the California Critical Thinking Dispositions Inventory (Facione, 1996), or the Ennis-Weir Critical Thinking Essay Test (Ennis & Weir, 1985). These and similar standardized tests have many appealing strengths. For example, they have been developed and refined by teams of brilliant researchers. They have been used for decades with hundreds of thousands of people from around the world. They are relatively well-known and prestigious tests, meaning that if you publish your research using these tests, some of that gravitas can rub off onto your work. Also, studies find that the work that has gone into making these tests has paid off, as many have been found to be valid and reliable measures of CT (e.g., Gadzella & Baloğlu, 2003; Sosu, 2013; Yeh, 2002).

However, it is not easy to use such tests in the ELT context. Professionally made tests must be purchased, and some might not be able to afford this expense. The English language level on these tests is intended for native English speakers, and many were trialed with a majority of middle and upper-class Caucasian university undergraduates in the United States. This will have linguistic and cultural implications for your learners. Numerous studies provide compelling evidence that such tests may pose linguistic challenges, which then result in artificially low scores (Floyd, 2011; Lun et al., 2010; Takano & Noda, 1993). Depending on the proficiency level of your learners, you will either need to investigate whether there are translations of your chosen test, to make your own translation, or to find someone who can translate the test for you. If you have a wide range of languages represented in your class, making translations for everyone may be neither practical nor possible. And even if you are working with learners with high levels of proficiency, research has also found that a lack of assumed background cultural knowledge can still result in lower CT scores, even among native English speakers from different ethnic and class groups (Ennis, 1993; Evans & Waites, 1981; Gunderson & Siegel, 2001; Hyytinen et al., 2015). Ku (2009) adds that because these tests focus on certain aspects of critical thinking to the exclusion of others, there is a further risk of their negatively assessing students coming from cultures that have emphasized other critical thinking skills that may not have been addressed by the chosen test.

It may be the case that none of these concerns affect you and your learners, and, if so, a professionally made test might be a quick and easy way to start your exploration. For most language teachers, however, we think that a better approach would be to create your own assessment tool based on some of the critical thinking skills, logical fallacies, and dispositions in the activities this book. The advantage would be in having a measurement tool written at a language level appropriate for your learners, and one that would complement your language course. It would serve as a diagnostic tool for discovering your learners' needs and it would prime your students for the type of problems and issues they will encounter later in the course. The disadvantages are that making this assessment tool will take a lot of work. You will need to decide the format for measurement, write clear questions, and check for reliability. One way to lighten the load is to conduct an Internet search for examples of practice tests found on the websites of the companies who sell standardized CT tests. You can then create your own questions that follow a similar format. Making your own test will still be challenging, but we think it is well worth the effort.

After deciding on the assessment tool, the next step of qualitative verification will depend partly on whether you have chosen a standardized assessment tool or something that you have created on your own. If using the standardized test, identify one of the several dispositions, logical fallacies, or other issues indicated, which seem to be prevalent among your learners. Then assign a writing assignment to your learners that asks them to explain some of the reasons for their opinions or thoughts on this issue of interest. If your students have problems with writing essays, then you should interview some of them in a nonthreatening manner. This might be a one-on-one interview for some, but for others it might be in the safety of a focus group. If you can get informed consent to record the interview, do it, and later transcribe it. Then code either your interviews (or essays) for any underlying themes, practices, or beliefs that emerge.

If you have used your own test or assessment tool, as in the example shown earlier in Figure 4.6, provide space for short answers so students can explain the reasoning behind their responses. This qualitative data can then be coded, depending on the length and quality of their answer. Based on the way in which you have set up a scale for numerically measuring the answers in your questionnaire or assessment tool, you may be able to link different themes to the groups of students representing different bands of responses. Even if this isn't possible, other surprises may occur.

Consider another hypothetical study, one in which an English teacher of German high school students (called a gymnasium in Germany) is curious to know more about the sorts of CT dispositions that resonate with her learners. One question (see Table 4.3) explores the degree to which her students are willing to maintain an open mind and to listen empathetically to different perspectives on an issue. She found that even among those who agreed with the statement, the qualitative reasons given by several seemed to express an idea of listening in order to change the other person's mind. This, of course, is sophistic use of CT skills of the type we discussed earlier in this book, and not being truly open-minded, thoughtful listeners. The teacher also finds that the class was nearly split down the middle on the question, with many who disagreed, bringing up extreme examples of certain people who did not represent their political, philosophical, or social worldview. The teacher then follows

TABLE 4.3 Sample First Stage of Data Display from Hypothetical Study

Question	Quantitative Response	Qualitative Samples
5. It is important to listen to people so that we can better understand their viewpoints, especially when we disagree strongly with them.	Agree: 56%	'It is important to understand why we disagree.' 'Maybe they know more than me.' 'If I understand them better, maybe later I can convince them.'
	Disagree: 44%	'It depends on the person. For example, if the person is religious, I won't waste my time listening.' 'Why should I listen to some crazy conspiracy theory? Some people are just stupid.'

up on this data with a few recorded focus group interviews, and codes the transcripts. This further verifies that the students were expressing attitudes that she coded as 'listening in order to win,' 'cancelling the thought criminals,' and 'not acknowledging one's own assumptions,' among others. She also identifies a smaller group of learners who did express attitudes representative of an empathetic openness to understanding another person's point of view.

The teacher reflects on the qualitative and quantitative data, and, in the integrated display, summarizes her students' barrier to better critical thinking as 'tribalism.' At this stage, she begins to think of ways to encourage her learners out of their echo chamber, and to express this in the form of an action research question.

Formulating a specific research question that includes aspects of the action plan and problem can be challenging. In Figure 4.8, we have provided you with a template that can help to focus your thoughts and to create a doable research question. This template can be used with either the exploratory or explanatory cyclical AR designs, though for the exploratory version, the main question in the beginning would start only with 'What' or 'Does.' Here, our goal is explanation, which is why one would start with 'How do/does' or 'What are the ways in which' a particular teaching approach, strategy, or set of activities either affect or solve the issue that you have identified as a potential barrier to critical thinking among your learners, who are situated within a specific educational context.

Turning again to our English teacher in the hypothetical study, she recognizes that several German students demonstrate a willingness and capacity for listen empathetically. She devises a set of activities that allows these students to serve as peer guides. During the activities, these students lead the group by sharing their ideas, reasons, and strategies for empathetic listening with other students. Based on the template in Figure 4.8, the teacher embeds the action plan within the research question, which she expresses as 'How does the sharing of student strategies for empathetic listening impact the problem of tribalism among students of English in a rural German gymnasium?' After a period of plan implementation, the teacher conducts another qualitative study to ask the students how these activities have affected their attitudes. This would be most easily carried out, in our opinion, as an essay assignment. Then, for

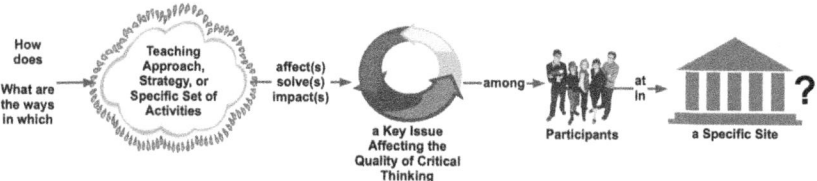

FIGURE 4.8 Template for Creating Research Questions

verification, another assessment tool, one that investigates the same concerns as before but expressed as different questions and situations, would be given to the learners to see if the quantitative measure either corroborates or conflicts with what is expressed in the qualitative data.

If you were conducting this study and found further discrepancies, this would lead to a round of AR to search for solutions with your learners. But if the qualitative and quantitative data complement each other, your students may have progressed in their critical thinking. You could then go back to data from your first quantitative exploration to see if there were any other potential issues with your learners' critical thinking skills. You could then choose another, and repeat the progressive explanatory AR procedures. This is what we meant earlier about how such an assessment tool could act as a needs analysis for informing you as to which CT skills you should emphasize in your classes.

C. Final Caveats and Suggestions

The critical theorist Max Horkheimer (1947/2003, p. 15) once wrote about the tendency in modern industrial societies to reduce the search for knowledge to mechanistic processes. Process thinking, as we call it, happens when someone believes that 'the assiduous application of rigorous method will yield sound fact – as if empirical methodology were some form of meat grinder from which truth could be turned out like so many sausages' (Gergen, 1985, p. 273). We would urge you not to approach the research of CT with the attitude of a methodological sausage-maker. Not only would that be the *wurst* of strategies, it is fundamentally uncritical in its approach.[1] While we are confident that the steps we have described in our PEAR approach can help you to find your focus and structure your search, following the procedures of these research designs alone cannot provide you with the answers that you are looking for. You will still have to think critically about what you are doing and what you are learning during your investigation. In addition, once you are in the middle of an investigation, it is important for you to expect the unexpected. Be prepared for the possibility of going through all the procedures and not finding problems or solutions right away. Discovering what is happening with your students' CT skills often takes time and extra effort, but if you maintain your sense of critical awareness, plan carefully, and flexibly apply the ideas that we have suggested in this section, we believe eventually you will succeed either in gaining new teaching insights, helping your students become better critical thinkers, or a combination of both.

---

1 *Wurst* is a German word for sausage, and it is a play on the English word 'worst,' which sounds similar to *wurst*.

D. Making a Contribution

The late Robert Burden, an educational psychologist who started a movement of 'Thinking Schools' throughout the UK, observed that the difficulties we often face when investigating CT skills has meant that 'our overall understanding of the experience of thinking in situ is under-researched and poorly understood' (Burden, 2015, p. 302). While true, we would also add that difficult does not mean impossible. We sense an opportunity here – to explore areas of critical thinking that others may have overlooked. While we have seen in this section how simply giving students a questionnaire asking how they feel about their critical thinking is not enough, carefully crafted critical thinking research is doable. If we devote ourselves to approaching our investigations in a thoughtful, methodical, and informed manner, we will be able make helpful contributions not only to second-language education but also to the work of educators in other fields.

By 'making helpful contributions' we mean that you should share your findings with others through presentations at teaching conferences and by publishing in educational journals. After successfully completing a few cycles of AR as we have described in this section, you will have plenty of data to explain, insights to share, and stories to tell. All of this will be of great interest to us, your colleagues. We believe that no research is really finished until it is shared, so we encourage you to take this important step and contribute what you have learned to improve CT education in the ELT community.

E. Concluding Thoughts

As we come to the end, it is a good place to think about all the ground that we have covered together. We started with a rationale for the teaching of critical thinking and considered some of the debate that surrounds whether critical thinking skills can be taught to second-language learners. We learned about the basics of informal logic and were introduced to a cycle for teaching CT. We studied some of the common logical fallacies that are often encountered in daily life. This was punctuated by our use of a logical fallacy at the end of our argument, which, you learned later, in the second part of this book, to be the Sunk Cost Fallacy.

In the second part, we put meat on the bones of our theoretical discussion to provide you with practical and engaging activities for improving your students' CT skills within the context of second-language learning. The third section offered ideas on how to implement these activities in your teaching environment, as well as suggestions for using them as part of a broader curriculum or language course.

And so, here we are at the end of our journey. Or is it the beginning? We wish you well as you strive to foster better critical thinking among your students. In doing so, know that you are helping your learners to develop skills that will improve their lives, even as they use those skills to help improve their communities. By working together on the task of teaching critical thinking, we are not only making a lasting contribution to ELT, but we are also working together to make the world a better place.

REFERENCES

Allman, P. (2001). *Revolutionary Social Transformation: Democratic Hopes, Political Possibilities and Critical Education.* Bergin & Garvey.
Almossawi, A. (2013). *An Illustrated Book of Bad Arguments.* JasperCollins Publishers.
Arkes, H., & Blumer, C. (1985). The psychology of sunk cost. *Organizational Behavior and Human Decision Processes, 35,* 124–140.
Arum, R., & Roksa, J. (2011). *Academically Adrift: Limited Learning on College Campuses.* University of Chicago Press.
Asimov, I. (1988). *The Relativity of Wrong.* Windsor Publishing Corp.
Atkinson, D. (1997). A critical approach to critical thinking in TESOL. *TESOL Quarterly, 31*(1), 71–94. https://doi.org/10.2307/3587975
Bacon, F. (1868/2011). Progress of philosophical speculations (preface to indended treatise de interpretatione naturae). In J. Spedding, R. Ellis, & D. Heath (Eds.), *The Works of Francis Bacon (The Cambridge Library Collection) (Vol. Volume 10: The Letters and the Life 3).* Cambridge University Press/Longmans, Green, Reader and Dyer.
Bailin, S., Case, R., Coombs, J., & Daniels, L. (1999). Common misconceptions of critical thinking. *Journal of Curriculum Studies, 31*(3), 269–283. https://doi.org/10.1080/002202799183124
Barkun, M. (2003). *A Culture of Conspiracy: Apocalyptic Visions in Contemporary America.* University of California Press.
Bergdahl, L., & Langmann, E. (2018). Time for values: Responding educationally to the call from the past. *Studies in Philosophy and Education, 37*(4), 367–382. https://doi.org/10.1007/s11217-017-9591-2
Bluedorn, N., & Bluedorn, H. (2015). *The Fallacy Detective: Thirty-Eight Lessons on How to Recognize Bad Reasoning (Workbook Print Edition)* (4th ed.). Christian Logic.
Blunt, S. (2016). Critical realism and grounded theory: Analysing the adoption of outcomes for disabled children using the retroduction framework. *Qualitative Social Work, 17*(2), 176–194.
Boon, A. (2011). Negotiated syllabuses: Do you want to? In I.S.P. Nation & J. Macalister (Eds.), *Case Studies in Language Curriculum Design* (pp. 166–177). Routledge.

Boon, A. (2012). Here we are, now motivate us. *Modern English Teacher, 21*(1), 56–61.
Boon, A. (2020). *Research & Write*. Halico.
Bowell, T., & Kemp, G. (2015). *Critical Thinking: A Concise Guide* (4th ed.). Routledge.
Browne, M.N., & Keeley, S. (2007). *Asking the Right Questions: A Guide to Critical Thinking* (8th ed.). Pearson Prentice Hall.
Burden, R. (2015). Do they really work? Evidence for the efficacy of thinking skills approaches in affecting learning outcomes: The need for a broader perspective. In R. Wegerif, L. Li, & J. Kaufman (Eds.), *The Routledge International Handbook of Research on Teaching Thinking* (pp. 291–304). Routledge.
Burns, A. (2010). *Doing Action Research in English Language Teaching: A Guide for Practitioners*. Routledge.
Burns, A. (2019). Generating action research topics. In G. Barkhuizen (Ed.), *Qualitative Research Topics in Language Teacher Education* (pp. 167–173). Routledge.
Butler, H. (2012). Halpern critical thinking assessment predicts real-world outcomes of critical thinking. *Applied Cognitive Psychology, 26*(5), 721–729.
Cavender, N., & Kahane, H. (2010). *Logic and Contemporary Rhetoric: The Use of Reason in Everyday Life* (11th ed.). Wadsworth Cengage Learning.
Charmaz, K. (1983). The grounded theory method: An explication and interpretation. In R. Emerson (Ed.), *Contemporary Field Research* (pp. 109–126). Little, Brown, and Company.
Chase, B. (2013). *Pathways: Listening, Speaking & Critical Thinking*. National Geographic Learning and Cengage Learning.
Chase, R., & Johanssen, K. (2012). *Pathways 1: Listening, Speaking, and Critical Thinking*. Cengage Learning. https://books.google.co.jp/books?id=3C3_XwAACAAJ
Cottrell, S. (2005). *Critical Thinking Skills: Developing Effective Analysis and Argument*. Palgrave Macmillan.
Cowie, N. (2011). Emotions that experienced English as a Foreign Language (EFL) teachers feel about their students, their colleagues and their work. *Teaching and Teacher Education, 27*(1), 235–242. https://doi.org/10.1016/j.tate.2010.08.006
Creswell, J. (2015). *A Concise Introduction for Mixed Methods Research*. Sage Publications, Inc.
Creswell, J. (2020). *New Directions in Advancing the Methodology of Mixed Methods Research*. In MAXQDA International Conference 2020, Berlin, Germany. https://conference.maxqda.com/wp/wp-content/uploads/sites/2/2020/03/MQIC-2020-Method-Keynote-Creswell-200224.pdf
Creswell, J., & Plano Clark, V. (2018). *Designing and Conducting Mixed Methods Research* (3rd ed.). Sage Publications, Inc.
Damasio, A. (1994). *Descartes' Error: Emotion, Reason, and the Human Brain*. Avon Books.
Davidson, B., & Dunham, R. (1997). Assessing EFL student progress in critical thinking with the Ennis-Weir critical thinking essay tes. *JALT Journal, 19*(1), 43–57.
Davies, M., & Barnett, R. (Eds.). (2015). *The Palgrave Handbook of Critical Thinking in Higher Education*. Palgrave Macmillan.
Davies, W. (2019). *Nervous States: Democracy and the Decline of Reason*. W.W. Norton & Company.
Denzin, N. (1991). *Images of Postmodern Society: Social Theory and Contemporary Cinema*. Newbury Park.
Dewey, J. (1910). *How We Think*. D.C. Heath & Co., Publishers.
Ding, A., & Bruce, I. (2017). *The English for Academic Purposes Practitioner: Operating on the Edge of Academia*. Palgrave Machmillan.
Dummett, P., & Hughes, J. (2019). *Critical Thinking in ELT: A Working Model for the Classroom*. National Geographic Learning.

Duron, R., Limbach, B., & Waugh, W. (2006). Critical thinking framework for any discipline. *International Journal of Teaching and Learning in Higher Education, 17*(2), 160–166.

Edge, J. (Ed.) (2001). *Action Research*. TESOL.

Elder, L., & Paul, R. (2013). *30 Days to Better Thinking and Better Living Through Critical Thinking: A Guide for Improving Every Aspect of Your Life, Revised and Expanded*. Pearson Education, Inc.

Elfatihi, M. (2017). A rationale for the integration of critical thinking skills in EFL/ESL instruction. *Higher Education of Social Science, 12*(2), 26–31.

Enfield, N. (2017). Junk cognition: A science-based guide offers tips for exploiting and overcoming faulty decision-making. *Science, 357*(6358), 1361.

Ennis, R. (1985). A logical basis for measuring critical thinking skills. *Educational Leadership, 43*(2), 44–48.

Ennis, R. (1991). Critical thinking: A streamlined conception. *Teaching Philosophy, 21*(1), 15–33.

Ennis, R. (1993). Critical thinking assessment. *Theory into Practice, 32*(3), 179–186. https://doi.org/10.1080/00405849309543594

Ennis, R. (1996). Critical thinking dispositions: Their nature and assessability. *Informal Logic, 18*(2 & 3), 165–182.

Ennis, R., & Weir, E. (1985). *The Ennis-Weir Critical Thinking Essay Test*. Critical Thinking Press and Software.

Evans, B., & Waites, B. (1981). *IQ and Mental Testing: An Unnatural Science and its Social History*. The Macmillian Press, LTD.

Facione, P. (1996). *The California Critical Thinking Disposition Inventory*. California Academic Press.

Facione, P. (2000). The disposition toward critical thinking: Its character, measurement, and relationship to critical thinking skill. *Informal Logic, 21*(1), 61–84.

Facione, P., Sanchez, C., Facione, N., & Gainen, J. (1995). The disposition towards critical thinking. *The Journal of General Education, 44*(1), 1–25. http://www.jstor.org/stable/27797240

Fisher, A. (2005). *Critical Thinking: An Introduction*. Cambridge University Press.

Floyd, C. (2011). Critical thinking in a second language. *Higher Education Research & Development, 30*(3), 289–302.

Fong, G., Krantz, D., & Nisbett, R. (1986). The effects of statistical training on thinking about everyday problems. *Cognitive Psychology, 18*(3), 253–292. https://doi.org/10.1016/0010-0285(86)90001-0

Fox, H. (1994). *Listening to the World: Cultural Issues in Academic Writing*. National Council of Teachers of English.

Gadzella, B., & Baloğlu, M. (2003). Psychometric properties of Watson-Glaser critical thinking appraisal for a sample of education majors. *Psychological Reports, 92*(3_suppl), 1249–1254. https://doi.org/10.2466/pr0.2003.92.3c.1249

Gann, D. (2016). Multi-step process for critical thinking instruction step one: Explicit instruction through product delivered content. *Tokyo University of Science Research Journal, 48*, 157–171.

Gergen, K. (1985). The social constructionist movement in modern psychology. *American Psychologist, 40*(3), 266–275.

Glaser, E. (1941). *An Experiment in the Development of Critical Thinking*. B. o. Publications.

Goodwin, M., & Sommervold, C. (2012). *Creativity, Critical Thinking, and Communication: Strategies to Increase Students' Skills*. Rowman & Littlefield.

Grim, P. (2013). *The Philosopher's Toolkit: How to be the Most Rational Person in Any Room*. The Great Courses.

Gunderson, L., & Siegel, L. (2001). The Evils of the use of IQ tests to define learning disabilities in first- and second-language learners. *The Reading Teacher, 55*(1), 48–55. www.jstor.org/stable/20205010

Hadley, G. (2015). *English for Academic Purposes in Neoliberal Universities: A Critical Grounded Theory*. Springer. http://link.springer.com/book/10.1007%2F978-3-319-10449-2

Hadley, G. (Ed.) (2003). *Action Research in Action*. RELC.

Halpern, D. (2014). *Thought and Knowledge: An Introduction to Critical Thinking* (5th ed.). Psychology Press.

Harvey, D. (1990). *The Condition of Postmodernity: An Enquiry into the Origins of Cultural Change*. Blackwell Publishers.

Holmes, N., Wieman, C., & Bonn, D. (2015). Teaching critical thinking. *Proceedings of the National Academy of Sciences, 112*(36), 11199–11204. https://doi.org/10.1073/pnas.1505329112

Horkheimer, M. (1947/2003). *Eclipse of Reason*. Continuum.

Houston, H. (2009). *Provoking Thought: Memory and Thinking in ELT*. Anthemeria Press.

Howe, E. (2007). Canadian and Japanese teachers' conceptions of critical thinking: A comparative study. *Teachers and Teaching: Theory and Practice, 10*(5), 505–525.

Hunter, D. (2009). *A Practical Guide to Critical Thinking: Deciding What to Do and Believe*. Wiley.

Hyers, L. (2018). *Diary Methods*. Oxford University Press.

Hyytinen, H., Nissinen, K., Ursin, J., Toom, A., & Lindblom-Ylänne, S. (2015). Problematising the equivalence of the test results of performance-based critical thinking tests for undergraduate students. *Studies in Educational Evaluation, 44*, 1–8. https://doi.org/10.1016/j.stueduc.2014.11.001

Ivie, S. (1989). Idols of the mind. *The Educational Forum, 53*(3), 281–289. https://doi.org/10.1080/00131728909335610

Johnston, B. (1997). Do EFL teachers have careers? *TESOL Quarterly, 31*(4), 681–712. http://links.jstor.org/sici?sici=0039-8322%28199724%2931%3A4%3C681%3ADETHC%3E2.0.CO%3B2-J

Jones, T., Chapman, G., Cleese, J., Gilliam, T., Idle, E., & Palin, M. (1979). *Monty Python's The Life of Brian (of Nazareth)*. Monty Python (Comedy troupe), Anchor Bay Entertainment, Inc.

Judge, B., Jones, P., & McCreery, E. (2009). *Critical Thinking Skills for Education Students*. Learning Matters.

Keeley, S., Shemberg, K., Cowell, B., & Zinnbauer, B. (1995). Coping with student resistance to critical thinking. *College Teaching, 43*(4), 140–145. https://doi.org/10.1080/87567555.1995.9925537

Kemmis, S., & McTaggart, R. (1988). *The Action Research Planner*. Deakin University Press.

Ketabi, S., Zabihi, R., & Ghadiri, M. (2013). Critical thinking across the ELT curriculum: A mixed-methods approach to analyzing L2 teachers' attitudes towards critical thinking instruction. *International Journal of Research Studies in Education, 2*(3), 15–24.

Kosonen, P., & Winne, P. (1995). Effects of teaching statistical laws on reasoning about everyday problems. *Journal of Educational Psychology, 87*(1), 33–46.

Kramsch, C. (2006). From communicative competence to symbolic competence. *The Modern Language Journal, 90*(2), 249–252.

Ku, K.Y.-L. (2009). Assessing students' critical thinking performance: Urging for measurements using multi-response format. *Thinking Skills and Creativity, 4*(1), 70–76. https://doi.org/10.1016/j.tsc.2009.02.001

Kurfiss, J. (1988). *Critical Thinking: Theory, Research, Practice, and Possibilities* (Vol. 2). ASHE-ERIC Clearing House on HIgher Education Report, The George Washington University.

Lau, J. (2011). *An Introduction to Critical Thinking and Creativity: Think More, Think Better.* Wiley.

Lewin, K. (1946). Action research and minority problems. *Journal of Social Issues, 2*, 34–46.

Lin, Y. (2018). *Developing Critical Thinking in EFL Classes: An Infusion Approach.* Springer Nature.

Lipman, M. (2003). *Thinking in Education.* Cambridge University Press.

Lun, M.-C., Fischer, R., & Ward, C. (2010). Exploring cultural differences in critical thinking: Is it about my thinking style or the language I speak? *Learning and Individual Differences, 20*(6), 604–616. https://doi.org/10.1016/j.lindif.2010.07.001

Maher, B., & Haugnes, N. (1998). *NorthStar: Focus on Reading and Writing, Basic.* Longman.

Marin, L., & Halpern, D. (2011). Pedagogy for developing critical thinking in adolescents: Explicit instruction produces greatest gains. *Thinking Skills and Creativity, 6*(1), 1–13. https://doi.org/10.1016/j.tsc.2010.08.002

Marin, M., & de la Pava, L. (2017). Conceptions of critical thinking from university EFL teachers. *English Language Teaching, 10*(7), 78–88.

Martin, M., Wilkinson, J., McPhee, A., McQueen, I., McConnell, F., & Baron, S. (2006). Implementing critical skills in UK schools. *Journal of Education for Teaching, 32*(4), 423–434. https://doi.org/10.1080/02607470600982076

McPeck, J. (1981). *Critical Thinking and Eduation.* St. Martin's Press.

McPeck, J. (1990). Critical thinking and subject specificity: A reply to Ennis. *Educational Researcher, 19*(4), 10–12. https://doi.org/10.3102/0013189x019004010

Melles, G. (2009). Teaching and evaluation of critical appraisal skills to postgraduate ESL engineering students. *Innovations in Education and Teaching International, 46*(2), 161–170. https://doi.org/10.1080/14703290902843810

Mok, J. (2010). The new role of English language teachers: Developing students' critical thinking in Hong Kong secondary school classrooms. *The Asian EFL Journal Quarterly, 12*(2), 262–287.

Moore, T. (2011). *Critical Thinking and Language: The Challenge of Generic Skills and Disciplinary Discourses.* Continuum.

Moore, T. (2013). Critical thinking: Seven definitions in search of a concept. *Studies in Higher Education, 38*(4), 506–522. https://doi.org/10.1080/03075079.2011.586995

Naiditch, F. (Ed.) (2016). *Developing Critical Thinking: From Theory to Classroom Practice.* Rowman & Littlefield.

Najafi, K., & Fettig, C. (2014). *Pathways Foundations: Listening, Speaking, & Critical Thinking* (2nd ed.). National Geographic Learning.

Norris, S., & Ennis, R. (1989). *Evaluating Critical Thinking.* Thinking Press & Software.

Norton, B. (1997). Language, identity, and the ownership of English. *TESOL Quarterly, 31*(3), 409–429. https://doi.org/10.2307/3587831

Norton, B. (2001). Non-participation, imagined communities and the language classroom. In M. Breen (Ed.), *Learner Contributions to Language Learning: New Directions in Research* (pp. 159–171). Pearson Education.

Norton-Peirce, B. (1995). Social identity, investment, and language learning*. *TESOL Quarterly, 29*(1), 9–31. https://doi.org/10.2307/3587803

Numrich, C. (2010). *Raise the Issues: An Integrated Approach to Critical Thinking* (3rd ed.). Pearson Longman.

O'Hare, L., & McGuinness, C. (2009). Measuring critical thinking, intelligence, and academic performance in psychology undergraduates. *The Irish Journal of Psychology, 30*(3–4), 123–131. https://doi.org/10.1080/03033910.2009.10446304

Paul, R. (1981). Teaching critical thinking in the 'strong' sense: A focus on self-deception, world views, and a dialectical mode of analysis. *Informal Logic*, 4(2), 2–7.

Paul, R., & Elder, L. (2002). *Critical Thinking: Tools for Taking Charge of Your Professional and Personal Life*. Financial Times Prentice Hall.

Paul, R., & Elder, L. (2006). *The Miniature Guide to Critical Thinking: Concepts and Tools* (4th ed.). Foundation for Critical Thinking.

Peters, M. (2018). Education in a post-truth world. In M. Peters, S. Rider, M. Hyvönen, & T. Besley (Eds.), *Post-Truth, Fake News: Viral Modernity & Higher Education* (pp. 145–150). Springer Nature.

Powers, D., & Enright, M. (1987). Analytical reasoning skills in graduate study: Perceptions of faculty in six fields. *The Journal of Higher Education*, 58(6), 658–682. https://doi.org/10.1080/00221546.1987.11778292

Quantz, R. (2016). *Sociocultural Studies in Education: Critical Thinking for Democracy*. Routledge.

Ramanathan, V., & Atkinson, D. (1999). Individualism, academic writing, and ELS writers. *Journal of Second Language Writing*, 8(1), 45–75.

Ramanathan, V., & Kaplan, R. (1996). Audience and voice in current L1 composition texts: Some implications for ESL student writers. *Journal of Second Language Writing*, 5(1), 21–34. https://doi.org/10.1016/S1060-3743(96)90013-2

Rear, D. (2017). Reframing the debate on Asian students and critical thinking: Implications for Western universities. *Journal of Contemporary Issues in Education*, 12(2), 18–33.

Rider, S. (2018). On knowing how to tell the truth. In M. Peters, S. Rider, M. Hyvönen, & T. Besley (Eds.), *Post-Truth, Fake News: Viral Modernity & Higher Education* (pp. 27–42). Springer Nature.

Rose, H., McKinley, J., & Briggs Baffoe-Djan, J. (2019). *Data Collection Research Methods in Applied Linguistics*. Bloombury.

Sagan, C. (1996). *The Demon-Haunted World*. Random House Publishing Company.

Said, E. (1978/2003). *Orientalism*. Penguin Books.

Saldaña, J. (2016). *The Coding Manual for Qualitative Researchers* (3rd ed.). Sage Publications, Ltd.

Schmidt, M. (1987). On classifications of fallacies. *Informal Logic*, 8(2), 57–66.

Schuster, E. (2014). *Critical Thinking in Language Learning*. CreateSpace.

Scull, S. (1987). *Critical Reading & Writing for Advanced Students*. Prentice Hall.

Shermer, M. (2011). *The Believing Brain: From Ghosts and Gods to Politics and Conspiracies: How We Construct Beliefs and Reinforce Them as Truths*. Times Books.

Shirkhani, S., & Fahim, M. (2011). Enhancing critical thinking In foreign language learners. *Procedia: Social and Behavioral Sciences*, 29, 111–115. https://doi.org/10.1016/j.sbspro.2011.11.214

Sosu, E. (2013). The development and psychometric validation of a Critical Thinking Disposition Scale. *Thinking Skills and Creativity*, 9, 107–119. https://doi.org/10.1016/j.tsc.2012.09.002

Specter, M. (2009). *Denialism: How Irrational Thinking Hinders Scientific Progress, Harms the Planet, and Threatens Our Lives*. Penguin Press.

Stanovich, K., & West, R. (2008). On the relative independence of thinking biases and cognitive ability. *Journal of Personality and Social Psychology*, 94(4), 672–695. https://doi.org/10.1037/0022-3514.94.4.672

Takano, Y., & Noda, A. (1993). A temporary decline of thinking ability during foreign language processing. *Journal of Cross-Cultural Psychology*, 24(4), 445–462.

Tashakkori, A., & Creswell, J. (2007). Editorial: The new era of mixed methods. *Journal of Mixed Methods Research*, 1(1), 3–7. https://doi.org/10.1177/2345678906293042

Thompson, G. (2019). Is critical thinking a part of liberal education. In K. Dharamsi & J. Zimmer (Eds.), *Liberal Education and the Idea of the University: Arguments and Reflections* (pp. 121–134).Vernon Press.

Topping, K., & Trickey, S. (2015). Philosophy for children: Short and long term effects. In R. Wegerif, L. Li, & J. Kaufman (Eds.), *The Routledge International Handbook of Research on Teaching Thinking* (pp. 103–112). Routledge.

Tsui, L. (2002). Fostering critical thinking through effective pedagogy. *The Journal of Higher Education, 73*(6), 740–763. https://doi.org/10.1080/00221546.2002.11777179

Varghese, M., Morgan, B., Johnston, B., & Johnson, K. (2005). Theorizing language teacher identity: Three perspectives and beyond. *Journal of Language, Identity & Education, 4*(1), 21–44. http://www.informaworld.com/10.1207/s15327701jlie0401_2

Viner, K. (2016, 12 July). How technology disrupted the truth. *The Guardian*, https://www.theguardian.com/media/2016/jul/2012/how-technology-disrupted-the-truth. Accessed 2024 February 2019.

Walters, K. (1994). Critical thinking, rationality, and the Vulcanization of students. In K. Walters (Ed.), *Re-Thinking Reason: New Perspectives in Critical Thinking* (pp. 61–80). SUNY Press.

Watson, G., & Glaser, E. (2002). *Watson-Glaser Critical Thinking Appraisal: UK Edition*. Pearson Assessment.

White, N., Peterson, S., Jordan, N., & Sowton, C. (2019). *Unlock Level 1 Listening, Speaking & Critical Thinking Student's Book, Mob App and Online Workbook w/ Downloadable Audio and Video* (2nd ed.). Cambridge University Press.

Yeh, M.-L. (2002). Assessing the reliability and validity of the Chinese version of the California critical thinking disposition inventory. *International Journal of Nursing Studies, 39*(2), 123–132. https://doi.org/https://doi.org/10.1016/S0020-7489(01)00019-0

Zollo, F., & Quattrochiochi, W. (2018). Misinformation spreading on facebook. In S. Lehmann & Y.Y. Ahn (Eds.), *Complex Spreading Phenomena in Social Systems* (pp. 177–196). Springer.

INDEX

ability 4, 10–12, 60, 125, 259, 284
achievement 44, 102, 296
action research (AR) 327–328;
    progressive explanatory action
    research 331–337, 337–344
actualization 9, 16–17, 26
Ad Hominem 24, 92, 171–179
Allman, P. 6
Almossawi, A. 22
ambiguity 20, 22–23, 25, 27, 229
analysis 7, 10, 14, 33, 88, 322, 337, 344
Appeal to Emotion 25, 92, 236–245
Appealing to Improper Authority 23
argumentation 17–18, 21, 26, 29, 71, 320,
    335; *see also* counterargumentation
Aristotle 22
Arkes, H. 165
Arum, R. 6
Asimov, I. 95, 155–157
assessment inventories 6, 26, 340–341
assumptions 1–2, 8, 11, 16, 18–27, 29,
    32–34, 41–42, 88–89, 91, 93, 197–198,
    246–250, 253–256, 263, 265–274,
    280, 290, 292, 294–295, 307, 309,
    315–316, 319, 321–322, 336–337, 343
attitudes 12–13, 343–344

backchanneling 46, 52–53
Bailin, S. 26
Baloğlu, M. 340
Bandwagon Fallacy 23
Barkun, M. 3

Barnett, R. 4, 15, 22
Begging the Question 24, 96, 111–120
believability 28, 277
Bergdahl, L. 6
Bluedorn, N. 7, 26
Blumer, C. 165
Boon, A. 33, 78, 317, 324
Bowell, T. 4, 10, 15, 21–22, 26
Browne, M.N. 12, 22, 26–27
Bruce, I. 6, 315–316

causation 94, 128–132
Cavender, N. 18, 22, 27
Charmaz, K. 333
Circular Reasoning 24, 92, 189–198
clarification 38–39, 67, 71
Classifications 22–25
cognition 12, 15, 20–21, 26
collaboration 6, 16–17, 26
Common Belief Fallacy 25, 93, 283–289
communication 5, 7, 11, 14, 16
compassion 241, 243–244
consequences 102, 107, 111, 293
contradictions 1, 24, 27, 93, 247,
    257–258, 260–263
correlation 94, 128, 130–132
Cottrell, S. 4, 9–10, 15, 23
counterargumentation 136, 157, 297
Cowie, N. 6
Creswell, J. 329–331
critical thinking 1; balancing thought and
    emotion 15–16; common questions

2–17; criticality 5; dispositional view 10; distinctions from cynical thinking 23; distinctions from problem-solving 26; limited presence in English language education 16–17; Orientalist critique 12–15; skill-based view 10–11; sociopolitical factors 3–6; Spock Metaphor 13, 15
Critical Thinking Cycle 29–30, 32–34, 85–87; developing dispositions 34–45; reasoning 60–72; receiving 46–49; responding 73–85
Critical Thinking Instruction 27–30, 317–325; implementation 321–324; pedagogic extensions 324–325; sequencing 27; syllabus design 317–321; teaching applications 28–30, 321
curriculum 5–6, 11, 345

Damasio, A. 15–16
Darwin, C. 281–282
Denzin, N. 3
dictation 67, 149–150
Ding, A. 6
discourse 5, 10, 18, 28, 322
Dummett, P. 15–16
Dunham, R. 11
Duron, R. 1, 11

Elfatihi, M. 7
Either/Or Fallacy 7, 17, 21, 25, 92, 209–217
emotion 4, 13, 15–16, 25, 92, 170, 236–245, 339
empathy 7, 243–244, 342–343
Enfield, N. 21
English for Academic Purposes (EAP) 6
English Language Teaching (ELT) 1, 3, 8, 11, 15–17, 30, 327, 332, 341, 345–346
Ennis, R. 10, 14, 27, 340–341
Enright, M. 17
Equivocation 25, 92, 95, 170, 227–235
exaggeration 169, 199–200, 203
exploration 329, 336, 340–341, 344

Facione, P. 10, 340
Fahim, M. 7
faith 116, 232–233
False Equivalence 25, 92, 148–157
Faulty Conclusions 22, 93–95, 322
fearmongering 94, 108–109, 111
feedback 26, 49, 53, 59, 76, 82

Fettig, C. 16
Fong, G. 11
Formal Fallacies 22

Gann, D. 17
Gambler's Fallacy 24, 93, 250–256
generalization 23, 25, 91, 94–95, 132, 134–141, 318, 335
Genetic Fallacy 24, 93, 274–282
Gergen, K. 344
Glaser, E. 12, 340
Goodwin, M. 16
grammar 24–25, 114, 278
guilt 169, 177–179, 243–244
Gunderson, L. 341

Hadley, G. 6, 327
Halpern, D. 11–12, 15
Hasty Generalization 25, 91, 132–140
Haugnes, N. 16
Horkheimer, M. 344
Howe, E. 14
Hunter, D. 15, 22
Hyers, L. 332
Hyytinen, H. 341

Ignorance Fallacy 25, 93, 249, 298–307
Illogicality 24, 99, 124, 130, 336
imagination 41–42, 128, 131, 176, 270, 283
improvement 6, 11, 273, 326–327
induction 27
inferences 329, 334–335, 337–339
Informal Fallacies 22
integrated research design 329–331
integration 7, 9, 17, 326, 329–331, 334, 336–337, 343
intelligence 26, 136
interaction 5, 10, 26, 29, 85, 327
Introducing to Learners 88–93
intuition 13, 15, 20
investment 9–10, 28; *see also* motivation
irrationality 5, 18, 166, 255
irrelevance 95, 161–163, 165, 178, 181, 187
Ivie, S. 5

Johanssen, K. 8
judgment 7, 14, 18, 23, 27, 333

Kahane, H. 18, 22, 27
Kaplan, R. 12–13
Keeley, S. 12, 15, 22, 26–27
Kemmis, S. 327
Kemp, G. 4, 10, 15, 21–22, 26

Ketabi, S. 1
Kosonen, P. 11
Kramsch, C. 7
Kurfiss, J. 4–5, 8, 11, 26

Langmann, E. 6
Lau, J. 26
Lewin, K. 327
Lin, Y. 8, 11
Lipman, M. 26
logic 5, 7, 13, 15–17, 22, 26, 60, 65, 80, 94, 96–98, 101–102, 306, 318, 345
Logical Fallacies 21
Logical Paradox 24, 93, 257–264

Maher, B. 16
McGuinness, C. 26
McPeck, J. 4, 10
McTaggart, R. 327
measurement 230, 329, 341
Melles, G. 13
metaphor 15, 18, 21, 32, 330
methodology 326–327, 344
Mistaken Assumptions 22, 246–249, 322
mixed methods research (MMR) 328–329, 331, 334
Mok, J. 1
motivation 8–9, 326; *see also* investment

Naiditch, F. 4, 16
Naturalistic Fallacy 25, 93, 307–316
Noda, A. 341
Non-Sequitur 24, 91, 96–102
Norris, S. 14, 27
Norton-Pierce, B. 9
Numrich, C. 16

Orientalism 13–14
othering 13
overgeneralizing 334–335, 338

paradox 24, 93, 247, 257–258, 261–265
pedagogy 4–5, 7, 15, 18, 32, 324
Peters, M. 5–6
Plano Clark, V. 329, 331
Post Hoc Fallacy 24, 91, 121–131
premises 13, 18–20, 22, 60, 63, 91–92, 99, 102, 110–112, 115, 118–119, 189, 193–194, 197–198, 232, 318
Probability Paradox 24, 91, 103–110
process thinking 344
proficiency 1, 3, 7–8, 33–34, 45, 80, 89, 93, 123, 134, 163, 246, 323, 337, 341

proof 23, 25, 35, 67–70, 72, 91, 94, 132, 135, 139, 278, 302, 325
propositions 5, 18

qualitative research 328–330; coding 333; diary study 332–333
quantitative research 328–330, 334–340, 342–344; questionnaires 326, 336, 342, 345
Quantz, R. 6
Quattrochiochi, W. 4
Questionable Reasoning 22, 168–170, 322

Ramanathan, V. 12–13
rationality 15–16
Red Herring 24, 92, 180–188
reliability 19, 24, 34–36, 280, 318, 320, 340–341
research question construction 343
Roksa, J. 6
roleplay 183, 185

Sagan, C. 14
Saldaña, J. 333
sausage-making 344; *see also* process thinking
Schmidt, M. 22
Scull, S. 16
Shermer, M. 14
Shirkhani, S. 7
Siegel, L. 341
Single Cause Fallacy 25, 92, 141–147
Slippery Slope Fallacy 25, 93, 290–297
Sommervold, C. 16
sophistry 60, 71, 342
Specter, M. 14
Stacking the Deck 25, 92, 218–226
Stanovich, K. 26
statistics 240, 244, 255, 278
stereotyping 13, 41–42, 140
Strawman Fallacy 15, 21, 24, 92, 199–208
Sunk Cost Fallacy 25, 92, 158–167, 345
Sweeping Generalizations 23

Takano, Y. 341
Tashakkori, A. 329
techniques 11, 23, 46, 52, 108, 336
theorization 5, 17–18, 125, 281–282, 307, 342
Thompson, G. 6
TOEFL 24, 90–91, 96, 98, 101

Topping, K. 15
Trickey, S. 15
truth 3–5, 10–11, 20–21, 24, 93, 117, 235, 266, 269, 271, 296, 298, 344
truthiness 5
Tsui, L. 26
Tu Quoque 23

Unwarranted Assumptions 24, 93, 265–273

validity 1, 3, 8, 14, 20, 22, 32, 106, 157
Varghese, M. 6

verification 329–330, 334, 336, 341, 344
Viner, K. 5

Waites, B. 341
Walters, K. 13, 15
Watson, G. 340
Weir, E. 340
wikiality 5
Winne, P. 11

Yeh, M.-L. 340

Zollo, F. 4